2016

Sunday Scriptures and Scripture Insights

Rev. J. Philip Horrigan
Lisa M. Orchen
Ed Langlois

ALSO AVAILABLE IN A LARGE PRINT EDITION

LTP
LITURGY
TRAINING
PUBLICATIONS

Nihil Obstat
Very Reverend Daniel A. Smilanic, JCD
Vicar for Canonical Services
Archdiocese of Chicago
March 16, 2015

Imprimatur
Very Reverend Ronald A. Hicks
Vicar General
Archdiocese of Chicago
March 16, 2015

AT HOME WITH THE WORD® 2016 © 2015 Archdiocese of Chicago: Liturgy Training Publications, 3949 South Racine Avenue, Chicago, IL 60609; 1-800-933-1800; fax 1-800-933-7094; e-mail orders@ltp.org; website www.LTP.org. All rights reserved.

The cover art for this year's *At Home with the Word*® is by P.M. Cerezo Barredo, CMF. The interior art is by Kathy Ann Sullivan. This book was edited by Lorie Simmons; Michaela Tudela was the production editor; Kari Nicholls was the production artist.

As a publisher, LTP works toward responsible stewardship of the environment.

We printed the text of *At Home with the Word*® with soy-based ink on paper certified to the SFI (Sustainable Forestry Initiative) Certified Sourcing Standard, and Chain-of-Custody, confirming that the paper manufacturer takes a responsible approach to obtaining and managing the fiber.

The wood fiber required for the making of this paper includes recycled content and was obtained from 100% Responsible sources.

Renewable and carbon-neutral biomass fuels are used for the energy needed in the paper manufacturing process, reducing the use of fossil fuels.

Printed in the United States of America.

ISBN 978-1-61671-197-9

AHW16

Welcome to At Home with the Word® 2016

THE AUTHORS OF THE INTRODUCTIONS

Martin F. Connell teaches liturgical theology at St. John's University in Collegeville, Minnesota. Michael Cameron teaches Scripture and history of Christianity in the theology department at the University of Portland in Oregon.

SCRIPTURE READINGS

For each Sunday, you will find the three readings and Responsorial Psalm from the *Lectionary for Mass*, from which readings are proclaimed in Roman Catholic churches in the United States.

SCRIPTURE INSIGHTS

J. Philip Horrigan, DMIN, is a presbyter of the Archdiocese of Kingston, Ontario, Canada, and works as an independent author and liturgical design consultant from his home office in Chicago. He holds master's degrees in education and theology and a doctor of ministry degree in liturgical studies from Catholic Theological Union, Chicago. The former director of the art and architecture department in the Office for Divine Worship, Archdiocese of Chicago, he is also an adjunct instructor in the Word and Worship faculty of Catholic Theological Union, Chicago.

Phil is a contributing author for a variety of liturgical publications and a frequent presenter at conferences and workshops on various topics related to the building and renovation of worship spaces, the liturgical environment, the history and components of liturgical design, sacramental theology, the spiritual and ecclesial dimensions of liturgical ministries, and the pastoral implications of liturgical rituals, documents, and praxis. Because the Scriptures are fundamental to all aspects of liturgy, Phil's Scripture Insights in this edition of *At Home with the Word®* continue a life-long process of reflection and writing about them.

PRACTICE OF FAITH, HOPE, CHARITY

Two authors wrote the Practices.

Ed Langlois has been a staff writer for the *Catholic Sentinel*, the newspaper of the Archdiocese of Portland, Oregon, since 1993. He graduated from Colorado College with a degree in English, studied theology at Notre Dame University, and is now completing a master of arts in pastoral ministry from the University of Portland. Ed's newspaper writing has focused on church-government relations, social issues like assisted suicide and poverty, Catholic schools, and religious life. He is a husband and a father who commutes to work on a bicycle. Ed has written the Practices for Easter and those from the Tenth to the Twenty-Fourth Sundays in Ordinary Time.

Lisa Orchen is a writer who has served in many pastoral roles over the past twenty years: hospital chaplain, director of campus ministry, pastoral associate, retreat leader, and catechist in the Catechesis of the Good Shepherd. She holds a master of divinity from the University of Notre Dame. Lisa lives in Connecticut with her husband and two children. She has written Practices for Advent, Christmas, Ordinary Time in winter, Most Holy Trinity and Most Holy Body and Blood, and the Twenty-Fifth Sunday in Ordinary Time through Our Lord Jesus Christ, King of the Universe.

WEEKDAY READINGS

See the opening of each liturgical time for a list of Scripture texts read at Mass on weekdays and on feasts falling on weekdays.

ART FOR 2016

On the cover, Fr. Maximino Cerezo Barredo depicts the vision of the prophet, Isaiah, in which he is called by God to his ministry. We hear this reading on the Fifth Sunday in Ordinary Time, (February 7 of this liturgical year). A Claretian priest who lives in Salamanca, Spain, Fr. Maximino has been creating art since his studies in the early 1960s. He has specialized in religious art, especially murals, in Spain and in Central and Latin America. In the interior art, Kathy Ann Sullivan uses a scratch board technique to evoke the liturgical seasons, from our ancestors in faith on the Jesse tree to the oil lamps for Ordinary Time in the fall. Kathy Ann designed the scenes in the baptismal font at St. Mary's Cathedral, Colorado Springs.

Table of Contents

The Lectionary

by Martin F. Connell

WHAT IS A LECTIONARY?

A Lectionary is an ordered selection of readings, chosen from both testaments of the Bible, for proclamation in the assembly gathered for worship. Lectionaries have been used for Christian worship since the fourth century. Before the invention of the printing press in the fifteenth century, the selection and order of the readings differed somewhat from church to church, often reflecting the issues that were important to the local communities of the time.

For the four centuries between the Council of Trent (1545–1563) and the Second Vatican Council (1963–1965), the readings in most Catholic churches varied little from year to year and were proclaimed in Latin, a language that many no longer understood. The Second Vatican Council brought dramatic changes. It allowed the language of the people to be used in the liturgy and initiated a revision of the Lectionary. The Bible became far more accessible to Catholics and once again a vibrant source of our faith and tradition.

THE THREE-YEAR LECTIONARY CYCLE

The new Lectionary that appeared in 1970 introduced a three-year plan that allowed a fuller selection of readings from the Bible. During Year A, the Gospel readings for Ordinary Time are taken from Matthew, for Year B from Mark, and for Year C from Luke. The Sundays in this liturgical year, 2016, begin with the First Sunday of Advent, November 29, 2015, and end with Our Lord Jesus Christ, King of the Universe, November 20, 2016. It is Year C, the year of Luke.

YEAR C: THE GOSPEL ACCORDING TO LUKE

Most of the Gospel readings proclaimed in your Sunday assembly this year and printed in *At Home with the Word® 2016* are from the Gospel according to Luke. The introduction to the Gospel according to Luke on page 8 and the Scripture Insights for each week will help you recognize and appreciate the contribution this Gospel account makes to our faith.

THE GOSPEL ACCORDING TO JOHN

You might ask, What about the Fourth Gospel? The Gospel according to John is not assigned a year of its own because it constitutes so much of our reading during certain seasons and times of the year.

The readings for Year A on the Third, Fourth, and Fifth Sundays of Lent are from the Gospel according to John, and they are proclaimed every year in parishes celebrating the Rite of Christian Initiation of Adults (RCIA) when the elect are present. These three wonderful stories from John—the woman at the well (on the Third Sunday), the man born blind (on the Fourth Sunday), and the raising of Lazarus (on the Fifth Sunday)—accompany the celebration of the Scrutinies in the process of Christian initiation. During Years B and C, you will find two sets of readings on these Sundays in *At Home with the Word®*: one set for Sunday Masses at which the Scrutinies of the RCIA are celebrated, and another set for Masses at which they are not celebrated.

The Gospel according to John also appears for the Mass of the Lord's Supper on Holy Thursday and for the long Passion reading on Good Friday. And it is proclaimed on most of the Sundays of the Easter season.

THE DIFFERENCE BETWEEN THE BIBLE AND THE LECTIONARY

Because the Lectionary uses selections from the Bible, arranged according to the seasons and feasts of the liturgical year, the assembly often hears a selection of texts "out of order" from their position in the Bible. However, the overall shape of the Lectionary comes from the ancient Church practice of *lectio continua*, a Latin term that describes the successive reading through books of the Bible from Sunday to Sunday.

You can see *lectio continua* in practice if you consider the Gospel texts for the Tenth Sunday in Ordinary Time, June 5, through the Feast of Our

Lord Jesus Christ, King of the Universe, November 20. Though not every verse is included (and excepting Sundays when feasts interrupt the flow of Matthew with other Gospel texts), the Lectionary moves from chapter 7 in Luke through chapter 23.

Although Christians hold the Gospels in particular reverence, the first two readings provide strong teaching as well and comprise nearly two-thirds of the material in the Lectionary. The First Reading often echoes some image or idea in the Gospel, as is the Church's intention. The Second Reading often stands on its own and comes from a letter of Paul or another letter from the New Testament. Notice, for example, that the Second Readings from early June through November take us through parts of Galatians, Colossians, Hebrews, Philemon, 1 and 2 Timothy, and 2 Thessalonians. The stretch of Ordinary Time in summer and autumn provides a perfect opportunity for sustained attention to one or a few sections of the Bible.

UNITY WITH OTHER CHRISTIAN CHURCHES IN THE WORD OF GOD

The basic plan of the Lectionary for Catholics is universal. The readings proclaimed in your parish on a particular Sunday are the same as those proclaimed in Catholic churches all over the globe. The Lectionary is one of the main things that makes our liturgy so "catholic," or universal.

The revision of the Roman Catholic Lectionary has been so well received that other Christian churches have begun to follow its three-year cycle. Catholics and their neighbors who attend other Christian churches often hear the same Word of God proclaimed and preached in the Sunday gathering. We may not talk about the Sunday readings with our neighbors and therefore don't realize that their readers read the same Scripture passages and their preachers preach on the same scriptural texts. This is really a remarkable change when you consider how very far apart from one another Catholic and Protestant Churches were before the Second Vatican Council.

Although Roman Catholics in the United States always hear the *New American Bible* translation in their liturgy, and that is what you will find in this book, the Church has approved other translations for study, such as the *New Revised Standard Version* (NRSV) and the *New Jerusalem Bible*. When preparing to hear the readings on Sunday, it is helpful to read more than one translation, and also to read more than the Lectionary passage so that you understand the context in which it occurs in the Bible. Consulting various Bibles, and perhaps a few Bible study tools, will enrich your preparation. (See Studying and Praying Scripture on page 10.)

May your experience of the liturgy in your parish be deepened by the preparations you make with this book, and may the time you spend with Scripture during the liturgical year help you feel ever more "at home with the Word" of God.

Introduction to the Gospel according to Luke

by Michael Cameron

The Gospel according to Luke, together with its sequel, the Acts of the Apostles, presents a breathtaking narrative of early Christianity, from Gabriel announcing the birth of John the Baptist in Jerusalem to the Apostle Paul announcing the Gospel of Jesus in Rome. This majestically conceived, magnificently crafted epic makes up about a quarter of the New Testament.

Luke was a second-generation Christian who may have been a Gentile admirer of Judaism before his conversion. He was well educated, traveled widely, wrote excellent Greek, and was influenced by contemporary modes of writing history. He echoes the atmosphere, the language, and at times even the style of the Old Testament. Luke tells us directly that he is handing on what contemporaries of Jesus have reported (1:1–4). Writing about fifty years after Jesus' time, he incorporates many stories and sayings from Mark, from a source also known to Matthew, and from his own traditions. Nevertheless, he shapes the traditions according to his own rich perspective.

Luke is a theologian with a historical bent, possessing a strong sense of the salvation story's development through three phases of time. *The time of Israel* is the period of "the law and the prophets" (16:16) from the creation to the appearance of John the Baptist. The entire Old Testament portrayed Israel growing in the knowledge of God and awaiting the future "redemption of Jerusalem" (2:38). Luke's account represents this time poetically through the infancy narrative (chapters 1 and 2), with its unforgettable characters who represent Old Testament piety at its best. *The time of Jesus* encompasses his baptism to his Ascension (chapters 3 to 24), when salvation is definitively accomplished in the words and works of the Messiah, especially his Death and Resurrection in Jerusalem (24:44–47). Luke accentuates the dramatic immediacy of salvation by a strategic use of the word *today* (fulfillment "today," 4:21; salvation "today," 19:9; paradise "today," 23:43). *The time of the church* stretches from Pentecost until Jesus returns. Anticipated in 24:48, this period begins to unfold in the 28 chapters of Acts of the Apostles.

Luke's work has a distinctive, sweet air, a beautiful mildness. His naturally humane outlook finds deep resonance with Jesus' concern for people's healing and salvation. In contrast to Mark's rough prophet, Matthew's wise teacher, and John's mystical divine, Luke's Jesus is the herald of healing peace. From the early scene announcing "liberty to captives" (4:17–19) to the last healing of the slave of the high priest who arrested him (22:50–51), Luke's Jesus is the good and gentle Savior. At the same time, Luke is blunt about Jesus' severe demands on those who become his disciples (14:25–33; 17:7–10), who must take up their cross daily (9:23) and leave *everything* to follow him, a favorite idea (5:11, 28; 14:33).

Luke is an exquisite storyteller, with a keen eye for deep characters, pungent storylines, poignant ironies, and heartwarming endings. As with all such masters, his pen's slightest stroke speaks volumes, as when Jesus agonizes while the disciples sleep "from grief" (22:45), or Peter denies Jesus a third time and "the Lord turned and looked at Peter" (22:61). Luke's arresting vignettes anticipate the stained glass storytelling of great medieval cathedrals. It is not accidental that artists have often rendered Luke as a portrait painter, or that the Church has made Luke patron saint of artists.

Luke contains certain features that the other Gospel accounts omit or mention only in passing. Joy is a distinct emphasis (1:14, 47; 2:10; 10:17, 21; 15:7, 10; 19:37; 24:41), as are prayer (3:21; 6:12; 11:5–8; 18:1–8; 23:46), the Holy Spirit (1:15, 41, 67; 2:27; 4:18; 10:21; 11:13), Jesus' friendships with women (7:36–50; 8:2–3; 10:38–42; 23:27–31; 23:55), and his teaching on hospitality (9:49–50; 10:25–37; 14:12–14; 15:4) and right attitude about wealth (6:24–25; 12:13–21; 16:19–31). If Luke's account of the Gospel had somehow not survived, our loss would be incalculable.

Luke alone gives us the stories of Jesus' infancy narrative, including the birth of John the Baptist, the angel Gabriel's Annunciation to Mary (1:26–38), and her visitation to Elizabeth (1:39–45); the liturgical songs of Mary (1:46–55, the *Magnificat*) and Zechariah (1:67–79, the Benedictus); he draws *images* of the crowded inn at Bethlehem, Jesus lying in the manger, shepherds frightened by angels singing "Peace on Earth" (2:1–20), hoary Simeon exclaiming his praise (2:28–32, the *Nunc Dimittis*), old Anna prophesying redemption, (2:36–38), the young Jesus cross-examining the scholars (2:46), and Mary keeping in her heart the mysteries about her son (2:19, 51).

Luke's memorable *characters* include the judgmental Pharisee Simon (7:39–47), the hungry learner Mary (10:39), the repentant taxman Zacchaeus (19:1–10), and the distraught disciple Cleopas (24:18–24). Special *dramas* abound: Jesus raised up a widow's only son at his funeral, then "gave him to his mother" (7:11–17), healed the woman bent double for eighteen years (13:10–17), and cured ten lepers among whom the Samaritan alone returned to say thanks (17:11–19). He painted a host of affecting *scenes*: Jesus reading in his home synagogue (4:16–20), Peter repenting at Jesus' knees (5:8), the woman bathing Jesus' feet with her tears (7:38), Jesus praying with sweat "like drops of blood" (22:44).

Further, Luke transmitted many unique *sayings* of Jesus: "One's life does not consist of possessions" (12:15). "Do not be afraid any longer, little flock" (12:32). "The kingdom of God is among you" (17:21). "Father, forgive them, they know not what they do" (23:34). "Today you will be with me in Paradise" (23:43). And many well-known parables are found only in Luke: the Good Samaritan (10:29–37), the Woman's Lost Coin (15:8–10), the Prodigal Son (15:11–32), the Rich Man and Lazarus (16:19–31), the Widow and the Unjust Judge (18:1–8), the Pharisee and the Tax Collector (18:9–14).

Luke's first sentences in the prologue (1:1–4) address an otherwise unknown figure named Theophilus (the name means "God's friend"), who symbolizes any Christian seeking a deeper understanding of Jesus. For each reader who takes up his "orderly sequence" with serious intent, Luke has a single stirring aim. Literally translated, it reads, "that you may come to know a deep assurance about the teachings you have received."

Studying and Praying Scripture

by Michael Cameron

A recent study claimed that only twenty-two percent of American Catholics read the Bible regularly, and just 8 percent are involved in Scripture groups. Not many know how profoundly biblical the Roman Catholic Church has been from its very roots, having "always venerated the divine Scriptures as she venerated the Body of the Lord" (*Dei Verbum* [*Dogmatic Constitution on Divine Revelation*], 21). How may Catholics learn to read Scripture? This essay sketches a path for seekers.

PREPARING TO READ

Become an apprentice to the Bible. Even a novice can reach a good level of understanding, but at a cost: the Bible yields its riches to those who give themselves to the search for understanding. Start by reading daily, even if only for a few minutes. Join a group that reads and discusses Scripture together.

You will need tools. Think of yourself as a prospector for the Bible's gold. Nuggets on the ground are easily picked up, but the really rich veins lie beneath the surface. Digging requires study, commitment, and skills.

Invest in tools that reap the harvest of others' labors. Buy a study Bible with introductions, explanatory notes, and maps. Use another translation for devotional reading and comparison. Take advantage of a Bible dictionary with detailed information on biblical books, concepts, geography, outlines, customs, and other topics. Bible concordances will help you find all occurrences of particular words. A dictionary of biblical theology will give guidance on major theological ideas. A Bible atlas will give a sense of the locations and movements in the biblical stories. Recent church documents on the Bible offer rich instruction to seekers.

READING FOR KNOWLEDGE

Get to know historical contexts suggested by a passage. Learn all you can about the Bible's basic storyline, its "salvation history," beginning with Israel and continuing in the Church. Salvation by God's

grace, obedience to God's will, and judgment on sin are basic to both Old and New Testaments. Learn particularly about the covenants with Abraham and David that emphasize God's grace. The covenant with Moses presumes God's grace and emphasizes obedience. Both covenant traditions re-emerge and are fulfilled in the new covenant in Jesus, who pours out his life to save all people (grace) but is extremely demanding of his disciples (obedience).

Read entire books of the Bible in order to gain a sense of the whole cloth from which the snippets of the Sunday Lectionary are cut. Try to imagine what the books meant for their original authors and audiences. Ask how and why a book was put together: What is its structure, outline, main themes, literary forms, overall purpose?

Get to know the Old Testament narratives and the psalms, but learn the Gospel accounts especially. The Lectionary's yearly focus on Matthew, Mark, or Luke offers an opportunity to learn each one. John is the focus during the Church's special seasons.

READING FOR WISDOM

Read as one who seeks God, like the writer of Psalm 119. Ask what the text is asking you to believe, do, or hope for. Jesus's powerful proclamation in Mark 1:15 gives a strong framework: "This is the time of fulfillment" (now is the time to be attentive and ready to act); "the kingdom of God is at hand" (God is about to speak and act); "repent" (be willing to change your mind and move with fresh direction); "believe in the gospel" (embrace the grace that has already embraced you).

Read books straight through, a self-contained section at a time, carefully, slowly, and meditatively. Stop where natural breaks occur at the end of stories or sequences of thought.

Beware the sense that you already know what a text is going to say. Read attentively, asking what God is teaching you through this text at this minute about your life or about your communities—family, church, work, neighborhood, nation. Trust the Holy Spirit to guide you to what you need.

READING FOR WORSHIP

The goal of reading the Bible is not learning new facts or getting merely private inspiration for living, but entering into deeper communion with God. Allow the Bible to teach you to pray by giving you the words to use in prayer. The psalms are especially apt for this, but any part of the Bible may be prayed. This practice, dating back more than fifteen hundred years, is called *lectio divina*, Latin for "sacred reading."

Read Scripture in relation to the Eucharist. The Bible both prepares for Jesus's real presence and helps us understand it. The same Jesus who healed the lepers, stilled the storm, and embraced the children is present in the Word and the Sacrament.

The Bible is a library of spiritual treasures waiting to be discovered. The Church intends that this treasury be "widely available to the Christian faithful" (*Dei Verbum* [*Dogmatic Constitution on Divine Revelation*], 22).

RESOURCES

Brown, Raymond E., ss. *101 Questions and Answers on the Bible*. Paulist Press, 2003.

Casey, Michael. *Sacred Reading: The Ancient Art of Lectio Divina*. Liguori/Triumph Books, 1996.

Frigge, Marielle, OSB. *Beginning Biblical Studies*. Winona, MN: Anselm Academic, 2013.

Hahn, Scott, ed. *Catholic Bible Dictionary*. Doubleday, 2009.

Magrassi, Mariano, OSB. *Praying the Bible: An Introduction to Lectio Divina*. Liturgical Press, 1998.

New Collegeville Bible Commentary Series. Collegeville, MN: Liturgical Press. (Short books on individual books of the Bible, various dates.)

Paprocki, Joe. *The Bible Blueprint, A Catholic's Guide to Understanding and Embracing God's Word. Chicago*: Loyola Press, 2009.

The Bible Documents: A Parish Resource. Chicago: Liturgy Training Publications, 2001.

The Catholic Study Bible, 2nd Edition. General editor, Donald Senior, CP. New York: Oxford, 2011.

Advent

Prayer before Reading the Word

In this and every year,
in this and every place,
O God everlasting,
your Word resounds in the wilderness of Advent,
calling us to stand upon the height
and to behold the splendor of your beauty.

Fill in the valleys of our neglect;
bring low our mountains of self-centeredness.
Prepare in our hearts
your way of righteousness and peace.
Let our love become a harvest of goodness,
which you will bring to completion
for the day of Christ Jesus,
who was, who is, and who is to come,
your Son who lives and reigns with you
in the unity of the Holy Spirit,
one God, for ever and ever. Amen.

Prayer after Reading the Word

God of holiness,
whose promises stand through all generations,
fulfill the longings of a humanity
weighed down by confusion and burdened
            with fear.

Raise up our heads and strengthen our hearts,
that we may proclaim to all people
the Good News of your presence in our midst.
May we delight to share with them
your peace, which surpasses all understanding.

We ask this through our Lord Jesus Christ,
            your Son,
who lives and reigns with you
in the unity of the Holy Spirit,
one God, for ever and ever. Amen.

Weekday Readings

November 30: Feast of St. Andrew, Apostle
    Romans 10:9–18; Matthew 4:18–22
December 1: *Isaiah 11:1–10; Luke 10:21–24*
December 2: *Isaiah 25:6–10a; Matthew 15:29–37*
December 3: *Isaiah 26:1–6; Matthew 7:21, 24–27*
December 4: *Isaiah 29:17–24; Matthew 9:27–31*
December 5: *Isaiah 30:19–21, 23–26; Matthew 9:35—10:1, 5a, 6–8*

December 7: *Isaiah 35:1–10; Luke 5:17–26*
December 8: Solemnity of the Immaculate Conception
    of the Blessed Virgin Mary
    Genesis 3:9–15, 20; Ephesians 1:3–6, 11–12;
    Luke 1:26–38
December 9: *Isaiah 40:25–31; Matthew 11:28–30*
December 10: *Isaiah 41:13–20; Matthew 11:11–15*
December 11: *Isaiah 48:17–19; Matthew 11:16–19*
December 12: Feast of Our Lady of Guadalupe
    Zechariah 2:14–17; Luke 1:26–38

December 14: *Numbers 24:2–7, 15–17a; Matthew 21:23–27*
December 15: *Zephaniah 3:1–2, 9–13; Matthew 21:28–32*
December 16: *Isaiah 45:6b–8, 18, 21b–25; Luke 7:18b–23*
December 17: *Genesis 49:2, 8–10; Matthew 1:1–17*
December 18: *Jeremiah 23:5–8; Matthew 1:18–25*
December 19: *Judges 13:2–7, 24–25a; Luke 1:5–25*

December 21: *Song of Songs 2:8–14 or Zephaniah 3:14–18a; Luke 1:39–45*
December 22: *1 Samuel 1:24–28; Luke 1:46–56*
December 23: *Malachi 3:1–4, 23–24; Luke 1:57–66*
December 24: *Morning: 2 Samuel 7:1–5, 8b–12, 14a, 16; Luke 1:67–79*

READING I *Jeremiah 33:14–16*

The days are coming, says the LORD, when I will fulfill the promise I made to the house of Israel and Judah. In those days, in that time, I will raise up for David a just shoot; he shall do what is right and just in the land. In those days Judah shall be safe and Jerusalem shall dwell secure; this is what they shall call her: "The LORD our justice."

RESPONSORIAL PSALM
Psalm 25:4–5, 8–9, 10, 14 (1b)

R. To you, O Lord, I lift my soul.

Your ways, O LORD, make known to me;
    teach me your paths,
guide me in your truth and teach me,
    for you are God my savior,
    and for you I wait all the day.   R.

Good and upright is the LORD;
    thus he shows sinners the way.
He guides the humble to justice,
    and teaches the humble his way.   R.

All the paths of the LORD are kindness
            and constancy
    toward those who keep his covenant and
            his decrees.
The friendship of the LORD is with those who
            fear him,
    and his covenant, for their instruction.   R.

READING II *1 Thessalonians 3:12—4:2*

Brothers and sisters: May the Lord make you increase and abound in love for one another and for all, just as we have for you, so as to strengthen your hearts, to be blameless in holiness before our God and Father at the coming of our Lord Jesus with all his holy ones. Amen.

Finally, brothers and sisters, we earnestly ask and exhort you in the Lord Jesus that, as you received from us how you should conduct yourselves to please God—and as you are conducting yourselves—you do so even more. For you know what instructions we gave you through the Lord Jesus.

GOSPEL *Luke 21:25–28, 34–36*

Jesus said to his disciples: "There will be signs in the sun, the moon, and the stars, and on earth nations will be in dismay, perplexed by the roaring of the sea and the waves. People will die of fright in anticipation of what is coming upon the world, for the powers of the heavens will be shaken. And then they will see the Son of Man coming in a cloud with power and great glory. But when these signs begin to happen, stand erect and raise your heads because your redemption is at hand.

"Beware that your hearts do not become drowsy from carousing and drunkenness and the anxieties of daily life, and that day catch you by surprise like a trap. For that day will assault everyone who lives on the face of the earth. Be vigilant at all times and pray that you have the strength to escape the tribulations that are imminent and to stand before the Son of Man."

Practice of Hope

Advent calls our attention in two directions: backward to recall the birth of Jesus and forward to anticipate his second coming. During Advent the Church invites us to prepare to celebrate both Jesus' birth and his promise to return at the end of time. ◆ A Jesse Tree highlights the ancestry of Jesus. Set up a small tree for Advent and hang symbols of the people and events that foreshadowed his birth. Consult http://www.catholicculture.org /culture/liturgicalyear/activities/ and click on "Advent" for guidance on how to get started. ◆ As a household, mark the days through Advent with an Advent calendar, by lighting the appropriate candle on an Advent wreath, and with daily reading of Scripture or seasonal stories. ◆ On November 30, the Church celebrates the Feast of St. Andrew. Andrew was the first Apostle called by Jesus away from his life as a fisherman, and he suffered a martyr's death for his courageous evangelization. Prepare a fish dinner and reflect on your own readiness for Jesus' call.

Download more questions and activities for families, Christian initiation groups, and other adult groups at http://www.ltp.org/t-productsupplements.aspx.

Scripture Insights

The season of Advent is shaped by two distinct threads in the tapestry of Scripture readings: God's promise to bring forth a Messiah and the people's preparations for the Messiah, both as an infant and as the Lord returning at the end of time. Throughout the Advent readings we see God's promise unfolding for the people of Israel. They are charged to be ready, and that exhortation is for us in our time as well. The prophets, the Apostle Paul, and Jesus are giving us directions for our Advent journey.

Today, Jeremiah proclaims the promise of the Lord God: a "just shoot" will come forth to do what "is right and just" for the people. God's promise will be for the entire house of Israel.

In the Responsorial Psalm, the Lord will lead and instruct the faithful in the way of "kindness and constancy." It is a prayer for those who seek divine guidance so as to live in the Lord's friendship.

Paul prays that the Thessalonians will live in this friendship; that they will "be blameless in holiness." He exhorts them to strive to conduct themselves in a pleasing way. His words encourage us to conduct our lives in a way that will be one with "all his holy ones," ready for the coming of the Lord Jesus.

The cosmic predictions of Jesus are serious and foreboding; they get our attention. Scripture scholars tell us that this is not literal language, but a figure of speech that communicates a profound spiritual message. This style of prophetic preaching awakens us to God intervening in human affairs. The coming of the Son of Man will indeed transform the world and its peoples. How shall we prepare for such an astonishing event? Jesus tells us to be vigilant—not because God intends to frighten or destroy us, but because God has great things in store for those whom God redeems.

◆ How does each of these readings help us prepare for the coming of the Lord?

◆ How can members of your parish or your family mark the unfolding of Advent?

◆ What personal spiritual exercise would help you to be vigilant to the presence of God in the world?

December 6, 2015 <small>Second Sunday of Advent</small>

Reading I *Baruch 5:1–9*

Jerusalem, take off your robe of mourning
    and misery;
  put on the splendor of glory from
      God forever:
wrapped in the cloak of justice from God,
  bear on your head the mitre
  that displays the glory of the eternal name.
For God will show all the earth your splendor:
  you will be named by God forever
  the peace of justice, the glory of God's worship.

Up, Jerusalem! stand upon the heights;
  look to the east and see your children
gathered from the east and the west
  at the word of the Holy One,
  rejoicing that they are remembered by God.
Led away on foot by their enemies they left you:
  but God will bring them back to you
  borne aloft in glory as on royal thrones.
For God has commanded
  that every lofty mountain be made low,
and that the age-old depths and gorges
  be filled to level ground,
  that Israel may advance secure in the glory
    of God.
The forests and every fragrant kind of tree
  have overshadowed Israel at God's command;
for God is leading Israel in joy
  by the light of his glory,
  with his mercy and justice for company.

Responsorial Psalm
Psalm 126:1–2, 2–3, 4–5, 6 (3)

R. The Lord has done great things for us; we are
      filled with joy.

When the Lord brought back the captives of Zion,
  we were like men dreaming.
Then our mouth was filled with laughter,
  and our tongue with rejoicing. R.

Then they said among the nations,
  "The Lord has done great things for them."
The Lord has done great things for us;
  we are glad indeed. R.

Restore our fortunes, O Lord,
  like the torrents in the southern desert.
Those who sow in tears
  shall reap rejoicing. R.

Although they go forth weeping,
  carrying the seed to be sown,
they shall come back rejoicing,
  carrying their sheaves. R.

Reading II *Philippians 1:4–6, 8–11*

Brothers and sisters: I pray always with joy in my
every prayer for all of you, because of your partnership for the gospel from the first day until now.
I am confident of this, that the one who began a
good work in you will continue to complete it until
the day of Christ Jesus. God is my witness, how
I long for all of you with the affection of Christ
Jesus. And this is my prayer: that your love may
increase ever more and more in knowledge and
every kind of perception, to discern what is of
value, so that you may be pure and blameless for
the day of Christ, filled with the fruit of righteousness that comes through Jesus Christ for the glory
and praise of God.

Gospel *Luke 3:1–6*

In the fifteenth year of the reign of Tiberius Caesar,
when Pontius Pilate was governor of Judea, and
Herod was tetrarch of Galilee, and his brother
Philip tetrarch of the region of Ituraea and
Trachonitis, and Lysanias was tetrarch of Abilene,
during the high priesthood of Annas and Caiaphas,
the word of God came to John the son of Zechariah
in the desert. John went throughout the whole
region of the Jordan, proclaiming a baptism of
repentance for the forgiveness of sins, as it is written in the book of the words of the prophet Isaiah: /
*A voice of one crying out in the desert: / "Prepare
the way of the Lord, / make straight his paths. /
Every valley shall be filled / and every mountain
and hill shall be made low. / The winding roads
shall be made straight, / and the rough ways made
smooth, / and all flesh shall see the salvation of God."*

Practice of Charity

This year the optional memorial of St. Nicholas (December 6) falls on the Second Sunday of Advent, and so we don't celebrate the day liturgically. However, we can still remember St. Nicholas in our homes during the coming week. This saint lived in the fourth century and was bishop of Myra (modern-day Turkey). He has been remembered mainly in legends about his anonymous acts of charity for the poor. ◆ This week, care for the poor first of all in your family prayers, mentioning specific situations, local and international, that you hear about in the news. ◆ As a household, go through closets looking for unused warm clothing to contribute to a clothing drive. ◆ In the spirit of St. Nicholas, plan your own secret gift for a person or agency in need this Advent.

Download more questions and activities for families, Christian initiation groups, and other adult groups at http://www.ltp.org/t-productsupplements.aspx.

Scripture Insights

In Baruch's intensely joyful proclamation, Jerusalem is portrayed as a mother who rejoices at seeing her children gathered by the Word of God. The tone is jubilant because God who has commanded that the earth be prepared for all of Israel to "advance secure in the glory of God." The prophet's words call us also to put aside any anxiety or mourning, like a robe we can discard. We are to wrap ourselves in God's justice and rejoice in the light of God's glory.

The theme of rejoicing continues in the Responsorial Psalm, and that is the Lord's doing, for even those who "sow in tears" shall "reap rejoicing."

Paul's letter to the Philippians speaks of his "joy" for their "partnership" with him in announcing the Gospel. He prays for the Christians of Philippi, that their "love may increase ever more and more." They need increased love to be ready for "the day of Christ." Paul seemed to expect that "the day of Christ" would come soon and his exhortation is urgent. The return of the Lord did not happen in Paul's time, but his words are encouraging and timely for us. We need to be constantly striving to live "pure and blameless lives" in the presence of the Lord who dwells among us. We are always preparing for his return in glory.

The Gospel touches on different time scenarios. Luke's references to current political leaders place the in-breaking of God in human history and announce that the coming of the Messiah will alter human affairs. John the Baptist's message introduces the long view of salvation history: the Messiah will fulfill the prophecies of Isaiah. John stands in the line of the prophets, announcing God's plan for those who have been waiting in hope. The repentance he urges is the proper posture for all those preparing to welcome the Messiah, and the liturgical time of Advent is our time to heed John's message in our own hearts.

◆ Where do you find the theme of repentance in the other readings?

◆ How does your parish provide ways to celebrate repentance?

◆ How will a spirit of repentance shape your Advent spirituality?

17

READING I *Zephaniah 3:14–18a*

Shout for joy, O daughter Zion!
  Sing joyfully, O Israel!
Be glad and exult with all your heart,
  O daughter Jerusalem!
The LORD has removed the judgment
        against you,
  he has turned away your enemies;
the King of Israel, the LORD, is in your midst,
  you have no further misfortune to fear.
On that day, it shall be said to Jerusalem:
  Fear not, O Zion, be not discouraged!
The LORD, your God, is in your midst,
  a mighty savior;
he will rejoice over you with gladness,
  and renew you in his love,
he will sing joyfully because of you,
  as one sings at festivals.

RESPONSORIAL PSALM
Isaiah 12:2–3, 4, 5–6 (6)

R. Cry out with joy and gladness:
  for among you is the great and Holy One
      of Israel.

God indeed is my savior;
  I am confident and unafraid.
My strength and my courage is the LORD,
  and he has been my savior.
With joy you will draw water
  at the fountain of salvation.   R.

Give thanks to the LORD, acclaim his name;
  among the nations make known his deeds,
  proclaim how exalted is his name.   R.

Sing praise to the LORD for his glorious
        achievement;
  let this be known throughout all the earth.
Shout with exultation, O city of Zion,
  for great in your midst
  is the Holy One of Israel!   R.

READING II *Philippians 4:4–7*

Brothers and sisters: Rejoice in the Lord always. I shall say it again: rejoice! Your kindness should be known to all. The Lord is near. Have no anxiety at all, but in everything, by prayer and petition, with thanksgiving, make your requests known to God. Then the peace of God that surpasses all understanding will guard your hearts and minds in Christ Jesus.

GOSPEL *Luke 3:10–18*

The crowds asked John the Baptist, "What should we do?" He said to them in reply, "Whoever has two cloaks should share with the person who has none. And whoever has food should do likewise." Even tax collectors came to be baptized and they said to him, "Teacher, what should we do?" He answered them, "Stop collecting more than what is prescribed." Soldiers also asked him, "And what is it that we should do?" He told them, "Do not practice extortion, do not falsely accuse anyone, and be satisfied with your wages."

Now the people were filled with expectation, and all were asking in their hearts whether John might be the Christ. John answered them all, saying, "I am baptizing you with water, but one mightier than I is coming. I am not worthy to loosen the thongs of his sandals. He will baptize you with the Holy Spirit and fire. His winnowing fan is in his hand to clear his threshing floor and to gather the wheat into his barn, but the chaff he will burn with unquenchable fire." Exhorting them in many other ways, he preached good news to the people.

Practice of Hope

The rose candle on that will be lit on the Advent wreath today reminds us that the Church marks the Third Sunday of Advent as "Gaudete Sunday," and the Scriptures call us to be a joyful people. ♦ This week when you gather to light the candles of your Advent wreath, pray the joyful words of today's Responsorial Psalm. ♦ Plant wheat or grass seeds in a shallow container. By Christmas Eve they will have grown several inches and can be cut and placed in the crib of your household nativity set. The wheat serves as new "hay" for the Christ child. ♦ The crowds and tax collectors in Luke's Gospel ask John, "What should we do?" He instructs them to make choices rooted in justice and charity. Make a charitable gift or do a deed of justice this week. Visit Catholic Relief Services at www.crs.org for good ideas.

Download more questions and activities for families, Christian initiation groups, and other adult groups at http://www.ltp.org/t-productsupplements.aspx.

Scripture Insights

There can be no mistaking the message of the prophet Zephaniah to the people of Israel. The phrases, "shout for joy," "sing joyfully," and "be glad and exult" are delivered as commands to the people because "the King of Israel, the LORD, is in your midst." This Third Sunday of Advent was once referred to as "Gaudete Sunday," the Sunday to rejoice. Although Advent has a certain penitential character, still we are called to rejoice because God does indeed dwell among us. Zephaniah makes it clear that the reason for rejoicing rests in the action of God on behalf of God's own people. Their enemies have been defeated and there will be no more "misfortune to fear." This same message brings us comfort.

The Responsorial Psalm for today is actually a passage from the prophet Isaiah and not from the Book of Psalms. The refrain reiterates the theme of joy; and once again the reason for such joy is because the "great and Holy One of Israel" is in the midst of the people. This spirit of joy leads to thanks—a natural reaction for the ancient Israelites and for us. When we acknowledge that "God indeed is my savior" we are filled with joy and gratitude.

The Second Reading is another passage from the Letter to the Philippians in which Paul continues to exhort the people to rejoice and assures them that "the Lord is near." Grounded in such joy and awareness of God's presence, the people are empowered to behave in new ways: "Your kindness should be known to all."

The text from Luke's Gospel is one of the longer passages not centered on a teaching of Jesus, but of John the Baptist. Three different groups—the crowds, the tax collectors, and the soldiers—are responding to John's warning in the previous verse (9) that any tree not producing good fruit will be thrown into the fire. But in today's reading (beginning with verse 10) we hear only their questions and John's answers, group by group. Note that John does not tell them to change their vocation or profession; instead he tells them that they need to change the way they act as soldiers, or tax collectors, or members of their community. They are to express their repentance by being more compassionate, considerate, and honest in all they do. Now willing to do these things, they are filled with great expectation; they are ready to welcome the One that John announces.

♦ How do you think John would answer your question: "What should I do?"

♦ How do you bring joy to others?

♦ In what ways do you sense a renewed awareness of Christ during Advent?

READING I *Micah 5:1–4a*

Thus says the LORD:
You, Bethlehem-Ephrathah,
   too small to be among the clans of Judah,
from you shall come forth for me
   one who is to be ruler in Israel;
whose origin is from of old,
   from ancient times.
Therefore the Lord will give them up,
         until the time
   when she who is to give birth has borne,
and the rest of his kindred shall return
   to the children of Israel.
He shall stand firm and shepherd his flock
   by the strength of the LORD,
   in the majestic name of the LORD, his God;
and they shall remain, for now his greatness
   shall reach to the ends of the earth;
   he shall be peace.

RESPONSORIAL PSALM
Psalm 80:2–3, 15–16, 18–19 (4)

R. Lord, make us turn to you; let us see your face
   and we shall be saved.

O shepherd of Israel, hearken,
   from your throne upon the cherubim,
         shine forth.
Rouse your power,
   and come to save us.   R.

Once again, O LORD of hosts,
   look down from heaven, and see;
take care of this vine,
   and protect what your right hand has planted,
   the son of man whom you yourself
         made strong.   R.

May your help be with the man of your right hand,
   with the son of man whom you yourself
         made strong.
Then we will no more withdraw from you;
   give us new life, and we will call upon
         your name.   R.

READING II *Hebrews 10:5–10*

Brothers and sisters:
When Christ came into the world, he said:
   "Sacrifice and offering you did not desire,
      but a body you prepared for me;
   in holocausts and sin offerings you took
            no delight.
   Then I said, 'As is written of me in the scroll,
      behold, I come to do your will, O God.'"

First he says, "Sacrifices and offerings, holocausts and sin offerings, you neither desired nor delighted in." These are offered according to the law. Then he says, "Behold, I come to do your will." He takes away the first to establish the second. By this "will," we have been consecrated through the offering of the body of Jesus Christ once for all.

GOSPEL *Luke 1:39–45*

Mary set out and traveled to the hill country in haste to a town of Judah, where she entered the house of Zechariah and greeted Elizabeth. When Elizabeth heard Mary's greeting, the infant leaped in her womb, and Elizabeth, filled with the Holy Spirit, cried out in a loud voice and said, "Blessed are you among women, and blessed is the fruit of your womb. And how does this happen to me, that the mother of my Lord should come to me? For at the moment the sound of your greeting reached my ears, the infant in my womb leaped for joy. Blessed are you who believed that what was spoken to you by the Lord would be fulfilled."

Practice of Faith

Long before the birth of Jesus, the prophet Micah foretold that the very tiny town of Bethlehem would witness the birth of the long-awaited savior. The name *Jesus* means "savior." In the sixth century, St. Gregory the Great reminded us that the name, "Bethlehem," means "house of bread." Jesus, our savior, was born in the "House of Bread" in fulfillment of the prophecy and would eventually become our "Bread of Life." ◆ Reflect on the daily news and look for some examples of the miraculous way God allows great things to occur in the most humble of places. ◆ Share stories about the birth of each member of your household. Talk about their birthplace and the special reasons their birth names were chosen. ◆ Bless your household nativity set. Visit http://www.usccbpublishing.org/client/client_pdfs/creche.pdf for a beautiful blessing prayer published by the United States Catholic Conference of Bishops (USCCB).

Download more questions and activities for families, Christian initiation groups, and other adult groups at http://www.ltp.org/t-productsupplements.aspx.

Scripture Insights

Micah is the fourth Hebrew prophet we hear from this Advent. He announces the Word of God to the people of Bethlehem-Ephrathah, telling of a new ruler in Israel, who hails not from royalty but from this humble village. The new ruler will act as a shepherd and will rule by the "strength of the Lord." This prophecy became part of the literature related to the coming of the Messiah, and Christians later applied it to the arrival of Jesus, the Good Shepherd of the flock of Israel.

The Responsorial Psalm picks up the shepherd image, "O shepherd of Israel" and calls on him to "come to save us." We find other powerful images of God in this psalm: "Lord of hosts," the one who cares for the vineyard, the one who sits on the throne of heaven, and the one who gives new life. Jesus will later take up the shepherd image and in his parables will attribute the keeper of the vineyard image to his Father.

The author of the Letter to the Hebrews recalls Jesus' teaching on sacrifice, including his own sacrifice, as the offering of his body "once for all." Even now during Advent, this text shifts our thinking for a moment to the end of Jesus' life. The one who would come to be shepherd will eventually be the lamb of sacrifice. Such will be the depth of love that the shepherd will have for his flock.

Luke describes the encounter of Mary and Elizabeth and their greetings of joy and hospitality. The tenderness of this scene engages our own joy and desire to make ready for the coming of the Savior-Messiah into our everyday lives. This meeting of Elizabeth, the mother of John the Baptist (often called the Precursor) and the mother of the one whom John announced represents the meeting of a peoples' hope with the fulfillment of that hope.

◆ What signs of Jesus' future mission do you note in the readings today?

◆ What signs or events in your parish show that the Church is preparing to celebrate the coming of Christ?

◆ How have you been able to help others receive this Good News of the birth of Christ?

Christmas Time

Prayer before Reading the Word

By the light of a star, O God of the universe,
you guided the nations to the Light of the world.

Until this Redeemer comes again in glory,
we, with the Magi, seek the face of the Savior.
Summon us with all those who thirst now
to the banquet of love.
May our hunger be filled and our thirst
                be quenched
with your Word of truth.

We ask this through our Lord Jesus Christ,
                your Son,
who lives and reigns with you
in the unity of the Holy Spirit,
one God, for ever and ever. Amen.

Prayer after Reading the Word

In the beginning, O God, was your Word,
and now in time your Word becomes flesh.
The Light that shines unconquered
through the darkness of the ages,
and has made his dwelling place among us,
transforming earth's gloom into heaven's glory.

As we behold upon the mountains
the messenger who announces your peace,
touch our lips as well that we may lift up our voices
as bearers of Good News and heralds of salvation.

We ask this through our Lord Jesus Christ,
Emmanuel, God-with-us,
your Son, who lives and reigns with you
in the unity of the Holy Spirit,
God, for ever and ever. Amen.

December 25: Solemnity of the Nativity of the Lord
   Day: Isaiah 52:7–10; Hebrews 1:1–6; John 1:1–18
December 26: Feast of St. Stephen
   Acts 6:8–10; 7:54–59; Matthew 10:17–22

December 28: Feast of the Holy Innocents
   1 John 1:5—2:2; Matthew 2:13–18
December 29: Fifth Day within the Octave
   of the Nativity of the Lord
   1 John 2:3–11; Luke 2:22–35
December 30: Sixth Day within the Octave of the
   Nativity of the Lord
   1 John 2:12–17; Luke 2:36–40
December 31: Seventh Day within the Octave of the
   Nativity of the Lord
   1 John 2:18–21; John 1:1–18
January 1: Solemnity of Mary, the Holy Mother of God
   Numbers 6:22–27; Galatians 4:4–7; Luke 2:16–21
January 2: *1 John 2:22–28; John 1:19–28*

January 4: *1 John 3:22—4:6; Matthew 4:12–17, 23–25*
   January 5: 1 John 4:7–10; Mark 6.34–44
January 6: *1 John 4:11–18; Mark 6:45–52*
January 7: *1 John 4:19—5:4; Luke 4:14–22a*
January 8: *1 John 5:5–13; Luke 5:12–16*
January 9: *1 John 5:14-21; John 3:22–30*

READING I *Isaiah 62:11–12*

See, the LORD proclaims
   to the ends of the earth:
Say to daughter Zion,
   your savior comes!
Here is his reward with him,
   his recompense before him.
They shall be called the holy people,
   the redeemed of the LORD,
And you shall be called "Frequented,"
   a city that is not forsaken.

RESPONSORIAL PSALM
Psalm 97:1, 6, 11–12

R. A light will shine on us this day: the Lord is
       born for us.

The LORD is king; let the earth rejoice;
   let the many islands be glad.
The heavens proclaim his justice,
   and all peoples see his glory.   R.

Light dawns for the just;
   and gladness, for the upright of heart.
Be glad in the LORD, you just,
   and give thanks to his holy name.   R.

READING II *Titus 3:4–7*

Beloved:
  When the kindness and generous love
   of God our savior appeared,
not because of any righteous deeds
      we had done
   but because of his mercy,
he saved us through the bath of rebirth
   and renewal by the Holy Spirit,
whom he richly poured out on us
   through Jesus Christ our savior,
so that we might be justified by his grace
   and become heirs in hope of eternal life.

GOSPEL *Luke 2:15–20*

When the angels went away from them to heaven, the shepherds said to one another, "Let us go, then, to Bethlehem to see this thing that has taken place, which the Lord has made known to us." So they went in haste and found Mary and Joseph, and the infant lying in the manger. When they saw this, they made known the message that had been told them about this child. All who heard it were amazed by what had been told them by the shepherds. And Mary kept all these things, reflecting on them in her heart. Then the shepherds returned, glorifying and praising God for all they had heard and seen, just as it had been told to them.

Practice of Faith

During the Christmas Mass at Dawn, the Church proclaims in psalmody, "A light will shine on us this day: the Lord is born for us." As dawn breaks on early Christmas morning and lights flicker on early in homes filled with excited children, we remember the image of Jesus as the "light" coming into the world, overcoming the darkness once and for all. ◆ At some point this morning when the household is gathered, take turns reading the Gospel aloud. End with a Christmas carol about the Savior's birth. ◆ People of Irish ancestry sometimes place lit candles in their windows as a message that Mary, Joseph, and Jesus would be welcomed in their search for shelter. Light candles in your home, and pray for families who are refugees this Christmas. ◆ Extend Christmas hospitality by inviting a family member or neighbor who would otherwise be alone to join your household for a Christmas meal.

Download more questions and activities for families, Christian initiation groups, and other adult groups at http://www.ltp.org/t-productsupplements.aspx.

Scripture Insights

The First Reading for the four Masses for the Nativity is from the prophet Isaiah. Although passages from other prophets were proclaimed during Advent, Isaiah is generally regarded as the one whose prophecies best lead into the events and theology associated with the Advent-Christmas season. In today's text the Lord proclaims that the Savior comes, a proclamation meant to be heard to the "ends of the earth." This announcement is the very heart of Christmas: God's people have been redeemed. It is an exclamation of what has come about; there is no more waiting.

"The Lord is born for us," we sing in the refrain of the Responsorial Psalm. The psalmist imagines the whole earth rejoicing in the light of this cosmic event: the islands, the heavens, and the peoples will proclaim justice and see the Lord's glory.

Whether it was indeed Paul who wrote the letter to Titus, as some scholars believe, or someone writing in Paul's name, as others argue, we hear today that all the peaceable behavior asked of the new Christians is possible because Jesus Christ appeared in their midst and saved them through his grace and the renewal of the Holy Spirit. Christ has appeared, not as a reward for any righteous deeds, but because of God's mercy.

The Gospel reading for the Mass at Dawn follows the shepherds to the stable after they have heard the angels' announcement. (This Mass was once called the Shepherds' Mass.) Stunned and empowered by what they have heard, the shepherds hurry to discover the reason for the angels' joy. Once they have seen, they become evangelizers; they bear good news (*evangelium*), and all who hear it are "amazed." We are left with a couple of questions: what did they really "see," and what did they tell the others that brought such amazement? Rather than explain it, perhaps we are meant to reflect on it (with Mary) and rejoice!

◆ What actual message do you imagine the shepherds telling others?

◆ What is the Good News you hear in each of today's readings?

◆ How can you be the bearer of Good News?

December 27, 2015

FEAST OF THE HOLY FAMILY OF JESUS, MARY, AND JOSEPH

READING I *1 Samuel 1:20–22, 24–28*

Alternate reading: Sirach 3:2–6, 12–14

In those days Hannah conceived, and at the end of her term bore a son whom she called Samuel, since she had asked the LORD for him. The next time her husband Elkanah was going up with the rest of his household to offer the customary sacrifice to the LORD and to fulfill his vows, Hannah did not go, explaining to her husband, "Once the child is weaned, I will take him to appear before the LORD and to remain there forever; I will offer him as a perpetual nazirite."

Once Samuel was weaned, Hannah brought him up with her, along with a three-year-old bull, an ephah of flour, and a skin of wine, and presented him at the temple of the LORD in Shiloh. After the boy's father had sacrificed the young bull, Hannah, his mother, approached Eli and said: "Pardon, my lord! As you live, my lord, I am the woman who stood near you here, praying to the LORD. I prayed for this child, and the LORD granted my request. Now I, in turn, give him to the LORD; as long as he lives, he shall be dedicated to the LORD." Hannah left Samuel there.

RESPONSORIAL PSALM
Psalm 84:2–3, 5–6, 9–10 *(see 5a)*

Alternate Psalm: Psalm 128:1–2, 3, 4–5 (see 1)

R. Blessed are they who dwell in your house,
    O Lord.

How lovely is your dwelling place,
    O LORD of hosts!
  My soul yearns and pines for the courts
      of the LORD.
My heart and my flesh cry out for the
    living God.   R.

Happy they who dwell in your house!
  Continually they praise you.
Happy the men whose strength you are!
  Their hearts are set upon the pilgrimage.   R.

O LORD of hosts, hear our prayer;
  hearken, O God of Jacob!
O God, behold our shield,
  and look upon the face of your anointed.   R.

READING II *1 John 3:1–2, 21–24*

Alternate reading: Colossians 3:12–21 or 3:12–17

Beloved: See what love the Father has bestowed on us that we may be called the children of God. And so we are. The reason the world does not know us is that it did not know him. Beloved, we are God's children now; what we shall be has not yet been revealed. We do know that when it is revealed we shall be like him, for we shall see him as he is.

Beloved, if our hearts do not condemn us, we have confidence in God and receive from him whatever we ask, because we keep his commandments and do what pleases him. And his commandment is this: we should believe in the name of his Son, Jesus Christ, and love one another just as he commanded us. Those who keep his commandments remain in him, and he in them, and the way we know that he remains in us is from the Spirit he gave us.

GOSPEL *Luke 2:41–52*

Each year Jesus' parents went to Jerusalem for the feast of Passover, and when he was twelve years old, they went up according to festival custom. After they had completed its days, as they were returning, the boy Jesus remained behind in Jerusalem, but his parents did not know it. Thinking that he was in the caravan, they journeyed for a day and looked for him among their relatives and acquaintances, but not finding him, they returned to Jerusalem to look for him. After three days they found him in the temple, sitting in the midst of the teachers, listening to them and asking them questions, and all who heard him were astounded at his understanding and his answers. When his parents saw him, they were astonished, and his mother said to him, "Son, why have you done this to us? Your father and I have been looking for you with great anxiety." And he said to them, "Why were you looking for me? Did you not know that I must be in my Father's house?" But they did not understand what he said to them. He went down with them and came to Nazareth, and was obedient to them; and his mother kept all these things in her heart. And Jesus advanced in wisdom and age and favor before God and man.

Practice of Faith

Today's Gospel lets us feel the paralyzing panic that consumes Mary and Joseph (and any parent) who has lost sight of a child. When she and Joseph finally find Jesus in the Temple, Mary speaks of the "great anxiety" all parents sometimes feel about their children. ◆ The United States Conference of Catholic Bishops supports parents in their ministry as family caregivers. See suggested resources at http://www.usccb.org/issues-and-action /marriage-and-family/parents-and-parenting. ◆ The Knights of Columbus Museum in New Haven, Connecticut, displays an annual Christmas exhibit of nativity scenes from around the world. Take a virtual tour of the beautiful exhibit at www. kofcmuseum.org/en. ◆ January 1 is the Solemnity of Mary, the Holy Mother of God, as well as the World Day of Peace. Visit http://w2.vatican.va /content/francesco/en/messages/peace/index.html to read the Pope's annual New Year's Day Message to the world. ◆ Today's Responsorial Psalm tells of the blessings of dwelling in the Lord's house. Consider how your house could become more like God's.

Download more questions and activities for families, Christian initiation groups, and other adult groups at http://www.ltp.org/t-productsupplements.aspx.

Scripture Insights

Today we enter Hannah's poignant story halfway through. In the verses preceding this reading, she is miserable because of her barrenness, she pours out her soul to God in the temple at Shiloh, praying for a child. The priest, Eli, mistakes her fervency for drunkenness, but she explains herself eloquently and leaves full of faith. When the child is granted, Hannah responds to God's generosity by giving the child back to the Lord as a nazirite, one consecrated to the Lord's service. Samuel will become a great prophet.

The Responsorial Psalm uses the very human image of "house" to describe the "dwelling place" of the Lord. Singing that psalm, we join the psalmist in yearning for the blessing of living in the Lord's house, desiring its strength for our own pilgrimage.

In John's letter, we Christians are called beloved children of God whom the world cannot recognize since it could not recognize Christ. Like Samuel, set apart for God's service and the child Jesus in today's Gospel, going about his daily life with his parents, we are to stay grounded in our identity, believing in Jesus Christ and loving one another until the future shall be revealed.

There are few fears in life greater than that of parents when they realize that their child is missing. Jesus' parents share this anxiety when they discover that he is not among the others who have gone up to Jerusalem. But this family crisis is also an enticing teaching about Jesus' identity and mission. Although Luke tells us that Jesus is only twelve years old, already he has a premonition that his place is "in my Father's house." Nonetheless, he returns to the home of his human parents, and we are left to ponder with his mother the process he undergoes as he grows "in wisdom and age and favor before God."

◆ What insights do these readings offer about the role of parents in our relationship with God?

◆ What are your fears and blessings related to your family?

◆ How do you understand "the way we know that he remains in us is from the Spirit he gave us?"

READING I *Isaiah 60:1–6*

Rise up in splendor, Jerusalem! Your light
    has come,
  the glory of the Lord shines upon you.
See, darkness covers the earth,
  and thick clouds cover the peoples;
but upon you the LORD shines,
  and over you appears his glory.
Nations shall walk by your light,
  and kings by your shining radiance.
Raise your eyes and look about;
  they all gather and come to you:
your sons come from afar,
  and your daughters in the arms of their nurses.

Then you shall be radiant at what you see,
  your heart shall throb and overflow,
for the riches of the sea shall be emptied out
    before you,
  the wealth of nations shall be brought to you.
Caravans of camels shall fill you,
  dromedaries from Midian and Ephah;
all from Sheba shall come
  bearing gold and frankincense,
  and proclaiming the praises of the LORD.

RESPONSORIAL PSALM *Psalm 72:1–2, 7–8, 10–11, 12–13 (see 11)*

R. Lord, every nation on earth will adore you.

O God, with your judgment endow the king,
  and with your justice the king's son;
he shall govern your people with justice
  and your afflicted ones with judgment. R.

Justice shall flower in his days,
  and profound peace, till the moon be no more.
May he rule from sea to sea,
  and from the River to the ends of
    the earth. R.

The kings of Tarshish and the Isles shall offer gifts;
  the kings of Arabia and Seba shall
    bring tribute.
All kings shall pay him homage,
  all nations shall serve him. R.

For he shall rescue the poor when he cries out,
  and the afflicted when he has no one to
    help him.
He shall have pity for the lowly and the poor;
  the lives of the poor he shall save. R.

READING II *Ephesians 3:2–3a, 5–6*

Brothers and sisters: You have heard of the stewardship of God's grace that was given to me for your benefit, namely, that the mystery was made known to me by revelation. It was not made known to people in other generations as it has now been revealed to his holy apostles and prophets by the Spirit: that the Gentiles are coheirs, members of the same body, and copartners in the promise in Christ Jesus through the gospel.

GOSPEL *Matthew 2:1–12*

When Jesus was born in Bethlehem of Judea, in the days of King Herod, behold, magi from the east arrived in Jerusalem, saying, "Where is the newborn king of the Jews? We saw his star at its rising and have come to do him homage." When King Herod heard this, he was greatly troubled, and all Jerusalem with him. Assembling all the chief priests and the scribes of the people, he inquired of them where the Christ was to be born. They said to him, "In Bethlehem of Judea, for thus it has been written through the prophet:

And you, Bethlehem, land of Judah, / are by no means least among the rulers of Judah; / since from you shall come a ruler, / who is to shepherd my people Israel."

Then Herod called the magi secretly and ascertained from them the time of the star's appearance. He sent them to Bethlehem and said, "Go and search diligently for the child. When you have found him, bring me word, that I too may go and do him homage." After their audience with the king they set out. And behold, the star that they had seen at its rising preceded them, until it came and stopped over the place where the child was. They were overjoyed at seeing the star, and on entering the house they saw the child with Mary his mother. They prostrated themselves and did him homage. Then they opened their treasures and offered him gifts of gold, frankincense, and myrrh. And having been warned in a dream not to return to Herod, they departed for their country by another way.

Practice of Hope

Today we celebrate the Solemnity of the Epiphany, the appearance of Christ to the Gentiles, told in the story of the Magi following the bright star that led to the newborn King. Little is known about the three visitors from the east who paid the Holy Family such astonishing homage, but their story invites us to reflect on their willingness to journey so far to meet Jesus and their reverence for mystery. ◆ On a clear evening this week, go outside to appreciate the bright stars. Reflect on your own continuing journey toward Christ. ◆ Epiphany is a day for the annual blessing of our homes. Visit http://stmarys-waco.org/documents/EpiphanyHouseBlessing.pdf for a simple blessing ritual. ◆ The worldwide Church celebrates Migration Week early in January. Visit www.usccb.org/about/migration-and-refugee-services/national-migration-week/ to learn about the struggles of immigrants and how you can join the efforts of the local and national Church in helping the needs of refugees.

Download more questions and activities for families, Christian initiation groups, and other adult groups at http://www.ltp.org/t-productsupplements.aspx.

Scripture Insights

The Solemnity of the Epiphany was once called "Little Christmas," and the story of the Magi was one of the four "epiphanies" or manifestations that surrounded God's intervention in human history. The birth of Christ, his baptism, and the miracle of the wedding feast of Cana are the other three. Each of these signs gives a different insight on Christ's coming. How does Matthew tell his Epiphany story?

The coming of the Magi is a fulfillment of Isaiah's prophecy, and the realization of his claim that there will be a time of great joy. Isaiah exhorts the people of God, Jerusalem, to "rise up in splendor" because the glory of the Lord has shattered the darkness over them and they will be a light to the nations. Indeed, because of them the nations from afar shall gather and bring gifts, "proclaiming the praises of the Lord." The Responsorial Psalm echoes these praises. All the nations shall adore the Lord, and kings from afar will offer gifts and pay him homage.

The exotic visitors in the Gospel narrative fulfill Isaiah's words. They come "from the east," and are called simply "magi." Many scholars regard them as astronomers because they follow the mysterious star. As Isaiah foretold, they bring gifts of "gold, frankincense, and myrrh." Because three gifts are offered to the child, the tradition has assumed that there were three magi. Their arrival and their conversation with Herod, the temporal ruler, suggest that Jesus' birth will have an impact far beyond "Bethlehem of Judea."

Matthew tells us the Magi receive a warning not to return to Herod—a warning in a dream. In the Bible, dreams alert humans that certain occurrences are not what they seem. The Magi "departed for their country by another way." Once one encounters an "epiphany" of divine origins, life is changed.

◆ What do today's readings tell us about the identity of the child Jesus?

◆ What gift do you offer to the Lord this year?

◆ Can you name at least one "epiphany" in your life during the past year?

Reading I *Isaiah 40:1–5, 9–11*

Alternate reading: Isaiah 42:1–4, 6–7

Comfort, give comfort to my people,
    says your God.
Speak tenderly to Jerusalem, and proclaim
        to her
    that her service is at an end,
    her guilt is expiated;
indeed, she has received from the hand of
        the Lord
    double for all her sins.

    A voice cries out:
In the desert prepare the way of the Lord!
    Make straight in the wasteland a highway
        for our God!
Every valley shall be filled in,
    every mountain and hill shall
        be made low;
the rugged land shall be made a plain,
    the rough country, a broad valley.
Then the glory of the Lord shall be revealed,
    and all people shall see it together;
    for the mouth of the Lord has spoken.

Go up onto a high mountain,
    Zion, herald of glad tidings;
cry out at the top of your voice,
    Jerusalem, herald of good news!
Fear not to cry out
    and say to the cities of Judah:
    Here is your God!
Here comes with power
    the Lord God,
    who rules by a strong arm;
here is his reward with him,
    his recompense before him.
Like a shepherd he feeds his flock;
    in his arms he gathers the lambs,
carrying them in his bosom,
    and leading the ewes with care.

Responsorial Psalm *Psalm 104:1b–2, 3–4, 24–25, 27–28, 29–30 (1)*

Alternate Psalm: Psalm 29:1–2, 3–4, 3, 9–10 (11b)

R. O bless the Lord, my soul.

O Lord, my God, you are great indeed!
    You are clothed with majesty and glory,
robed in light as with a cloak.
    You have spread out the heavens like
        a tent-cloth.   R.

You have constructed your palace upon the waters.
    You make the clouds your chariot;
you travel on the wings of the wind.
    You make the winds your messengers,
and flaming fire your ministers.   R.

How manifold are your works, O Lord!
    In wisdom you have wrought them all—
the earth is full of your creatures;
    the sea also, great and wide,
in which are schools without number
    of living things both small and great.   R.

They look to you to give them food in due time.
    When you give it to them, they gather it;
when you open your hand, they are filled with
        good things.   R.

If you take away their breath, they perish and
        return to the dust.
    When you send forth your spirit, they
        are created,
and you renew the face of the earth.   R.

Reading II *Titus 2:11–14; 3:4–7*

Alternate reading: Acts 10:34–38

Beloved: The grace of God has appeared, saving all and training us to reject godless ways and worldly desires and to live temperately, justly, and devoutly in this age, as we await the blessed hope, the appearance of the glory of our great God and savior Jesus Christ, who gave himself for us to deliver us from all lawlessness and to cleanse for himself a people as his own, eager to do what is good.

When the kindness and generous love
  of God our savior appeared,
not because of any righteous deeds we had done
  but because of his mercy,
he saved us through the bath of rebirth
  and renewal by the Holy Spirit,
whom he richly poured out on us
  through Jesus Christ our savior,
so that we might be justified by his grace
  and become heirs in hope of eternal life.

GOSPEL *Luke 3:15–16, 21–22*

The people were filled with expectation, and all were asking in their hearts whether John might be the Christ. John answered them all, saying, "I am baptizing you with water, but one mightier than I is coming. I am not worthy to loosen the thongs of his sandals. He will baptize you with the Holy Spirit and fire."

After all the people had been baptized and Jesus also had been baptized and was praying, heaven was opened and the Holy Spirit descended upon him in bodily form like a dove. And a voice came from heaven, "You are my beloved Son; with you I am well pleased."

Practice of Faith

As the Christmas decorations are packed away for another year, the Gospel turns from Christ's infancy to his initiation into mission. The story of Jesus' baptism invites us to remember our own baptisms. This week, connect the Gospel to the baptism stories of all in your household. ◆ Pull out baptismal pictures, videos, and mementos, and retell the stories. ◆ At some appropriate time, talk about what our Baptism means. (For a refresher, consult the *Catechism of the Catholic Church*, paragraphs 1213–1284.) ◆ Give godparents and godchildren a candle and recall our baptismal command to keep the light of Christ burning brightly in our lives.

Download more questions and activities for families, Christian initiation groups, and other adult groups at http://www.ltp.org/t-productsupplements.aspx.

Scripture Insights

The Feast of the Baptism of the Lord marks a passage from Christmas Time to Ordinary Time. In the Gospel, where we have been following the story of Jesus coming into the world, we now witness his baptism—an act that will launch him on the work he came to do.

Although in the First Reading Isaiah was speaking to a different situation, his description of a voice crying out to prepare a way for the LORD reminds us of the cry of John the Baptist, seven hundred years later. Isaiah says that the LORD will come with power, "a strong arm," and yet he will be "like a shepherd," gathering the lambs in his arms. Jesus adopted that shepherd persona to describe himself to the people of his time.

The poetry of today's Responsorial Psalm has helped the faithful of every age appreciate and praise the majestic works of God: "spread out the heavens like a tent-cloth," "make the clouds your chariot," "renew the face of the earth." This is the God to whom our Baptism joins us.

We heard the last part of the Second Reading at the Christmas Mass at Dawn; now on this feast we focus on the "bath of rebirth and renewal by the Holy Spirit" that Christ "poured out on us." We learn that our own Baptism trains us "to reject godless ways and worldly desires and to live temperately, justly and devoutly."

In Luke's account of Jesus' baptism, John makes a distinction between the baptism he performs (a baptism for repentance) and the one Jesus will give—the one we received—(for transformation and mission). In the Gospel, we also hear the Father's joyful affirmation of his Son as "beloved"—something we may not remember hearing at our own Baptism. Today is a good time to listen to those words again and claim them.

◆ What new insight do any of these readings offer you about Baptism?

◆ At this moment, how would you name your particular ministry as a follower of Jesus?

◆ What challenges do you encounter in living out your identity as the "beloved" of the Father?

Ordinary Time, Winter

Prayer before Reading the Word

In you, O Lord our God,
we find our joy,
for through your Law and your Prophets
you formed a people in mercy and freedom,
in justice and righteousness.
You call us with your voice of flame.
Give us ears to hear,
lives to respond,
and voices to proclaim the Good News
              of salvation,
which we know in our Savior Jesus Christ,
who lives and reigns with you and the Holy Spirit,
one God, now and forever. Amen.

Prayer after Reading the Word

In your Word, Lord God,
you reveal your power to heal and save us.
Let this Good News echo throughout the world,
in every tongue and in every culture,
so that people everywhere may gladly embrace
the salvation and life you offer to all.
We ask this through our Lord Jesus Christ,
              your Son,
who lives and reigns with you
in the unity of the Holy Spirit,
one God, for ever and ever. Amen.

Weekday Readings

January 11: *1 Samuel 1:1–8; Mark 1:14–20*
January 12: *1 Samuel 1:9–20; Mark 1:21–28*
January 13: *1 Samuel 3:1–10, 19–20; Mark 1:29–39*
January 14: *1 Samuel 4:1–11; Mark 1:40–45*
January 15: *1 Samuel 8:4–7, 10–22a; Mark 2:1–12*
January 16: *1 Samuel 9:1–4, 17–19; 10:1a; Mark 2:13–17*

January 18: *1 Samuel 15:16–23; Mark 2:18–22*
January 19: *1 Samuel 16:1–13; Mark 2:23–28*
January 20: *1 Samuel 17:32–33, 37, 40–51; Mark 3:1–6*
January 21: *1 Samuel 18:6–9; 19:1–7; Mark 3:7–12*
January 22: Day of Prayer for the Legal Protection
   of Unborn Children
   1 Samuel 24:3–21; Mark 3:13–19
January 23: *2 Samuel 1:1–4, 11–12, 19, 23–27; Mark 3:20–21*

January 25: Feast of the Conversion of St. Paul the Apostle
   Acts 22:3–16 or 9:1–22; Mark 16:15–18
January 26: *2 Timothy 1:1–8 or Titus 1:1–5; Mark 3:31–35*
January 27: *2 Samuel 7:4–17; Mark 4:1–20*
January 28: *2 Samuel 7:18–19, 24–29; Mark 4:21–25*
January 29: *2 Samuel 11:1–4a, 5–10a, 13–17; Mark 4:26–34*
January 30: *2 Samuel 12:1–7a, 10–17; Mark 4:35–41*

February 1: *2 Samuel 15:13–14, 30; 16:5–13; Mark 5:1–20*
February 2: Feast of the Presentation of the Lord
   Malachi 3:1–4; Hebrews 2:14–18;
   Luke 2:22–40 or 2:22–32
February 3: *2 Samuel 24:2, 9–17; Mark 6:1–6*
February 4: *1 Kings 2:1–4, 10–12; Mark 6:7–13*
February 5: *Sirach 47:2–11; Mark 6:14–29*
February 6: *1 Kings 3:4–13; Mark 6:30–34*

February 8: *1 Kings 8:1–7, 9–13; Mark 6:53–56*
February 9: *1 Kings 8:22–23, 27–30; Mark 7:1–13*

READING I *Isaiah 62:1–5*

For Zion's sake I will not be silent,
   for Jerusalem's sake I will not be quiet,
until her vindication shines forth like the dawn
   and her victory like a burning torch.

Nations shall behold your vindication,
   and all the kings your glory;
you shall be called by a new name
   pronounced by the mouth of the LORD.
You shall be a glorious crown in the hand
      of the LORD,
   a royal diadem held by your God.
No more shall people call you "Forsaken,"
   or your land "Desolate,"
but you shall be called "My Delight,"
   and your land "Espoused."
For the LORD delights in you
   and makes your land his spouse.
As a young man marries a virgin,
   your Builder shall marry you;
and as a bridegroom rejoices in his bride
   so shall your God rejoice in you.

RESPONSORIAL PSALM
Psalm 96:1–2, 2–3, 7–8, 9–10 (3)

R. Proclaim his marvelous deeds to all the nations.

Sing to the LORD a new song;
   sing to the LORD, all you lands.
Sing to the LORD; bless his name.   R.

Announce his salvation, day after day.
Tell his glory among the nations;
   among all peoples, his wondrous deeds.   R.

Give to the LORD, you families of nations,
   give to the LORD glory and praise;
   give to the LORD the glory due his name!   R.

Worship the LORD in holy attire.
   Tremble before him, all the earth;
say among the nations: The LORD is king.
   He governs the peoples with equity.   R.

READING II *1 Corinthians 12:4–11*

Brothers and sisters: There are different kinds of spiritual gifts but the same Spirit; there are different forms of service but the same Lord; there are different workings but the same God who produces all of them in everyone. To each individual the manifestation of the Spirit is given for some benefit. To one is given through the Spirit the expression of wisdom; to another, the expression of knowledge according to the same Spirit; to another, faith by the same Spirit; to another, gifts of healing by the one Spirit; to another, mighty deeds; to another, prophecy; to another, discernment of spirits; to another, varieties of tongues; to another, interpretation of tongues. But one and the same Spirit produces all of these, distributing them individually to each person as he wishes.

GOSPEL *John 2:1–11*

There was a wedding at Cana in Galilee, and the mother of Jesus was there. Jesus and his disciples were also invited to the wedding. When the wine ran short, the mother of Jesus said to him, "They have no wine." And Jesus said to her, "Woman, how does your concern affect me? My hour has not yet come." His mother said to the servers, "Do whatever he tells you." Now there were six stone water jars there for Jewish ceremonial washings, each holding twenty to thirty gallons. Jesus told them, "Fill the jars with water." So they filled them to the brim. Then he told them, "Draw some out now and take it to the headwaiter." So they took it. And when the headwaiter tasted the water that had become wine, without knowing where it came from—although the servers who had drawn the water knew—, the headwaiter called the bridegroom and said to him, "Everyone serves good wine first, and then when people have drunk freely, an inferior one; but you have kept the good wine until now." Jesus did this as the beginning of his signs at Cana in Galilee and so revealed his glory, and his disciples began to believe in him.

Practice of Faith

Today St. Paul affirms that the Holy Spirit infuses each of us with distinctive spiritual gifts. ◆ Deepen your awareness of how the Holy Spirit has empowered you. Pray with 1 Corinthians 12:4–11 and consider which gifts you detect in yourself. ◆ Reflect on the gifts of people in your parish. Tell someone what you recognize in them that they might not have felt in themselves; tell another person how much you appreciate the way they share their gifts. ◆ Called together by the Holy Spirit, the Catholic Church joins Christians around the world in marking the International Week of Prayer for Christian Unity from January 18 to 25. Visit http://www.usccb.org/beliefs-and-teachings /ecumenical-and-interreligious/events/week-of -prayer-for-christian-unity.cfm to learn more and join the chain of prayer.

Download more questions and activities for families, Christian initiation groups, and other adult groups at http://www.ltp.org/t-productsupplements.aspx.

Scripture Insights

Each year the date of Easter determines the number of Sundays in Ordinary Time that fall between the Feast of the Baptism of the Lord and Ash Wednesday. This year we celebrate four Sundays in the winter portion of Ordinary Time.

In the First Reading, Isaiah makes the relationship between God and the people vivid and startlingly personal when he says, "The LORD delights in you and makes your land his spouse." God apparently wants to marry the entire community! So deep is God's love for Israel that he "will not be silent." God's love will transform the land and the people from being called "forsaken" and "desolate" to being "my delight" and "espoused." In the Responsorial Psalm, the people sing to the LORD a new song to celebrate the new, redeemed relationship God offers. The psalmist urges the community to give God glory and praise, and to mark this transformative moment by worshiping the LORD "in holy attire."

During these four Sundays of Ordinary Time the Church reads from Paul's First Letter to the Corinthians. Today Paul encourages the people, reminding them of the many gifts that the Spirit has bestowed upon them. But Paul wants them to understand that these gifts are intended to unify them, since all the gifts come from the one Spirit.

The wedding feast of Cana is the setting for Jesus' first miracle in his public ministry—another "epiphany," or manifestation of God's intervention in human affairs. Like the Gospel for Epiphany about the Magi and last week's Gospel about the baptism of Jesus, this story from John the Evangelist announces that God transforms the human condition. The changing of the water into wine is not intended to be an exhibition, but a "sign" of the glory of God that Jesus would continue to reveal throughout his mission.

◆ What transformations do you discern in each of today's readings?

◆ Is there a transformation needed in your own life, or one that has recently taken place?

◆ What signs of the glory of God do you see around you?

35

January 24, 2016 THIRD SUNDAY IN ORDINARY TIME

READING I Nehemiah 8:2–4a, 5–6, 8–10

Ezra the priest brought the law before the assembly, which consisted of men, women, and those children old enough to understand. Standing at one end of the open place that was before the Water Gate, he read out of the book from daybreak till midday, in the presence of the men, the women, and those children old enough to understand; and all the people listened attentively to the book of the law. Ezra the scribe stood on a wooden platform that had been made for the occasion. He opened the scroll so that all the people might see it—for he was standing higher up than any of the people—; and, as he opened it, all the people rose. Ezra blessed the LORD, the great God, and all the people, their hands raised high, answered, "Amen, amen!" Then they bowed down and prostrated themselves before the LORD, their faces to the ground. Ezra read plainly from the book of the law of God, interpreting it so that all could understand what was read. Then Nehemiah, that is, His Excellency, and Ezra the priest-scribe and the Levites who were instructing the people said to all the people: "Today is holy to the LORD your God. Do not be sad, and do not weep"—for all the people were weeping as they heard the words of the law. He said further: "Go, eat rich foods and drink sweet drinks, and allot portions to those who had nothing prepared; for today is holy to our LORD. Do not be saddened this day, for rejoicing in the LORD must be your strength!"

RESPONSORIAL PSALM Psalm 19:8, 9, 10, 15 (see John 6:63c)

R. Your words, Lord, are Spirit and life.

The law of the LORD is perfect,
  refreshing the soul;
the decree of the LORD is trustworthy,
  giving wisdom to the simple. R.

The precepts of the LORD are right,
  rejoicing the heart;
the command of the LORD is clear,
  enlightening the eye. R.

The fear of the LORD is pure,
  enduring forever;
the ordinances of the LORD are true,
  all of them just. R.

Let the words of my mouth and the thought
    of my heart
find favor before you,
O LORD, my rock and my redeemer. R.

READING II 1 Corinthians 12:12–14, 27

Longer: 1 Corinthians 12:12–30

Brothers and sisters: As a body is one though it has many parts, and all the parts of the body, though many, are one body, so also Christ. For in one Spirit we were all baptized into one body, whether Jews or Greeks, slaves or free persons, and we were all given to drink of one Spirit. Now the body is not a single part, but many. You are Christ's body, and individually parts of it.

GOSPEL Luke 1:1–4; 4:14–21

Since many have undertaken to compile a narrative of the events that have been fulfilled among us, just as those who were eyewitnesses from the beginning and ministers of the word have handed them down to us, I too have decided, after investigating everything accurately anew, to write it down in an orderly sequence for you, most excellent Theophilus, so that you may realize the certainty of the teachings you have received.

Jesus returned to Galilee in the power of the Spirit, and news of him spread throughout the whole region. He taught in their synagogues and was praised by all.

He came to Nazareth, where he had grown up, and went according to his custom into the synagogue on the sabbath day. He stood up to read and was handed a scroll of the prophet Isaiah. He unrolled the scroll and found the passage where it was written:

The Spirit of the Lord is upon me, / because he has anointed me / to bring glad tidings to the poor. / He has sent me to proclaim liberty to captives / and recovery of sight to the blind, / to let the oppressed go free, / and to proclaim a year acceptable to the Lord.

Rolling up the scroll, he handed it back to the attendant and sat down, and the eyes of all in the synagogue looked intently at him. He said to them, "Today this Scripture passage is fulfilled in your hearing."

Practice of Hope

On January 25 the Church commemorates the Conversion of St. Paul the Apostle. Like St. Paul, the founder of the American order, the Paulists, Isaac Hecker (1819–1888), experienced a conversion that led him to proclaim the Good News of Jesus Christ. ◆ Learn more about Fr. Hecker and his distinctively American style of evangelization through a book from your library, or at https://www.paulist.org/about/our-founder-path-sainthood or http://www.newadvent.org/cathen/07186a.htm. ◆ The Paulist community seeks to proclaim the Word of God in ways that will reach people through contemporary media. They bring the Word and the Catholic tradition to young adults through www.BustedHalo.com. Tell the young adults in your life about this spiritual resource. ◆ St. Paul affirmed and the United States Conference of Catholic Bishops speaks powerfully to the hopeful truth that each of us is called and gifted by the Holy Spirit in the service of God's people. Read the Bishops' document entitled *Called and Gifted*, which names how each of us is called to adult faith, to holiness, to community, and to mission. Visit http://www.usccb.org/about/laity-marriage-family-life-and-youth/laity/called-and-gifted-for-the-third-millennium.cfm to prayerfully read their statement and discern your own giftedness in the eyes of God.

Download more questions and activities for families, Christian initiation groups, and other adult groups at http://www.ltp.org/t-productsupplements.aspx.

Scripture Insights

The reading from Nehemiah recounts a liturgical event in the life of the Jewish community. The people had recently returned from the Babylonian exile, and had been bereft of their Scriptures for many years. On this day, Ezra the priest reads from the scroll, the "book of the law," and everyone listens attentively "from daybreak till midday." Their reaction is surprising: they weep. Nehemiah and Ezra charge the people not to weep but to rejoice at the proclamation of the Word of God. Quite appropriately then, in the Responsorial Psalm the psalmist announces, "the law of the Lord is perfect, refreshing the soul," and we sing "Your words, Lord, are Spirit and life." Surely this calls for rejoicing!

Today's Second Reading is part of Paul's lengthy exhortation to the Corinthians. To describe relations within the community of believers he draws an analogy to the physical body with its many parts. This familiar text reminds us of the richness of the life of the Church and everyone's responsibility for the common good. The body of the community, with its many parts, is the body of Christ.

Since we are in Year C of the Sunday Lectionary, our Gospel readings come from Luke. Today's text begins with the first four verses of chapter one and then skips to chapter four, omitting the infancy narratives we read during Christmas Time. Jesus is now an adult and he returns to the synagogue in Nazareth, where he reads from the scroll of the prophet, Isaiah. This dramatic moment marks the beginning of Jesus' public ministry and it allows Jesus to announce that his mission is the fulfillment of Isaiah's prophecy—the realization of the expectations of the Israelites. He boldly proclaims that what had been foretold is now unfolding "in your hearing."

◆ How do today's readings help you appreciate the role of Scripture in the Mass and in the life of the community?

◆ What do you believe is your gift in and for the Church as a member of the body of Christ?

◆ How do you offer those gifts to others?

January 31, 2016 FOURTH SUNDAY IN ORDINARY TIME

READING I *Jeremiah 1:4–5, 17–19*

The word of the LORD came to me, saying:
  Before I formed you in the womb I knew you,
    before you were born I dedicated you,
    a prophet to the nations I appointed you.

  But do you gird your loins;
    stand up and tell them
    all that I command you.
  Be not crushed on their account,
    as though I would leave you crushed
        before them;
  for it is I this day
    who have made you a fortified city,
  a pillar of iron, a wall of brass,
    against the whole land:
  against Judah's kings and princes,
    against its priests and people.
  They will fight against you but not prevail
        over you,
    for I am with you to deliver you, says the LORD.

RESPONSORIAL PSALM *Psalm 71:1–2, 3–4, 5–6, 15, 17 (see 15ab)*

R. I will sing of your salvation.

In you, O LORD, I take refuge;
  let me never be put to shame.
In your justice rescue me, and deliver me;
  incline your ear to me, and save me. R.

Be my rock of refuge,
  a stronghold to give me safety,
    for you are my rock and my fortress.
O my God, rescue me from the hand of
        the wicked. R.

For you are my hope, O Lord;
  my trust, O God, from my youth.
On you I depend from birth;
  from my mother's womb you are
        my strength. R.

My mouth shall declare your justice,
  day by day your salvation.
O God, you have taught me from my youth,
  and till the present I proclaim your
        wondrous deeds. R.

READING II *1 Corinthians 12:31—13:13*

Shorter: 1 Corinthians 13:4–13

Brothers and sisters: Strive eagerly for the greatest spiritual gifts. But I shall show you a still more excellent way.

If I speak in human and angelic tongues, but do not have love, I am a resounding gong or a clashing cymbal. And if I have the gift of prophecy, and comprehend all mysteries and all knowledge; if I have all faith so as to move mountains, but do not have love, I am nothing. If I give away everything I own, and if I hand my body over so that I may boast, but do not have love, I gain nothing.

Love is patient, love is kind. It is not jealous, it is not pompous, it is not inflated, it is not rude, it does not seek its own interests, it is not quick-tempered, it does not brood over injury, it does not rejoice over wrongdoing but rejoices with the truth. It bears all things, believes all things, hopes all things, endures all things.

Love never fails. If there are prophecies, they will be brought to nothing; if tongues, they will cease; if knowledge, it will be brought to nothing. For we know partially and we prophesy partially, but when the perfect comes, the partial will pass away. When I was a child, I used to talk as a child, think as a child, reason as a child; when I became a man, I put aside childish things. At present we see indistinctly, as in a mirror, but then face to face. At present I know partially; then I shall know fully, as I am fully known. So faith, hope, love remain, these three; but the greatest of these is love.

GOSPEL *Luke 4:21–30*

Jesus began speaking in the synagogue, saying: "Today this Scripture passage is fulfilled in your hearing." And all spoke highly of him and were amazed at the gracious words that came from his mouth. They also asked, "Isn't this the son of Joseph?" He said to them, "Surely you will quote me this proverb, 'Physician, cure yourself,' and say, 'Do here in your native place the things that we heard were done in Capernaum.'" And he said, "Amen, I say to you, no prophet is accepted in his own native place. Indeed, I tell you, there were many widows in Israel in the days of Elijah when the sky was closed for three and a half years and a severe famine spread over the entire land. It was to none of these that Elijah was sent, but only to a widow in Zarephath in the land of Sidon. Again, there were many lepers in Israel during the time of Elisha the prophet; yet not one of them was cleansed, but only Naaman the Syrian." When the people in the synagogue heard this, they were all filled with fury. They rose up, drove him out of the town, and led him to the brow of the hill on which their town had been built, to hurl him down headlong. But Jesus passed through the midst of them and went away.

Practice of Faith

Throughout history, God has chosen prophets to bring a message of truth spoken in love to God's people. Often, however, the prophet's message is not welcomed. ◆ Prayerfully consider why we are often resistant to the truth spoken in love. How can you open yourself more fully to the voice of prophets in our midst? ◆ Read chapter 2, section 1, of Pope Francis' *Joy of the Gospel*, "Some Challenges of Today's World." (Find the book in a library or the text at http://w2.vatican.va/content/francesco /en/apost_exhortations/documents/papa -francesco_esortazione-ap_20131124_evangelii -gaudium.html.) In what ways might this writing be regarded as prophetic? ◆ On the day of our Baptism, we are anointed with sacred chrism so that we may remain forever a member of Christ, who is Priest, Prophet, and King. As a member of the Body of Christ, listen deeply to the voice of God in your own life and courageously speak the truth of faith in love.

Download more questions and activities for families, Christian initiation groups, and other adult groups at http://www.ltp.org/t-productsupplements.aspx.

Scripture Insights

The prophet Jeremiah describes how the Lord called him—even as he was being formed in the womb. From that moment he was destined to be "a prophet to the nations." He was to preach "all that I command you." "Be not crushed" sounds ominous, but God promised to strengthen him as "a pillar of iron," and "a wall of brass." Jeremiah would prevail because the Lord God would be with him.

Today's Responsorial Psalm is the whole-hearted supplication of a solid believer. The psalmist asks the Lord to give him refuge from shame; to hear his plea, and be a "rock," a "stronghold." The Lord has been his strength "from my mother's womb;" indeed that trust leads him to "proclaim your wondrous deeds." Here is a model for dark days that we can rehearse in the liturgy.

The reading from Paul is surely one of his most familiar, poetic passages. Having reminded the Corinthians of all the gifts they possess as members of the body of Christ, he then asserts that these gifts amount to nothing if they are not rooted in love. For Paul, love is not an idea or feeling; it is an outward expression of what must be in the heart of those who follow the Lord.

Today's Gospel follows that of last Sunday when Jesus read from the scroll of the prophet Isaiah. The listeners' response is ambiguous. First they speak favorably about him, but soon the mood changes and they expel him from the town. They take offense when he reminds them of their history of faithlessness to the Word of God. After all, he is one of them; how dare he chastise them? By recounting this story near the beginning of Jesus' ministry, Luke alerts us to the opposing reactions that Jesus' message and mission will receive as he continues to preach the Word of God in their midst.

◆ Which description of love in Paul helps you most in your spiritual growth?

◆ What does Jesus have in common with Jeremiah?

◆ Has anyone you know ever refused to accept your faith?

READING I *Isaiah 6:1–2a, 3–8*

In the year King Uzziah died, I saw the Lord seated on a high and lofty throne, with the train of his garment filling the temple. Seraphim were stationed above.

They cried one to the other, "Holy, holy, holy is the LORD of hosts! All the earth is filled with his glory!" At the sound of that cry, the frame of the door shook and the house was filled with smoke.

Then I said, "Woe is me, I am doomed! For I am a man of unclean lips, living among a people of unclean lips; yet my eyes have seen the King, the LORD of hosts!" Then one of the seraphim flew to me, holding an ember that he had taken with tongs from the altar.

He touched my mouth with it, and said, "See, now that this has touched your lips, your wickedness is removed, your sin purged."

Then I heard the voice of the Lord saying, "Whom shall I send? Who will go for us?" "Here I am," I said; "send me!"

RESPONSORIAL PSALM
Psalm 138:1–2, 2–3, 4–5, 7–8 (1c)

R. In the sight of the angels I will sing your
    praises, Lord.

I will give thanks to you, O LORD, with all
        my heart,
    for you have heard the words of my mouth;
    in the presence of the angels I will sing
        your praise;
I will worship at your holy temple
    and give thanks to your name.   R.

Because of your kindness and your truth;
    for you have made great above all things
    your name and your promise.
When I called, you answered me;
    you built up strength within me.   R.

All the kings of the earth shall give thanks to
        you, O LORD,
    when they hear the words of your mouth;
and they shall sing of the ways of the LORD:
    "Great is the glory of the LORD."   R.

Your right hand saves me.
    The LORD will complete what he has done
            for me;
your kindness, O LORD, endures forever;
    forsake not the work of your hands.   R.

READING II *1 Corinthians 15:1–11*

Shorter: 1 Corinthians 15:3–8, 11

I am reminding you, brothers and sisters, of the gospel I preached to you, which you indeed received and in which you also stand. Through it you are also being saved, if you hold fast to the word I preached to you, unless you believed in vain. For I handed on to you as of first importance what I also received: that Christ died for our sins in accordance with the Scriptures; that he was buried; that he was raised on the third day in accordance with the Scriptures; that he appeared to Cephas, then to the Twelve. After that, he appeared to more than five hundred brothers at once, most of whom are still living, though some have fallen asleep. After that he appeared to James, then to all the apostles. Last of all, as to one born abnormally, he appeared to me. For I am the least of the apostles, not fit to be called an apostle, because I persecuted the church of God. But by the grace of God I am what I am, and his grace to me has not been ineffective. Indeed, I have toiled harder than all of them; not I, however, but the grace of God that is with me. Therefore, whether it be I or they, so we preach and so you believed.

GOSPEL *Luke 5:1–11*

While the crowd was pressing in on Jesus and listening to the word of God, he was standing by the Lake of Gennesaret. He saw two boats there alongside the lake; the fishermen had disembarked and were washing their nets. Getting into one of the boats, the one belonging to Simon, he asked him to put out a short distance from the shore. Then he sat down and taught the crowds from the boat. After he had finished speaking, he said to Simon, "Put out into deep water and lower your nets for a catch." Simon said in reply, "Master, we have worked hard all night and have caught nothing, but at your command I will lower the nets." When they had done this, they caught a great number of fish and their nets were tearing. They signaled to their partners in the other boat to come to help them. They came and filled both boats so that the boats were in danger of sinking. When Simon Peter saw this, he fell at the knees of Jesus and said, "Depart from me, Lord, for I am a sinful man." For astonishment at the catch of fish they had made seized him and all those with him, and likewise James and John, the sons of Zebedee, who were partners of Simon. Jesus said to Simon, "Do not be afraid; from now on you will be catching men." When they brought their boats to the shore, they left everything and followed him.

Practice of Faith

Today we hear the conversion stories of Isaiah, St. Paul, and St. Peter. As Lent begins this week, each of us is called to our own continuing conversion. ♦ Ash Wednesday serves as a doorway to a time of intense spiritual preparation leading to Easter and continuing until Pentecost. Make a deliberate plan to enter that doorway to Lent by arranging your calendar to attend Mass on Ash Wednesday. ♦ How is God calling you to journey through Lent? Begin to formulate ideas about how you will incorporate the spiritual practices of Lent—prayer, fasting, and almsgiving (acts of charity)—throughout the weeks ahead. ♦ As you prepare for Lent, draw a timeline of your life. Note any times that you experienced God's call. Choose one to write about in your journal and let your reflections lead you into Lent with an open heart.

Download more questions and activities for families, Christian initiation groups, and other adult groups at http://www.ltp.org/t-productsupplements.aspx.

Scripture Insights

The passage from the prophet Isaiah may well remind us of the reading from Jeremiah last week. It is another "call" story, though somewhat more dramatic. Here Isaiah finds himself in the very throne room of the LORD of hosts. He is "anointed" with the ember that touches his lips, his sense of unworthiness and sin are purged, and he boldly declares: "Here I am, send me!" The Responsorial Psalm places us with Isaiah at the foot of the throne: "In the sight of the angels I will sing your praises, Lord." Isaiah's sense of awe and gratitude becomes ours as we sing this psalm of praise.

The Second Reading from Paul is his autobiographical testimony of how he came to faith. He recalls how he came to be one of the Apostles, even though he characterizes himself as the least, and how, by God's favor, "I am what I am." Paul understands his vocation to the community of believers, that he "handed on to you as of first importance what I also received": that Christ "died for our sins," was buried, raised again on the third day, and appeared to various people. He returns to this statement in his other letters.

The first few verses of chapter five in Luke's Gospel recount the call of the first of Jesus' disciples. This "call" story has two layers. First, the crowd is anxious to hear the Word of God and they press around Jesus. As the story unfolds, the fishermen who are used to catching fish are invited to leave their nets and catch people. Those who would catch others must first be caught up in the Word of God. In order to do that they will need to leave their nets and their usual way of life, and follow the new life in and with the Lord.

♦ What similarities do you find in today's "call" stories?

♦ Was there a moment, or more than one moment, when you felt the call of the Lord?

♦ How do you understand your vocation in life to be a form of catching others for the Lord?

Lent

Prayer before Reading the Word

O Lord, great and faithful God,
it is good for us to be here!
Let us listen to your Son, your chosen One.

Shatter the hardness of our hearts
and open our minds to the wisdom of the Gospel,
that we may grasp the lessons you teach us daily
and bring forth the fruit of true
and continual conversion.

We ask this through the One
into whom we have been baptized,
our Lord Jesus Christ, your Son,
who lives and reigns with you
in the unity of the Holy Spirit,
one God, for ever and ever. Amen.

Prayer after Reading the Word

Infinite is your compassion, O God,
and gracious the pardon
that Jesus, the Teacher, offers
to every sinner who stands before him.

Gladden our hearts
at the Word that sends us on our way in peace;
and grant that we who have been found
   by your grace
may gladly welcome to the table of your family
all who long to find their way home.

We ask this through Christ,
our peace and reconciliation,
the Lord who lives and reigns with you
in the unity of the Holy Spirit,
one God, for ever and ever. Amen.

Weekday Readings

February 10: Ash Wednesday
   Joel 2:12–18; 2 Corinthians 5:20—6:2;
   Matthew 6:1–6, 16–18
February 11: *Deuteronomy 30:15–20; Luke 9:22–25*
February 12: *Isaiah 58:1–9a; Matthew 9:14–15*
February 13: *Isaiah 58:9b–14; Luke 5:27–32*

February 15: *Leviticus 19:1–2, 11–18; Matthew 25:31–46*
February 16: *Isaiah 55:10–11; Matthew 6:7–15*
February 17: *Jonah 3:1–10; Luke 11:29–32*
February 18: *Esther C:12, 14–16, 23–25; Matthew 7:7–12*
February 19: *Ezra 18:21–28; Matthew 5:20–26*
February 20: *Deuteronomy 26:16–19; Matthew 5:43–48*

February 22: Feast of the Chair of St. Peter the Apostle
   1 Peter 5:1–4; Matthew 16:13–19
February 23: *Isaiah 1:10, 16–20; Matthew 23:1–12*
February 24: *Jeremiah 18:18–20; Matthew 20:17–28*
February 25: *Jeremiah 17:5–10; Luke 16:19–31*
February 26: *Genesis 37:3–4, 12–13a, 17b–28a;*
   Matthew 21:33–43, 45–46
February 27: *Micah 7:14–15, 18–20; Luke 15:1–3, 11–32*

February 29: *2 Kings 5:1–15ab; Luke 4:24–30*
March 1: *Daniel 3:25, 34–43; Matthew 18:21–35*
March 2: *Deuteronomy 4:1, 5–9; Matthew 5:17–19*
March 3: *Jeremiah 7:23–28; Luke 11:14–23*
March 4: *Hosea 14:2–10; Mark 12:28–34*
March 5: *Hosea 6:1–6; Luke 18:9–14*

March 7: *Isaiah 65:17–21; John 4:43–54*
March 8: *Ezra 47:1–9, 12; John 5:1–16*
March 9: *Isaiah 49:8–15; John 5:17–30*
March 10: *Exodus 32:7–14; John 5:31–47*
March 11: *Wisdom 2:1a, 12–22; John 7:1–2, 10, 25–30*
March 12: *Jeremiah 11:18–20; John 7:40–53*

March 14: *Daniel 13:1–9, 15–17, 19–30, 33–62 or 13:41c–62;*
   John 8:12–20, or, if Year A readings are used on the Fifth
   Sunday of Lent, John 8:1–11
March 15: *Numbers 21:4–9; John 8:21–30*
March 16: *Daniel 3:14–20, 91–92, 95; John 8:31–42*
March 17: *Genesis 17:3–9; John 8:51–59*
March 18: *Jeremiah 20:10–13; John 10:31–42*
March 19: Solemnity of the St. Joseph,
   Spouse of the Blessed Virgin Mary
   2 Samuel 7:4–5a, 12–14a, 16; Romans 4:13, 16–18, 22;
   Matthew 1:16, 18–21, 24a or Luke 2:41–51a

March 21: *Isaiah 42:1–7; John 12:1–11*
March 22: *Isaiah 49:1–6; John 13:21–33, 36–38*
March 23: *Isaiah 50:4–9a; Matthew 26:14–25*

February 14, 2016 FIRST SUNDAY OF LENT

READING I *Deuteronomy 26:4–10*

Moses spoke to the people, saying: "The priest shall receive the basket from you and shall set it in front of the altar of the LORD, your God. Then you shall declare before the LORD, your God, 'My father was a wandering Aramean who went down to Egypt with a small household and lived there as an alien. But there he became a nation great, strong, and numerous. When the Egyptians maltreated and oppressed us, imposing hard labor upon us, we cried to the LORD, the God of our fathers, and he heard our cry and saw our affliction, our toil and our oppression. He brought us out of Egypt with his strong hand and outstretched arm, with terrifying power, with signs and wonders; and bringing us into this country, he gave us this land flowing with milk and honey. Therefore, I have now brought you the firstfruits of the products of the soil which you, O LORD, have given me.' And having set them before the LORD, your God, you shall bow down in his presence."

RESPONSORIAL PSALM *Psalm 91:1–2, 10–11, 12–13, 14–15 (see 15b)*

R. Be with me, Lord, when I am in trouble.

You who dwell in the shelter of the Most High,
    who abide in the shadow of the Almighty,
say to the LORD, "My refuge and fortress,
    my God, in whom I trust."   R.

No evil shall befall you,
    nor affliction come near your tent,
for to his angels he has given command
        about you,
that they guard you in all your ways.   R.

Upon their hands they shall bear you up,
    lest you dash your foot against a stone.
You shall tread upon the asp and the viper;
    you shall trample down the lion and
        the dragon.   R.

Because he clings to me, I will deliver him;
    I will set him on high because he
        acknowledges my name.

He shall call upon me, and I will answer him;
    I will be with him in distress;
I will deliver him and glorify him.   R.

READING II *Romans 10:8–13*

Brothers and sisters: What does Scripture say? / *The word is near you, / in your mouth and in your heart /* —that is, the word of faith that we preach —, for, if you confess with your mouth that Jesus is Lord and believe in your heart that God raised him from the dead, you will be saved. For one believes with the heart and so is justified, and one confesses with the mouth and so is saved. For the Scripture says, *No one who believes in him will be put to shame.* For there is no distinction between Jew and Greek; the same Lord is Lord of all, enriching all who call upon him. For "everyone who calls on the name of the Lord will be saved."

GOSPEL *Luke 4:1–13*

Filled with the Holy Spirit, Jesus returned from the Jordan and was led by the Spirit into the desert for forty days, to be tempted by the devil. He ate nothing during those days, and when they were over he was hungry. The devil said to him, "If you are the Son of God, command this stone to become bread." Jesus answered him, "It is written, *One does not live on bread alone.*" Then he took him up and showed him all the kingdoms of the world in a single instant. The devil said to him, "I shall give to you all this power and glory; for it has been handed over to me, and I may give it to whomever I wish. All this will be yours, if you worship me." Jesus said to him in reply, "It is written:
    *You shall worship the Lord,
        your God,
    and him alone shall you serve.*"

Then he led him to Jerusalem, made him stand on the parapet of the temple, and said to him, "If you are the Son of God, throw yourself down from here, for it is written:
    *He will command his angels concerning you,
        to guard you,*

and:

> *With their hands they will support you,*
> *lest you dash your foot against a stone."*

Jesus said to him in reply, "It also says, *You shall not put the Lord, your God, to the test."* When the devil had finished every temptation, he departed from him for a time.

Practice of Faith

Lenten fasting is modeled on Jesus' forty-day fast in the desert. Like Jesus, we fast to remember our dependence on God, and also to to be mindful of those around the world who have little or nothing to eat. ◆ As a gesture of solidarity with the poor, plan very simple, home-cooked, meatless meals for Fridays, and set aside the money usually spent for food and drink towards your local food bank or Operation Rice Bowl, sponsored by Catholic Relief Services. Visit www.crsricebowl.org to learn more. ◆ In addition to traditional forms of Lenten fasting, determine one area of your life that needs conversion. "Fast" from unhealthy behaviors and work on it during this period. ◆ This weekend, people who are preparing for initiation will participate in the Rite of Election in diocesan cathedrals around the world. Learn the names of the elect in your parish and pray for them daily in their final weeks of preparation for the Easter Sacraments of Baptism, Confirmation, and Eucharist.

Download more questions and activities for families, Christian initiation groups, and other adult groups at http://www.ltp.org/t-productsupplements.aspx.

Scripture Insights

Today's Scriptures all touch on the theme of remembering—a key strategy of the spiritual life, especially during Lent. In the First Reading we hear Moses' instructions for the offering of first fruits of the harvest. As the people present their offering they profess their faith by recalling everything God has done for them. Central to all God's care is this event: "He brought us out of Egypt with his strong hand and outstretched arm." Remembering solidifies the people's bond with God. In the Responsorial Psalm, we sing the words of a trusting people, asking for God's protection. How could anyone "abide in the shadow of the Almighty," trust, or cling to God without remembering God's deliverance in the past?

When Paul asks the Romans, "What does Scripture say?" he asks them to remember that *"the word is near . . . in your mouth and in your heart."* He reminds them that the way to salvation is to "confess with your mouth" and "believe in your heart" that Jesus was raised from the dead. This profession of faith is for anyone, whether Jew or Greek. Belief in the risen Lord justifies and saves.

After Jesus' baptism he is "led by the Spirit into the desert for forty days"—often the symbolic number used for periods of testing in Scripture, and the traditional number of days in Lent. Twice the tempter mocks Jesus: "If you are the Son of God. . . ." This was the identity pronounced over Jesus at his baptism by the "voice [that] came from heaven." The devil asks Jesus to forget being the kind of Son of God that would obey the will of the Father and instead be a Son of God with worldly power. Jesus' response shows that he remembers who he is; he recalls the words of Scripture that affirm his commitment to the mission of the Father.

◆ Which of the temptations of Jesus reminds you of what you find tempting?

◆ What favorite Scripture helps you in times of temptation?

◆ What offering will you make to the Lord during Lent?

February 21, 2016 SECOND SUNDAY OF LENT

READING I *Genesis 15:5–12, 17–18*

The Lord God took Abram outside and said, "Look up at the sky and count the stars, if you can. Just so," he added, "shall your descendants be." Abram put his faith in the LORD, who credited it to him as an act of righteousness.

He then said to him, "I am the LORD who brought you from Ur of the Chaldeans to give you this land as a possession." "O Lord GOD," he asked, "how am I to know that I shall possess it?" He answered him, "Bring me a three-year-old heifer, a three-year-old she-goat, a three-year-old ram, a turtledove, and a young pigeon." Abram brought him all these, split them in two, and placed each half opposite the other; but the birds he did not cut up. Birds of prey swooped down on the carcasses, but Abram stayed with them. As the sun was about to set, a trance fell upon Abram, and a deep, terrifying darkness enveloped him.

When the sun had set and it was dark, there appeared a smoking fire pot and a flaming torch, which passed between those pieces. It was on that occasion that the LORD made a covenant with Abram, saying: "To your descendants I give this land, from the Wadi of Egypt to the Great River, the Euphrates."

RESPONSORIAL PSALM
Psalm 27:1, 7–8, 8–9, 13–14 *(see 1a)*

R. The Lord is my light and my salvation.

The LORD is my light and my salvation;
   whom should I fear?
The LORD is my life's refuge;
   of whom should I be afraid? R.

Hear, O LORD, the sound of my call;
   have pity on me, and answer me.
Of you my heart speaks; you my glance seeks. R.

Your presence, O LORD, I seek.
   Hide not your face from me;
do not in anger repel your servant.
   You are my helper: cast me not off. R.

I believe that I shall see the bounty of the LORD
   in the land of the living.

Wait for the LORD with courage;
   be stouthearted, and wait for the LORD. R.

READING II *Philippians 3:17—4:1*

Shorter: Philippians 3:20—4:1

Join with others in being imitators of me, brothers and sisters, and observe those who thus conduct themselves according to the model you have in us. For many, as I have often told you and now tell you even in tears, conduct themselves as enemies of the cross of Christ. Their end is destruction. Their God is their stomach; their glory is in their "shame." Their minds are occupied with earthly things. But our citizenship is in heaven, and from it we also await a savior, the Lord Jesus Christ. He will change our lowly body to conform with his glorified body by the power that enables him also to bring all things into subjection to himself.

Therefore, my brothers and sisters, whom I love and long for, my joy and crown, in this way stand firm in the Lord.

GOSPEL *Luke 9:28b–36*

Jesus took Peter, John, and James and went up the mountain to pray. While he was praying, his face changed in appearance and his clothing became dazzling white. And behold, two men were conversing with him, Moses and Elijah, who appeared in glory and spoke of his exodus that he was going to accomplish in Jerusalem. Peter and his companions had been overcome by sleep, but becoming fully awake, they saw his glory and the two men standing with him. As they were about to part from him, Peter said to Jesus, "Master, it is good that we are here; let us make three tents, one for you, one for Moses, and one for Elijah." But he did not know what he was saying. While he was still speaking, a cloud came and cast a shadow over them, and they became frightened when they entered the cloud. Then from the cloud came a voice that said, "This is my chosen Son; listen to him." After the voice had spoken, Jesus was found alone. They fell silent and did not at that time tell anyone what they had seen.

Practice of Faith

As we hear in today's readings, prayer is the life-blood of our relationship with our loving God. Make daily prayer a priority during Lent. ◆ Discipline yourself to pause throughout the day and offer words of gratitude for all of the blessings given us by God. Set an alarm on your phone to remind you. ◆ Pray on behalf of others. Keep a list of people and concerns in need of God and spend time raising them to God in prayer every day. ◆ Pray in remembrance of Jesus' suffering and death. Set aside time to pray the Rosary and focus on the sorrowful mysteries of Jesus during these weeks of Lent. ◆ Pray with an open, listening heart. Allow time to sit in silence and listen to the voice of Jesus in response to your prayers of praise, gratitude, intercession, and remembrance.

Download more questions and activities for families, Christian initiation groups, and other adult groups at http://www.ltp.org/t-productsupplements.aspx.

Scripture Insights

In today's First Reading we listen in on God's intimate conversation with Abram (who will become Abraham, our father in faith). God promises descendants and Abram trusts the promise, yet he also asks for confirmation. God then instructs Abram in preparing a ritual to seal their covenant—an elaborate animal sacrifice in which God appears as a "smoking fire pot and a flaming torch." To the promise of descendants, the Lord then adds an expanse of land.

Like Abram in the First Reading, the psalmist begins by asserting his confidence in God—that "the Lord is my light and my salvation." Then in the comfort of that trust the psalmist asks for further assurance: "have pity . . . and answer me." The psalm ends with confidence reaffirmed: "I believe that I shall see the bounty of the Lord in the land of the living."

As Paul writes to the Philippians, he is deeply concerned about their fidelity to the Gospel. He has heard reports of some whose lifestyle makes them "enemies of the cross of Christ," and he urges them to be imitators of him instead—not to be taken in by those who "are occupied with earthly things." The passage closes with Paul encouraging the Philippians, "whom I love and long for" to "stand firm in the Lord."

On hearing that Jesus takes his companions up the mountain, we should expect something extraordinary, since in the Scriptures mountaintops are the setting for divine encounter. Jesus' Transfiguration is a theophany, a visible manifestation of his future glory. The appearance of Moses and Elijah places Jesus in the lineage of the Law and the Prophets, which he fulfills through his own mission. That mission will culminate in his suffering, death, and Resurrection. Despite Peter's plea that they stay on the mountain, Jesus sets out for Jerusalem.

◆ In what ways are Abram's and the disciples' experiences of God similar? different?

◆ Who or what would you identify as "enemies of the cross of Christ" today?

◆ Transfigured can also mean "transformed." How can Lent be a time of transformation for you?

47

READING I *Exodus 3:1–8a, 13–15*

Shorter: Exodus 1–3, 7–8, 12–17

Moses was tending the flock of his father-in-law Jethro, the priest of Midian. Leading the flock across the desert, he came to Horeb, the mountain of God. There an angel of the LORD appeared to Moses in fire flaming out of a bush. As he looked on, he was surprised to see that the bush, though on fire, was not consumed. So Moses decided, "I must go over to look at this remarkable sight, and see why the bush is not burned."

When the LORD saw him coming over to look at it more closely, God called out to him from the bush, "Moses! Moses!" He answered, "Here I am." God said, "Come no nearer! Remove the sandals from your feet, for the place where you stand is holy ground. I am the God of your fathers," he continued, "the God of Abraham, the God of Isaac, the God of Jacob." Moses hid his face, for he was afraid to look at God. But the LORD said, "I have witnessed the affliction of my people in Egypt and have heard their cry of complaint against their slave drivers, so I know well what they are suffering. Therefore I have come down to rescue them from the hands of the Egyptians and lead them out of that land into a good and spacious land, a land flowing with milk and honey."

Moses said to God, "But when I go to the Israelites and say to them, 'The God of your fathers has sent me to you,' if they ask me, 'What is his name?' what am I to tell them?" God replied, "I am who am." Then he added, "This is what you shall tell the Israelites: I AM sent me to you."

God spoke further to Moses, "Thus shall you say to the Israelites: The LORD, the God of your fathers, the God of Abraham, the God of Isaac, the God of Jacob, has sent me to you.

"This is my name forever; / thus am I to be remembered through all generations."

RESPONSORIAL PSALM
Psalm 103:1–2, 3–4, 6–7, 8, 11 (8a)

R. The Lord is kind and merciful.

Bless the LORD, O my soul;
    and all my being, bless his holy name.

Bless the LORD, O my soul,
    and forget not all his benefits.   R.

He pardons all your iniquities,
    he heals all your ills,
He redeems your life from destruction,
    he crowns you with kindness
            and compassion.   R.

The LORD secures justice
    and the rights of all the oppressed.
He has made known his ways to Moses,
    and his deeds to the children of Israel.   R.

Merciful and gracious is the LORD,
    slow to anger and abounding in kindness.
For as the heavens are high above the earth,
    so surpassing is his kindness toward those
            who fear him.   R.

READING II *1 Corinthians 10:1–6, 10–12*

I do not want you to be unaware, brothers and sisters, that our ancestors were all under the cloud and all passed through the sea, and all of them were baptized into Moses in the cloud and in the sea. All ate the same spiritual food, and all drank the same spiritual drink, for they drank from a spiritual rock that followed them, and the rock was the Christ. Yet God was not pleased with most of them, for they were struck down in the desert.

These things happened as examples for us, so that we might not desire evil things, as they did. Do not grumble as some of them did, and suffered death by the destroyer. These things happened to them as an example, and they have been written down as a warning to us, upon whom the end of the ages has come. Therefore, whoever thinks he is standing secure should take care not to fall.

GOSPEL *Luke 13:1–9*

Some people told Jesus about the Galileans whose blood Pilate had mingled with the blood of their sacrifices. Jesus said to them in reply, "Do you think that because these Galileans suffered in this way they were greater sinners than all other Galileans? By no means! But I tell you, if you do not repent, you will all perish as they did! Or those eighteen people who were killed when the tower at Siloam fell on them—do you think they were more guilty than everyone else who lived in Jerusalem? By no means! But I tell you, if you do not repent, you will all perish as they did!"

And he told them this parable: "There once was a person who had a fig tree planted in his orchard, and when he came in search of fruit on it but found none, he said to the gardener, 'For three years now I have come in search of fruit on this fig tree but have found none. So cut it down. Why should it exhaust the soil?' He said to him in reply, 'Sir, leave it for this year also, and I shall cultivate the ground around it and fertilize it; it may bear fruit in the future. If not you can cut it down.'"

Practice of Faith

In today's Gospel, Jesus calls the people of his time to repentance. The Hebrew word for *repentance* means "to turn around, retrace our steps, or change direction." The Greek word, *metanoia*, means "to radically change one's mind, outlook, and behaviors." Repentance, then, implies a change of heart and requires a conscious decision to be open to such change in all facets of our lives. ◆ The first step to *metanoia* is an inventory of what needs to change. Visit http://www.usccb.org/prayer-and-worship/sacraments-and-sacramentals/penance/examinations-of-conscience.cfm for examples of a personal examination of conscience. ◆ In response to Jesus' call to repentance and as an outward sign of *metanoia*, celebrate the Sacrament of Reconciliation, perhaps at your parish's Lenten penance service. ◆ The *Catechism of the Catholic Church* speaks beautifully of conversion as an ongoing process in paragraphs 1427–1429. Find the text at http://www.vatican.va/archive/ENG0015/_P49.HTM.

Download more questions and activities for families, Christian initiation groups, and other adult groups at http://www.ltp.org/t-productsupplements.aspx.

Scripture Insights

The geographical settings of Scripture stories are rarely incidental. For ancient peoples, mountains, as we saw last week, were the place of encounter with the deity, the place of revelation. It was on mountaintops that the Chosen People met their God and received instruction, as did Moses on Mt. Horeb in today's First Reading. God appears to Moses as something extraordinary within the ordinary landscape, and once he has Moses' attention, explains that he is "the God of your fathers." Moses is to be part of God's plan to save the people, and so Moses receives his mission. Like Abram, Moses needs more assurance—a name to give the people. God tells him to say, "I AM sent me to you" so that they will make God known "through all generations."

Today's Responsorial Psalm seems tailored to the First Reading as it recounts God's generous care: "He has made known his ways to Moses, and his deeds to the children of Israel." He is indeed "kind and merciful."

Paul instructs the believers in Corinth on their ancestors in faith who were "baptized into Moses"—a different sort of baptism than that of Christ. Nevertheless, Paul asserts, Christ was with the people all the while: "they drank from a spiritual rock that followed them, and the rock was the Christ." Still, God was not pleased with the grumbling of some of the Israelites, and that serves as a warning to the quarrelsome Corinthians.

Today's two-part Gospel presents Jesus' teachings on sin. His remarks about the two calamitous events are intended to counter popular belief that all misfortunes were punishments for sin. At the same time, everyone must take responsibility for turning away from sin. The parable of the fig tree illustrates God's great patience with our efforts and his mercy to those who accept his grace to bear fruit.

◆ What, from these readings, gives you insight for your lenten journey?

◆ How do you understand God's name, "I am who am"?

◆ What do you think are the fruits of your spiritual efforts?

READING I *Exodus 17:3–7*

In those days, in their thirst for water, the people grumbled against Moses, saying, "Why did you ever make us leave Egypt? Was it just to have us die here of thirst with our children and our live-stock?" So Moses cried out to the LORD, "What shall I do with this people? A little more and they will stone me!" The LORD answered Moses, "Go over there in front of the people, along with some of the elders of Israel, holding in your hand, as you go, the staff with which you struck the river. I will be standing there in front of you on the rock in Horeb. Strike the rock, and the water will flow from it for the people to drink." This Moses did, in the presence of the elders of Israel. The place was called Massah and Meribah, because the Israelites quarreled there and tested the LORD, say-ing, "Is the LORD in our midst or not?"

RESPONSORIAL PSALM
Psalm 95:1–2, 6–7, 8–9 (8)

R. If today you hear his voice, harden not
   your hearts.

Come, let us sing joyfully to the LORD;
   let us acclaim the Rock of our salvation.
Let us come into his presence with thanksgiving;
   let us joyfully sing psalms to him.

Come, let us bow down in worship;
   let us kneel before the LORD who made us.
For he is our God,
   and we are the people he shepherds, the flock
      he guides.

Oh, that today you would hear his voice:
   "Harden not your hearts as at Meribah,
   as in the day of Massah in the desert.
Where your fathers tempted me;
   they tested me though they had seen my works."

READING II *Romans 5:1–2, 5–8*

Brothers and sisters: Since we have been justified by faith, we have peace with God through our Lord Jesus Christ, through whom we have gained access by faith to this grace in which we stand, and we boast in hope of the glory of God.

And hope does not disappoint, because the love of God has been poured out into our hearts through the Holy Spirit who has been given to us. For Christ, while we were still helpless, died at the appointed time for the ungodly. Indeed, only with difficulty does one die for a just person, though perhaps for a good person one might even find courage to die. But God proves his love for us in that while we were still sinners Christ died for us.

GOSPEL
John 4:5–15, 19b–26, 39a, 40–42

Longer: John 4:5–42

Jesus came to a town of Samaria called Sychar, near the plot of land that Jacob had given to his son Joseph. Jacob's well was there. Jesus, tired from his journey, sat down there at the well. It was about noon.

A woman of Samaria came to draw water. Jesus said to her, "Give me a drink." His disciples had gone into the town to buy food. The Samaritan woman said to him, "How can you, a Jew, ask me, a Samaritan woman, for a drink?"—For Jews use nothing in common with Samaritans.—Jesus answered and said to her, "If you knew the gift of God and who is saying to you, 'Give me a drink,' you would have asked him and he would have given you living water." The woman said to him, "Sir, you do not even have a bucket and the cistern is deep; where then can you get this living water? Are you greater than our father Jacob, who gave us this cistern and drank from it himself with his children and his flocks?" Jesus answered and said to her, "Everyone who drinks this water will be thirsty again; but whoever drinks the water I shall give will never thirst; the water I shall give will become in him a spring of water welling up to eternal life." The woman said to him, "Sir, give me this water, so that I may not be thirsty or have to keep coming here to draw water.

"I can see that you are a prophet. Our ances-tors worshiped on this mountain; but you people say that the place to worship is in Jerusalem." Jesus said to her, "Believe me, woman, the hour is coming when you will worship the Father neither on this mountain nor in Jerusalem. You people worship what you do not understand; we worship what we understand, because salvation is from the Jews. But the hour is coming, and is now here, when true worshipers will worship the Father in Spirit and truth; and indeed the Father seeks such people to worship him. God is Spirit, and those who worship him must worship in Spirit and truth." The woman said to him, "I know that the Messiah is coming, the one called the Christ; when he comes, he will tell us everything." Jesus said to her, "I am he, the one speaking with you."

Many of the Samaritans of that town began to believe in him. When the Samaritans came to him, they invited him to stay with them; and he stayed there two days. Many more began to believe in him because of his word, and they said to the woman, "We no longer believe because of your word; for we have heard for ourselves, and we know that this is truly the savior of the world."

Practice of Hope

The key image in today's readings is living water. Christians first experience this living water through Baptism. During Lent the elect are preparing for Baptism, and the rest of us accompany them as we prepare to renew our baptismal vows at Easter. ◆ Rediscover the powerful reality of your Baptism. Focus your prayer this week on our baptismal promises so that you will be ready to renew them at Easter. ◆ On the Third, Fourth, and Fifth Sundays of Lent the elect experience the Scrutinies, during which the community asks God to remove obstacles that hinder living out the Gospel values. ◆ Baptism is central to Lenten spirituality. Notice how the symbol of water appears in the Sunday Scriptures during these weeks.

Download more questions and activities for families, Christian initiation groups, and other adult groups at http://www.ltp.org/t-productsupplements.aspx.

Scripture Insights

Today's readings from Year A are proclaimed when the First Scrutiny is celebrated for those preparing for Baptism at the Easter Vigil (the elect), and the readings are all about water. In spite of their liberation from slavery, the all-too-human Israelites are grumbling. Hardhearted because of their thirst and fear, they challenge Moses' leadership. Moses turns to God and his response is immediate and compassionate. The people were freed by walking through the waters of the Red Sea; now they will be refreshed by water gushing from the rock. God instructs Moses to use the same staff to strike the rock that he used to strike the river. Now the people have the answer to their question, "Is the LORD in our midst or not?"

In the Responsorial Psalm we can easily recognize elements of the story in the First Reading: "harden not your hearts," "Massah in the desert," "your fathers tempted me." In addition to the image of God as shepherd, the psalmist calls God "the Rock of our salvation"—and so God is the source of both living and salvation.

Paul instructs the Christians in Rome on one of his favorite themes: we are justified by the grace of God through Christ and not by our own effort. He asks: could you die even for a good person? Imagine, then, how astonishing it is that Christ died for us "while we were still sinners."

The story of Jesus' encounter with the Samaritan woman is the first in a trilogy of readings from John on the Third, Fourth and Fifth Sundays of Lent. Jesus' revelation "I am he, the one speaking with you" is one of several "I am" statements found in John's Gospel account. The entire story is rich with images of Baptism, Eucharist, and Reconciliation. In this intimate dialogue, Jesus reveals himself as the Messiah who comes from the Father to give water to all who thirst for eternal life.

◆ What baptismal images do you detect in these readings?

◆ How are the elect incorporated into the life of your parish?

◆ What do you still thirst for as you approach the celebration of Easter?

READING I *Joshua 5:9a, 10–12*

The LORD said to Joshua, "Today I have removed the reproach of Egypt from you."

While the Israelites were encamped at Gilgal on the plains of Jericho, they celebrated the Passover on the evening of the fourteenth of the month. On the day after the Passover, they ate of the produce of the land in the form of unleavened cakes and parched grain. On that same day after the Passover, on which they ate of the produce of the land, the manna ceased. No longer was there manna for the Israelites, who that year ate of the yield of the land of Canaan.

RESPONSORIAL PSALM
Psalm 34:2–3, 4–5, 6–7 (9a)

R. Taste and see the goodness of the Lord.

I will bless the LORD at all times;
    his praise shall be ever in my mouth.
Let my soul glory in the LORD;
    the lowly will hear me and be glad. R.

Glorify the LORD with me,
    let us together extol his name.
I sought the LORD, and he answered me
    and delivered me from all my fears. R.

Look to him that you may be radiant with joy,
    and your faces may not blush with shame.
When the poor one called out, the LORD heard,
    and from all his distress he saved him. R.

READING II *2 Corinthians 5:17–21*

Brothers and sisters: Whoever is in Christ is a new creation: the old things have passed away; behold, new things have come. And all this is from God, who has reconciled us to himself through Christ and given us the ministry of reconciliation, namely, God was reconciling the world to himself in Christ, not counting their trespasses against them and entrusting to us the message of reconciliation. So we are ambassadors for Christ, as if God were appealing through us. We implore you on behalf of Christ, be reconciled to God. For our sake he made him to be sin who did not know sin, so that we might become the righteousness of God in him.

GOSPEL *Luke 15:1–3, 11–32*

Tax collectors and sinners were all drawing near to listen to Jesus, but the Pharisees and scribes began to complain, saying, "This man welcomes sinners and eats with them." So to them Jesus addressed this parable: "A man had two sons, and the younger son said to his father, 'Father give me the share of your estate that should come to me.' So the father divided the property between them. After a few days, the younger son collected all his belongings and set off to a distant country where he squandered his inheritance on a life of dissipation. When he had freely spent everything, a severe famine struck that country, and he found himself in dire need. So he hired himself out to one of the local citizens who sent him to his farm to tend the swine. And he longed to eat his fill of the pods on which the swine fed, but nobody gave him any. Coming to his senses he thought, 'How many of my father's hired workers have more than enough food to eat, but here am I, dying from hunger. I shall get up and go to my father and I shall say to him, "Father, I have sinned against heaven and against you. I no longer deserve to be called your son; treat me as you would treat one of your hired workers."' So he got up and went back to his father. While he was still a long way off, his father caught sight of him, and was filled with compassion. He ran to his son, embraced him and kissed him. His son said to him, 'Father, I have sinned against heaven and against you; I no longer deserve to be called your son.' But his father ordered his servants, 'Quickly bring the finest robe and put it on him; put a ring on his finger and sandals on his feet. Take the fattened calf and slaughter it. Then let us celebrate with a feast, because this son of mine was dead, and has come to life again; he was lost, and has been found.' Then the celebration began. Now the older son had been out in the field and, on his way back, as he neared the house, he heard the sound of music and dancing. He called one of the servants and asked what this might mean. The servant said to him, 'Your brother has returned and your father has slaughtered the fattened calf because he has him back safe and sound.' He became angry, and when he refused to enter the house, his father came out and pleaded with him. He said to his father in reply, 'Look, all these years I served you and not once did I disobey your orders; yet you never gave me even a young goat to feast on with my friends. But when your son returns who swallowed up your property with prostitutes, for him you slaughter the fattened calf.' He said to him, 'My son, you are here with me always; everything I have is yours. But now we must celebrate and rejoice, because your brother was dead and has come to life again; he was lost and has been found.'"

Practice of Charity

Today's readings remind us that people facing hunger find it hard to know that God is present. God provided for the Israelites with "manna" from heaven. Today, as members of God's family, we are called provide for the hungry. ◆ Helping Hands is a program that provides nutritious meals for people in developing countries who are suffering from food shortages and famine. Learn how you can participate in ending hunger with your local community at http://helpinghands.crs.org/. ◆ Every extended family has a "black sheep." Try to locate and connect with someone you know who is "lost" to the family, and begin the steps to reconciliation. ◆ In three weeks it will be Easter. Purify your home as well as your life. In addition to spring cleaning, pick out one item every day between now and Easter that you no longer use or need. Donate these items to a local agency.

Download more questions and activities for families, Christian initiation groups, and other adult groups at http://www.ltp.org/t-productsupplements.aspx.

Scripture Insights

The events recorded in the Book of Joshua were especially important for the Israelites. At this point they have completed their pilgrimage. The Lord has "removed the reproach of Egypt"—the people have been freed from Egyptian slavery and are in the land of Canaan. They can worship their God. They do not need to rely on the manna God provided in their exile; now they can offer God the produce of their own work in thanksgiving.

In eating their own harvest in the promised land, the people could indeed "taste and see the goodness of the Lord," as the refrain of the psalm suggests. To "bless the LORD" (first verse) means simply to express delight in the Lord's blessings and gratitude for whatever those blessings might be.

Paul's powerful teaching for the Corinthians describes the mission of Jesus and his own ministry as reconciliation. "God was reconciling the world to himself in Christ"—it is a universal reconciliation. Christ will make all things new; the "old things have passed away." Paul understands that the continuation of God's reconciliation through Christ has been entrusted to him, and by analogy, to all those who are "in Christ." They (we) are "ambassadors for Christ."

The parable of the Prodigal Son is one of the most familiar in Jesus' teaching ministry, and it offers rich images and insights for Lent. Consider the many contrasts in the reading: the close-mindedness of the scribes and Pharisees and the openness of the Father's heart; the wayward but humbled younger son and his obedient but proud older brother; the grievous errors of the younger son and the extravagantly welcome response of his father; the son's self-description as no better than a hired hand and the father's insistence on calling him "my son." Any of these would stimulate reflection on this wonderful parable.

◆ What phrases in today's readings point to the celebration of the Paschal Mystery (the dying and rising of Christ)?

◆ Have you ever felt distant from the love of the Father?

◆ How are you an ambassador of reconciliation?

READING I
1 Samuel 16:1b, 6–7, 10–13a

The LORD said to Samuel: "Fill your horn with oil, and be on your way. I am sending you to Jesse of Bethlehem, for I have chosen my king from among his sons."

As Jesse and his sons came to the sacrifice, Samuel looked at Eliab and thought, "Surely the LORD's anointed is here before him." But the LORD said to Samuel: "Do not judge from his appearance or from his lofty stature, because I have rejected him. Not as man sees does God see, because man sees the appearance but the LORD looks into the heart." In the same way Jesse presented seven sons before Samuel, but Samuel said to Jesse, "The LORD has not chosen any one of these." Then Samuel asked Jesse, "Are these all the sons you have?" Jesse replied, "There is still the youngest, who is tending the sheep." Samuel said to Jesse, "Send for him; we will not begin the sacrificial banquet until he arrives here." Jesse sent and had the young man brought to them. He was ruddy, a youth handsome to behold and making a splendid appearance. The LORD said, "There—anoint him, for this is the one!" Then Samuel, with the horn of oil in hand, anointed David in the presence of his brothers; and from that day on, the spirit of the LORD rushed upon David.

READING II *Ephesians 5:8–14*

Brothers and sisters: You were once darkness, but now you are light in the Lord. Live as children of light, for light produces every kind of goodness and righteousness and truth. Try to learn what is pleasing to the Lord. Take no part in the fruitless works of darkness; rather expose them, for it is shameful even to mention the things done by them in secret; but everything exposed by the light becomes visible, for everything that becomes visible is light. Therefore, it says:
    "Awake, O sleeper,
    and arise from the dead,
    and Christ will give you light."

GOSPEL *John 9:1–41*
Shorter: John 9:1, 6–9, 13–17, 34–38

As Jesus passed by he saw a man blind from birth. His disciples asked him, "Rabbi, who sinned, this man or his parents, that he was born blind?" Jesus answered, "Neither he nor his parents sinned; it is so that the works of God might be made visible through him. We have to do the works of the one who sent me while it is day. Night is coming when no one can work. While I am in the world, I am the light of the world." When he had said this, he spat on the ground and made clay with the saliva, and smeared the clay on his eyes, and said to him, "Go wash in the Pool of Siloam"—which means Sent—. So he went and washed, and came back able to see.

His neighbors and those who had seen him earlier as a beggar said, "Isn't this the one who used to sit and beg?" Some said, "It is," but others said, "No, he just looks like him." He said, "I am." So they said to him, "How were your eyes opened?" He replied, "The man called Jesus made clay and anointed my eyes and told me, 'Go to Siloam and wash.' So I went there and washed and was able to see." And they said to him, "Where is he?" He said, "I don't know."

They brought the one who was once blind to the Pharisees. Now Jesus had made clay and opened his eyes on a sabbath. So then the Pharisees also asked him how he was able to see. He said to them, "He put clay on my eyes, and I washed, and now I can see." So some of the Pharisees said, "This man is not from God, because he does not keep the sabbath." But others said, "How can a sinful man do such signs?" And there was a division among them. So they said to the blind man again, "What do you have to say about him, since he opened your eyes?" He said, "He is a prophet."

Now the Jews did not believe that he had been blind and gained his sight until they summoned the parents of the one who had gained his sight. They asked them, "Is this your son, who you say was born blind? How does he now see?" His parents answered and said, "We know that this is our son and that he was born blind. We do not know how he sees now, nor do we know who opened his eyes. Ask him, he is of age; he can speak for himself." His parents said this because they were afraid of the Jews, for the Jews had already agreed that if anyone acknowledged him as the Christ, he would be expelled from the synagogue. For this reason his parents said, "He is of age; question him."

So a second time they called the man who had been blind and said to him, "Give God the praise! We know that this man is a sinner." He replied, "If he is a sinner, I do not know. One thing I do know is that I was blind and now I see." So they said to him, "What did he do to you? How did he open your eyes?" He answered them, "I told you already and you did not listen. Why do you want to hear it again? Do you want to become his disciples, too?" They ridiculed him and said, "You are that man's disciple; we are disciples of Moses! We know that God spoke to Moses, but we do not know where this one is from." The man answered and said to them, "This is what is so amazing, that you do not know where he is from, yet he opened my eyes. We know that God does not listen to sinners, but if one is devout and does his will, he listens to him. It is unheard of that anyone ever opened the eyes of a person born blind. If this man were not from God, he would not be able to do anything." They answered and said to him, "You were born totally in sin, and are you trying to teach us?" Then they threw him out.

When Jesus heard that they had thrown him out, he found him and said, "Do you believe in the Son of Man?" He answered and said, "Who is he, sir, that I may believe in him?" Jesus said to him, "You have seen him, and the one speaking with you is he." He said, "I do believe, Lord," and he worshiped him. Then Jesus said, "I came into this world for judgment, so that those who do not see might see, and those who do see might become blind."

Some of the Pharisees who were with him heard this and said to him, "Surely we are not also blind, are we?" Jesus said to them, "If you were blind, you would have no sin; but now you are saying, 'We see,' so your sin remains."

Scripture Insights

For Jews, David is especially beloved in the great story of the Chosen People. Christians have an additional attraction: the selection of the boy David as king prefigures the role of Jesus generations later. David is the eighth son of Jesse, and the first seven are rejected by God. The number seven was regarded as a sign of fulfillment or completeness. David is an unlikely choice because he is a shepherd. Yet David is clearly God's choice; his anointing is a sign of God's favor. The statement, "not as man sees does God see" will apply to much of Jesus' ministry.

Today's Responsorial Psalm echoes David's image as shepherd boy and Jesus' care for the man born blind, who is considered a lost sheep.

Paul contrasts the Ephesians' prebaptismal lives of sinfulness with their new lives by saying, "You were once darkness, but now you are light in the Lord." This new identity behooves them to live as children of the light who produce "every kind of goodness and righteousness and truth."

The story of the man born blind unfolds in a series of conversations: between Jesus and his disciples, Jesus and the blind man, and the Pharisees' interrogation of the blind man and his parents after the man has received his sight. Jesus' play on the words describing those who have sight as blind and those who are blind being able to see identifies the Pharisees perfectly. They have failed to see Jesus' identity ("this man is not from God"). John presents the story as another of the "I am" revelations of Jesus, this time in the context of a contrast between sight and blindness, darkness and light. Jesus is the one who dispels the darkness and gives sight to the blind, both physically and spiritually.

◆ What threads do you see connecting these readings with Easter?

◆ Have you noticed any "blind spots" in your spiritual outlook?

◆ When had you encountered a difficult situation that led you to "give God the praise?"

Download more questions and activities for families, Christian initiation groups, and other adult groups at http://www.ltp.org/t-productsupplements.aspx.

March 13, 2016 Fifth Sunday of Lent

Reading I *Isaiah 43:16–21*

Thus says the Lord,
  who opens a way in the sea
  and a path in the mighty waters,
who leads out chariots and horsemen,
  a powerful army,
till they lie prostrate together, never to rise,
  snuffed out and quenched like a wick.
Remember not the events of the past,
  the things of long ago consider not;
see, I am doing something new!
  Now it springs forth, do you not perceive it?
In the desert I make a way;
  in the wasteland, rivers.
Wild beasts honor me,
  jackals and ostriches,
for I put water in the desert
  and rivers in the wasteland
  for my chosen people to drink,
the people whom I formed for myself,
  that they might announce my praise.

Responsorial Psalm
Psalm 126:1–2, 2–3, 4–5, 6 (3)

R. The Lord has done great things for us; we are
      filled with joy.

When the Lord brought back the captives
            of Zion,
  we were like men dreaming.
Then our mouth was filled with laughter,
  and our tongue with rejoicing.   R.

Then they said among the nations,
  "The Lord has done great things for them."
The Lord has done great things for us;
  we are glad indeed.   R.

Restore our fortunes, O Lord,
  like the torrents in the southern desert.
Those that sow in tears
  shall reap rejoicing.   R.

Although they go forth weeping,
  carrying the seed to be sown,
they shall come back rejoicing,
  carrying their sheaves.   R.

Reading II *Philippians 3:8–14*

Brothers and sisters: I consider everything as a loss because of the supreme good of knowing Christ Jesus my Lord. For his sake I have accepted the loss of all things and I consider them so much rubbish, that I may gain Christ and be found in him, not having any righteousness of my own based on the law but that which comes through faith in Christ, the righteousness from God, depending on faith to know him and the power of his resurrection and the sharing of his sufferings by being conformed to his death, if somehow I may attain the resurrection from the dead.

It is not that I have already taken hold of it or have already attained perfect maturity, but I continue my pursuit in hope that I may possess it, since I have indeed been taken possession of by Christ Jesus. Brothers and sisters, I for my part do not consider myself to have taken possession. Just one thing: forgetting what lies behind but straining forward to what lies ahead, I continue my pursuit toward the goal, the prize of God's upward calling, in Christ Jesus.

Gospel *John 8:1–11*

Jesus went to the Mount of Olives. But early in the morning he arrived again in the temple area, and all the people started coming to him, and he sat down and taught them. Then the scribes and the Pharisees brought a woman who had been caught in adultery and made her stand in the middle. They said to him, "Teacher, this woman was caught in the very act of committing adultery. Now in the law, Moses commanded us to stone such women. So what do you say?" They said this to test him, so that they could have some charge to bring against him. Jesus bent down and began to write on the ground with his finger. But when they continued asking him, he straightened up and said to them, "Let the one among you who is without sin be the first to throw a stone at her." Again he bent down and wrote on the ground. And in response, they went away one by one, beginning with the elders. So he was left alone with the woman before him. Then Jesus straightened up and said to her,

"Woman, where are they? Has no one condemned you?" She replied, "No one, sir." Then Jesus said, "Neither do I condemn you. Go, and from now on do not sin any more."

Practice of Hope

There is a saying: "We cannot know the heart of another human being." The religious leaders tried to test Jesus and trick him into judging the woman publicly accused of adultery. Jesus responded by challenging every person in the crowd, and all of us, to look inward with a healthy dose of honest self-reflection. ◆ Embark on a different sort of fasting—from judging others. Instead, try to see others through the eyes of compassion, as Jesus modeled the practice. ◆ Reach out to someone you know who is recently divorced. Invite the person to coffee or over for dinner and offer a loving, listening heart. ◆ Remaining committed to the Sacrament of Marriage is not easy. A program called *Retrouvaille* offers a lifeline to marriages in trouble and the possibility of healing through the Paschal Mystery of Christ's death and Resurrection. Visit www.retrouvaille.org to learn about the hopeful assistance offered to those struggling in their marriages.

Download more questions and activities for families, Christian initiation groups, and other adult groups at http://www.ltp.org/t-productsupplements.aspx.

Scripture Insights

The people Isaiah addresses know their ancient history, that God's rescued them from subjection by the Egyptians. But they are also painfully aware of more recent events—their exile in Babylon. Isaiah calls on them to "remember not," to shift from the ancient rescue and focus on a new deliverance that God is preparing. This is not to disregard their history but to recognize a new future before them; they remain the Chosen People. The path through the "mighty waters" is a symbol of their regeneration as a people.

Today's psalm expresses the unbelievable joy over God's return of the captives from exile: "we were like men dreaming!" God's actions have changed their weeping to rejoicing and restored their fortunes like torrents of water over the desert.

Paul writes passionately about his conversion, "the supreme good of knowing Christ Jesus my Lord." Now that Paul has gained Christ in his life he considers his past as "so much rubbish." This was God's doing and not through any "righteousness" of his own. He knows his mission is not yet complete, and compares himself to an athlete who strains toward the goal. Near the end of his life he will return to this analogy when he confesses that he has run the race and kept the faith (2 Timothy 4:6–8).

The story of the woman caught in adultery is one of the most dramatic teachings about forgiveness in Jesus' ministry. The line "let the one among you who is without sin" has made its way into popular discourse on many occasions. According to the Law, adultery was punishable by stoning, and the scribes and Pharisees attempt to catch Jesus in a trap: will he uphold the Law or will he persist in his teaching on forgiveness? When they walk away they acknowledge their own judgment. Once again Jesus extends compassion to one who has sinned.

◆ How do you interpret the Lenten message in the Gospel story?

◆ In what ways does Paul's personal struggle remind you of a similar experience in your own life?

◆ What do you believe is "something new" that awaits you in your life in Christ?

READING I *Ezekiel 37:12–14*

Thus says the LORD God: O my people, I will open your graves and have you rise from them, and bring you back to the land of Israel. Then you shall know that I am the LORD, when I open your graves and have you rise from them, O my people! I will put my spirit in you that you may live, and I will settle you upon your land; thus you shall know that I am the LORD. I have promised, and I will do it, says the LORD.

RESPONSORIAL PSALM
Psalm 130:1–2, 3–4, 5–6, 7–8 (7)

R. With the Lord there is mercy, and fullness
    of redemption.

Out of the depths I cry to you, O LORD;
    LORD, hear my voice!
Let your ears be attentive
    to my voice in supplication. R.

If you, O LORD, mark iniquities,
    LORD, who can stand?
But with you is forgiveness
    that you may be revered. R.

I trust in the LORD;
    my soul trusts in his word.
More than sentinels wait for the dawn,
    let Israel wait for the LORD. R.

For with the LORD is kindness
    and with him is plenteous redemption;
and he will redeem Israel
    from all their iniquities. R.

READING II *Romans 8:8–11*

Brothers and sisters: Those who are in the flesh cannot please God. But you are not in the flesh; on the contrary, you are in the spirit, if only the Spirit of God dwells in you. Whoever does not have the Spirit of Christ does not belong to him. But if Christ is in you, although the body is dead because of sin, the spirit is alive because of righteousness. If the Spirit of the One who raised Jesus from the dead dwells in you, the One who raised Christ from the dead will give life to your mortal bodies also, through his Spirit dwelling in you.

GOSPEL
John 11:3–7, 17, 20–27, 33b–45

Longer: John 11:1–45

The sisters of Lazarus sent word to Jesus, saying, "Master, the one you love is ill." When Jesus heard this he said, "This illness is not to end in death, but is for the glory of God, that the Son of God may be glorified through it." Now Jesus loved Martha and her sister and Lazarus. So when he heard that he was ill, he remained for two days in the place where he was. Then after this he said to his disciples, "Let us go back to Judea."

When Jesus arrived, he found that Lazarus had already been in the tomb for four days. When Martha heard that Jesus was coming, she went to meet him; but Mary sat at home. Martha said to Jesus, "Lord, if you had been here, my brother would not have died. But even now I know that whatever you ask of God, God will give you." Jesus said to her, "Your brother will rise." Martha said, "I know he will rise, in the resurrection on the last day." Jesus told her, "I am the resurrection and the life; whoever believes in me, even if he dies, will live, and everyone who lives and believes in me will never die. Do you believe this?" She said to him, "Yes, Lord. I have come to believe that you are the Christ, the Son of God, the one who is coming into the world."

He became perturbed and deeply troubled, and said, "Where have you laid him?" They said to him, "Sir, come and see." And Jesus wept. So the Jews said, "See how he loved him." But some of them said, "Could not the one who opened the eyes of the blind man have done something so that this man would not have died?"

So Jesus, perturbed again, came to the tomb. It was a cave, and a stone lay across it. Jesus said, "Take away the stone." Martha, the dead man's sister, said to him, "Lord, by now there will be a stench; he has been dead for four days." Jesus said to her, "Did I not tell you that if you believe you will see the glory of God?" So they took away the stone. And Jesus raised his eyes and said, "Father, I thank you for hearing me. I know that you always hear me; but because of the crowd here I have said this, that they may believe that you sent me." And when he had said this, he cried out in a loud voice, "Lazarus, come out!" The dead man came out, tied hand and foot with burial bands, and his face was wrapped in a cloth. So Jesus said to them, "Untie him and let him go."

Now many of the Jews who had come to Mary and seen what he had done began to believe in him.

Practice of Hope

The Catholic Church offers the faithful a series of beautiful and comforting rituals for each stage in the process of dying. Throughout the *Order of Christian Funerals* we hear it proclaimed that "life is changed, not ended." While our earthly bodies return to dust, our spirit remains alive, in Christ. ◆ Many parishes, retreat centers, and funeral homes offer consolation to those who have lost a loved one through bereavement ministries. Discover the offerings for the bereaved in your local area and how you can support this life-giving ministry. ◆ Reach out to someone you know who is recently widowed. Accompany them on a visit to the cemetery and listen with an open heart to their cherished memories. ◆ During these last days of Lent, the "elect" are presented with two treasures of Christianity: The Creed and the Lord's Prayer. Dedicate some of your prayer time this week to meditating on these prayers in solidarity with all those preparing to die to their old selves and rise to new life in Christ through Baptism.

Download more questions and activities for families, Christian initiation groups, and other adult groups at http://www.ltp.org/t-productsupplements.aspx.

Scripture Insights

God's declaration through Ezekiel is a promise of new life for Israel as it waits in exile. The graves will be opened, the dead will rise, and the exiled will be brought "back to the land of Israel." God's promise extends over the living and the dead, and what the Lord has promised will be done.

Psalm 130 is one of the most expressive penitential psalms: "Out of the depths I cry to you, O LORD." Admitting that his sins are unpardonable, nevertheless the psalmist trusts that "with you is forgiveness." The sinner waits for the Lord like the sentinel waits for dawn, trusting that "With the Lord there is mercy, and fullness of redemption."

Paul is trying to teach the Romans the difference between living in the flesh (acting out of the limits of human nature) and living in the spirit (living in concert with the Spirit of God). Life in the spirit is impaired by our sin, but if Christ is in us, the Spirit of God who raised Jesus from the dead will "give life to [our] mortal bodies also."

The Gospel story of the death and raising of Lazarus is a prelude to the events of Jesus' own death and Resurrection. It includes another of the "I am" statements by Jesus. In speaking with Martha he proclaims, "I am the resurrection and the life." Those who believe in him will not be separated from him, even in death. In the midst of the story some bystanders taunt him, asking, "could not the one who opened the eyes of the blind man have done something . . . ?" In a similar way he will be mocked when he is on the cross: "If you are the King of the Jews, save yourself." But Jesus' intention is always to do the will of the Father and never to showcase his power.

◆ In the Gospel, what signs do you see of Jesus' human nature?

◆ In what ways does Martha seem to grasp Jesus' identity; in what ways does she not?

◆ When have you felt entombed and wished to hear Jesus calling "come out!"?

READING I *Isaiah 50:4–7*

The Lord GOD has given me
  a well-trained tongue,
that I might know how to speak to the weary
  a word that will rouse them.
Morning after morning
  he opens my ear that I may hear;
and I have not rebelled,
  have not turned back.
I gave my back to those who beat me,
  my cheeks to those who plucked my beard;
my face I did not shield
  from buffets and spitting.

The Lord GOD is my help,
  therefore I am not disgraced;
I have set my face like flint,
  knowing that I shall not be put to shame.

READING II *Philippians 2:6–11*

Christ Jesus, though he was in the form of God,
  did not regard equality with God
  something to be grasped.
Rather, he emptied himself,
  taking the form of a slave,
  coming in human likeness;
  and found human in appearance,
  he humbled himself,
  becoming obedient to the point of death,
  even death on a cross.
Because of this, God greatly exalted him
  and bestowed on him the name
  which is above every name,
  that at the name of Jesus
  every knee should bend,
  of those in heaven and on earth and under
      the earth,
  and every tongue confess that
  Jesus Christ is Lord,
  to the glory of God the Father.

GOSPEL *Luke 22:14—23:56*

Shorter: Luke 23:1–49

When the hour came, Jesus took his place at table with the apostles. He said to them, "I have eagerly desired to eat this Passover with you before I suffer, for, I tell you, I shall not eat it again until there is fulfillment in the kingdom of God." Then he took a cup, gave thanks, and said, "Take this and share it among yourselves; for I tell you that from this time on I shall not drink of the fruit of the vine until the kingdom of God comes." Then he took the bread, said the blessing, broke it, and gave it to them, saying, "This is my body, which will be given for you; do this in memory of me." And likewise the cup after they had eaten, saying, "This cup is the new covenant in my blood, which will be shed for you.

"And yet behold, the hand of the one who is to betray me is with me on the table; for the Son of Man indeed goes as it has been determined; but woe to that man by whom he is betrayed." And they began to debate among themselves who among them would do such a deed.

Then an argument broke out among them about which of them should be regarded as the greatest. He said to them, "The kings of the Gentiles lord it over them and those in authority over them are addressed as 'Benefactors'; but among you it shall not be so. Rather, let the greatest among you be as the youngest, and the leader as the servant. For who is greater: the one seated at table or the one who serves? Is it not the one seated at table? I am among you as the one who serves. It is you who have stood by me in my trials; and I confer a kingdom on you, just as my Father has conferred one on me, that you may eat and drink at my table in my kingdom; and you will sit on thrones judging the twelve tribes of Israel.

"Simon, Simon, behold Satan has demanded to sift all of you like wheat, but I have prayed that your own faith may not fail; and once you have turned back, you must strengthen your brothers." He said to him, "Lord, I am prepared to go to prison and to die with you." But he replied, "I tell you, Peter, before the cock crows this day, you will deny three times that you know me."

He said to them, "When I sent you forth without a money bag or a sack or sandals, were you in need of anything?" "No, nothing," they replied. He said to them, "But now one who has a money bag should take it, and likewise a sack, and one who does not have a sword should sell his cloak and buy one. For I tell you that this Scripture must be fulfilled in me, namely, *He was counted among the wicked*; and indeed what is written about me is coming to fulfillment." Then they said, "Lord, look, there are two swords here." But he replied, "It is enough!"

Then going out, he went, as was his custom, to the Mount of Olives, and the disciples followed him. When he arrived at the place he said to them, "Pray that you may not undergo the test." After withdrawing about a stone's throw from them and kneeling, he prayed, saying, "Father, if you are willing, take this cup away from me; still, not my will but yours be done." And to strengthen him an angel from heaven appeared to him. He was in such agony and he prayed so fervently that his sweat became like drops of blood falling on the ground. When he rose from prayer and returned to his disciples, he found them sleeping from grief. He said to them, "Why are you sleeping? Get up and pray that you may not undergo the test."

While he was still speaking, a crowd approached and in front was one of the Twelve, a man named Judas. He went up to Jesus to kiss him. Jesus said to him, "Judas, are you betraying the Son of Man with a kiss?" His disciples realized what was about to happen, and they asked, "Lord, shall we strike with a sword?" And one of them struck the high priest's servant and cut off his right ear. But Jesus said in reply, "Stop, no more of this!" Then he touched the servant's ear and healed him. And Jesus said to the chief priests and temple guards and elders who had come for him, "Have you come out as against a robber, with swords and clubs? Day after day I was with you in the temple area, and you did not seize me; but this is your hour, the time for the power of darkness."

After arresting him they led him away and took him into the house of the high priest; Peter was following at a distance. They lit a fire in the middle of the courtyard and sat around it, and Peter sat down with them. When a maid saw him seated in the light, she looked intently at him and said, "This man too was with him." But he denied it saying, "Woman, I do not know him." A short while later someone else saw him and said, "You too are one of them"; but Peter answered, "My friend, I am not." About an hour later, still another insisted, "Assuredly, this man too was with him, for he also is a Galilean." But Peter said, "My friend, I do not know what you are talking about." Just as he was saying this, the cock crowed, and the Lord turned and looked at Peter; and Peter remembered the word of the Lord, how he had said to him, "Before the cock crows today, you will deny me three times." He went out and began to weep bitterly.

The men who held Jesus in custody were ridiculing and beating him. They blindfolded him and questioned him, saying, "Prophesy! Who is it that struck you?" And they reviled him in saying many other things against him.

When day came the council of elders of the people met, both chief priests and scribes, and they brought him before their Sanhedrin. They said, "If you are the Christ, tell us," but he replied to them, "If I tell you, you will not believe, and if I question, you will not respond. But from this time on the Son of Man will be seated at the right hand of the power of God." They all asked, "Are you then the Son of God?" He replied to them, "You say that I am." Then they said, "What further need have we for testimony? We have heard it from his own mouth."

Then the whole assembly of them arose and brought him before Pilate. They brought charges against him, saying, "We found this man misleading our people; he opposes the payment of taxes to Caesar and maintains that he is the Christ, a king." Pilate asked him, "Are you the king of the Jews?" He said to him in reply, "You say so." Pilate then addressed the chief priests and the crowds, "I find this man not guilty." But they were adamant and said, "He is inciting the people with his teaching throughout all Judea, from Galilee where he began even to here."

On hearing this Pilate asked if the man was a Galilean; and upon learning that he was under

Herod's jurisdiction, he sent him to Herod, who was in Jerusalem at that time. Herod was very glad to see Jesus; he had been wanting to see him for a long time, for he had heard about him and had been hoping to see him perform some sign. He questioned him at length, but he gave him no answer. The chief priests and scribes, meanwhile, stood by accusing him harshly. Herod and his soldiers treated him contemptuously and mocked him, and after clothing him in resplendent garb, he sent him back to Pilate. Herod and Pilate became friends that very day, even though they had been enemies formerly. Pilate then summoned the chief priests, the rulers, and the people and said to them, "You brought this man to me and accused him of inciting the people to revolt. I have conducted my investigation in your presence and have not found this man guilty of the charges you have brought against him, nor did Herod, for he sent him back to us. So no capital crime has been committed by him. Therefore I shall have him flogged and then release him."

But all together they shouted out, "Away with this man! Release Barabbas to us."—Now Barabbas had been imprisoned for a rebellion that had taken place in the city and for murder.—Again Pilate addressed them, still wishing to release Jesus, but they continued their shouting, "Crucify him! Crucify him!" Pilate addressed them a third time, "What evil has this man done? I found him guilty of no capital crime. Therefore I shall have him flogged and then release him." With loud shouts, however, they persisted in calling for his crucifixion, and their voices prevailed. The verdict of Pilate was that their demand should be granted. So he released the man who had been imprisoned for rebellion and murder, for whom they asked, and he handed Jesus over to them to deal with as they wished.

As they led him away they took hold of a certain Simon, a Cyrenian, who was coming in from the country; and after laying the cross on him, they made him carry it behind Jesus. A large crowd of people followed Jesus, including many women who mourned and lamented him. Jesus turned to them and said, "Daughters of Jerusalem, do not weep for me; weep instead for yourselves and for your children for indeed, the days are coming when people will say, 'Blessed are the barren, the wombs that never bore and the breasts that never nursed.' At that time people will say to the mountains, 'Fall upon us!' and to the hills, 'Cover us!' for if these things are done when the wood is green what will happen when it is dry?" Now two others, both criminals, were led away with him to be executed.

When they came to the place called the Skull, they crucified him and the criminals there, one on his right, the other on his left. Then Jesus said, "Father, forgive them, they know not what they do." They divided his garments by casting lots. The people stood by and watched; the rulers, meanwhile, sneered at him and said, "He saved others, let him save himself if he is the chosen one, the Christ of God." Even the soldiers jeered at him. As they approached to offer him wine they called out, "If you are King of the Jews, save yourself." Above him there was an inscription that read, "This is the King of the Jews."

Now one of the criminals hanging there reviled Jesus, saying, "Are you not the Christ? Save yourself and us." The other, however, rebuking him, said in reply, "Have you no fear of God, for you are subject to the same condemnation? And indeed, we have been condemned justly, for the sentence we received corresponds to our crimes, but this man has done nothing criminal." Then he said, "Jesus, remember me when you come into your kingdom." He replied to him, "Amen, I say to you, today you will be with me in Paradise."

It was now about noon and darkness came over the whole land until three in the afternoon because of an eclipse of the sun. Then the veil of the temple was torn down the middle. Jesus cried out in a loud voice, "Father, into your hands I commend my spirit"; and when he had said this he breathed his last.

[Here all kneel and pause for a short time.]

The centurion who witnessed what had happened glorified God and said, "This man was innocent beyond doubt." When all the people who had gathered for this spectacle saw what had happened, they returned home beating their breasts; but all his acquaintances stood at a distance, including the women who had followed him from Galilee and saw these events.

Now there was a virtuous and righteous man named Joseph, who, though he was a member of the council, had not consented to their plan of action. He came from the Jewish town of Arimathea and was awaiting the kingdom of God. He went to Pilate and asked for the body of Jesus. After he had taken the body down, he wrapped it in a linen cloth and laid him in a rock-hewn tomb in which no one had yet been buried. It was the day of preparation, and the sabbath was about to begin. The women who had come from Galilee with him followed behind, and when they had seen the tomb and the way in which his body was laid in it, they returned and prepared spices and perfumed oils. Then they rested on the sabbath according to the commandment.

Practice of Faith

Palm Sunday draws us into Holy Week, which some people observe as a week-long retreat. ◆ Create a meditative tone in your home, with a red cloth, palm branches, Bible, crucifix or candle. ◆ To focus on spiritual essentials, fast in a spirit of penitence on Good. Plan to participate in the holiest liturgies of the year: the Mass of the Lord's Supper on Thursday evening, the Celebration of our Lord's Passion on Friday afternoon, and the Easter Vigil on Saturday evening or Mass on Easter Sunday morning.

Download more questions and activities for families, Christian initiation groups, and other adult groups at http://www.ltp.org/t-productsupplements.aspx.

Scripture Insights

Who is this person with the "well-trained tongue," described so sharply by Isaiah? He suffers grievously for proclaiming God's Word to a hostile people, and has much in common with a figure who appears in three other Isaiah passages, often called the Suffering Servant by Scripture scholars. The Servant trusts resolutely in God, sacrificing everything to fulfill his calling.

The haunting cry of the psalmist, "My God, my God, why have you abandoned me"? is that of Jesus from the Cross—Jesus faithfully praying this very psalm. In the verses of the Psalm and in the Isaiah reading, we Christians see images that remind us of Jesus and the Passion story, even though the texts were written hundreds of years earlier.

Paul's beautiful words about Christ also seem to carry echoes of Isaiah's Suffering Servant. Although Jesus has equality with God he willingly takes "the form of a slave" and becomes to the Father, "obedient to the point of death." In response, God exalts him above everything.

Luke is a master storyteller, and his account of the Passion of Jesus is a tapestry of locations, images, conversations, and details that engage the listener in the drama of Jesus' final hours. Luke's account begins with the Last Supper. The words and actions of Jesus at table prefigure his death and the coming of the Kingdom of God. In some sense Jesus is presented as a willing victim, which echoes the first two readings. Throughout his Gospel account Luke presents Jesus' ministry as one of compassion. On his journey to the Cross Jesus stops to comfort the weeping "daughters of Jerusalem" and on the Cross he extends the promise of eternal life to one of the thieves. The last words of the story summarize Jesus' life: he willingly hands over his spirit; his whole self is offered to the Father.

◆ What part of the Passion narrative do you find most moving this year?

◆ What do you consider to be your personal cross in life?

◆ How can you make the Triduum a spiritually enriching time?

Holy Thursday brings to an end the Forty Days of Lent, which make up the season of anticipation of the great Three Days. Composed of prayer, almsgiving, fasting, and the preparation of the catechumens for Baptism, the season of Lent is now brought to a close, and the Three Days begin as we approach the liturgy of Holy Thursday evening. As those to be initiated into the Church have prepared themselves for their entrance into the fullness of life, so have we been awakening in our hearts, minds, and bodies our own entrances into the life of Christ, experienced in the life of the Church.

Easter Triduum (Latin for "three days") is the center, the core, of the entire year for Christians. These Three Days mark the mystery around which our entire lives are played out. Adults in the community are invited to plan ahead so that the whole time from Thursday night until Easter Sunday is free of social engagements, free of entertainment, and free of meals except for the most basic nourishment. We measure these days—indeed, our very salvation in the life of God—in step with the catechumens themselves; we are revitalized as we support them along the way and participate in their initiation rites.

We are asked to fast on Good Friday and to continue fasting, if possible, all through Holy Saturday as strictly as we can so that we come to the Easter Vigil hungry and full of excitement, parched and longing to feel the sacred water of the font on our skin. We pare down distractions on Good Friday and Holy Saturday so that we may be free for prayer and anticipation, for reflection, preparation, and silence. The Church is getting ready for the great night of the Easter Vigil.

As one who has been initiated into the Church, as one whose life has been wedded to this community gathered at the table, you should anticipate the Triduum with concentration and vigor. With you, the whole Church knows that our presence for the liturgies of the Triduum is not just an invitation. Everyone is needed. We pull out all the stops for these days. As humans, wedded to humanity by the joys and travails of life and grafted onto the body of the Church by the sanctifying waters of Baptism, we lead the new members into new life in this community of faith.

To this end, the Three Days are seen not as three distinct liturgies, but as one movement. These days have been connected liturgically from the early days of the Christian Church. As members of this community, we should be personally committed to preparing for and attending the Triduum and its culmination in the Easter Vigil of Holy Saturday.

The Church proclaims the direction of the Triduum with the opening antiphon of Holy Thursday, which comes from Paul's Letter to the Galatians (6:14). With this verse the Church sets a spiritual environment into which we as committed Christians enter the Triduum:

> *We should glory in the cross*
> *of our Lord Jesus Christ, for he*
> *is our salvation, our life and*
> *resurrection; through him we*
> *are saved and made free.*

HOLY THURSDAY

On Thursday evening we enter into this Triduum together. Whether presider, lector, preacher, greeter, altar server, minister of the Eucharist, decorator, or person in the remote corner in the last pew of the church, we begin, as always, by hearkening to the Word of God. These are the Scriptures for the liturgy of Holy Thursday:

Exodus 12:1–8, 11–14
Ancient instructions for the meal of the Passover.

1 Corinthians 11:23–26
Eat the bread and drink the cup until the return of the Lord.

John 13:1–15
Jesus washes the feet of the disciples.

Then the priest, like Jesus, does something strange: he washes feet. Jesus gave us this image of what the Church is supposed to look like, feel like, act like. Our position—whether as observer, washer or washed, servant or served—may be difficult. Yet we learn from the discomfort, from the awkwardness.

Then we celebrate the Eucharist. Because it is connected to the other liturgies of the Triduum on Good Friday and Holy Saturday night, the evening liturgy of Holy Thursday has no ending. Whether we stay to pray awhile or leave, we are now in the quiet, peace, and glory of the Triduum.

GOOD FRIDAY

We gather quietly in community on Friday and again listen to the Word of God:

Isaiah 52:13—53:12
The servant of the Lord was crushed for our sins.

Hebrews 4:14–16; 5:7–9
The Son of God learned obedience through his suffering.

John 18:1—19:42
The Passion of Jesus Christ.

After the sermon, we pray at length for all the world's needs: for the Church; for the pope, the clergy and all the baptized; for those preparing for initiation; for the unity of Christians; for Jews; for non-Christians; for atheists; for all in public office; and for those in special need.

Then there is another once-a-year event: the holy cross is held up in our midst, and we come forward one by one to do reverence with a kiss, bow, or genuflection. This communal reverence of an instrument of torture recalls the painful price, in the past and today, of salvation, the way in which our redemption is wrought, the scourging and humiliation of Jesus Christ that bring direction and life back to a humanity that is lost and dead. During the adoration of the cross, we sing not only of the sorrow, but of the glory of the cross by which we have been saved.

Again, we bring to mind the words of Paul (Galatians 6:14), on which last night's entrance antiphon is loosely based: "May I never boast except in the cross of our Lord Jesus Christ, through which the world has been crucified to me, and I to the world."

We continue in fasting and prayer and vigil, in rest and quiet, through Saturday. This Saturday for us is God's rest at the end of creation. It is Christ's repose in the tomb. It is Christ's visit with the dead.

EASTER VIGIL

Hungry now, pared down to basics, lightheaded from vigilance and full of excitement, we, the already baptized, gather in darkness and light a new fire. From this blaze we light a great candle that will make this night bright for us and will burn throughout Easter Time.

We hearken again to the Word of God with some of the most powerful narratives and proclamations of our tradition:

Genesis 1:1—2:2
The creation of the world.

Genesis 22:1–18
The sacrifice of Isaac.

Exodus 14:15—15:1
The crossing of the Red Sea.

Isaiah 54:5–14
You will not be afraid.

Isaiah 55:1–11
Come, come to the water.

Baruch 3:9–15, 32—4:4
Walk by the light of wisdom.

Ezekiel 36:16–17a, 18–28
The Lord says: I will sprinkle water.

Romans 6:3–11
United with him in death.

Year A: Matthew 28:1–10, Year B: Mark 16:1–7, Year C: Luke 24:1–12
Jesus has been raised.

After the readings, we call on our saints to stand with us as we go to the font and the priest celebrant blesses the waters. The chosen of all times and all places attend to what is about to take place. The elect renounce evil, profess the faith of the Church, and are baptized and anointed.

All of us renew our Baptism. These are the moments when death and life meet, when we reject evil and make our promises to God. All of this is in the communion of the Church. So together we go to the table and celebrate the Easter Eucharist.

Prayer before Reading the Word

God of our ancestors,
you have raised up Jesus
and exalted him at your right hand
as Leader and Savior.

Open our minds to understand the Scriptures,
and, as with great joy we bless you in your temple,
make us witnesses who can proclaim
the repentance and forgiveness
you extend to all the nations
in the name of Jesus,
the Messiah, our great high priest,
who intercedes before you on our behalf,
living and reigning with you
in the unity of the Holy Spirit,
one God, for ever and ever. Amen.

Prayer after Reading the Word

O God, the fountain of joy and of peace,
into the hands of your risen Son
you have entrusted the destinies
of peoples and of nations.

Keep us safe in those arms
from which no one can snatch us,
that we may proclaim your Word
in peace and in persecution,
until at last we stand before the Lamb
with songs of praise on our lips.

We ask this through the Lord Jesus,
our Passover and our Peace,
who lives and reigns with you
in the unity of the Holy Spirit,
one God, for ever and ever. Amen.

Weekday Readings

March 28: Monday within the Octave of Easter
Acts 2:14, 22–33; Matthew 28:8–15
March 29: Tuesday within the Octave of Easter
Acts 2:36–41; John 20:11–18
March 30: Wednesday within the Octave of Easter
Acts 3:1–10; Luke 24:13–35
March 31: Thursday within the Octave of Easter
Acts 3:11–26; Luke 24:35–48
April 1: Friday within the Octave of Easter
Acts 4:1–12; John 21:1–14
April 2: Saturday within the Octave of Easter
Acts 4:13–21; Mark 16:9–15

April 4: Solemnity of the Annunciation of the Lord
Isaiah 7:10–14; 8:10; Hebrews 10:4–10; Luke 1:26–38
April 5: *Acts 4:32–37; John 3:7b–15*
April 6: *Acts 5:17–26; John 3:16–21*
April 7: *Acts 5:27–33; John 3:31–36*
April 8: *Acts 5:34–42; John 6:1–15*
April 9: *Acts 6:1–7; John 6:16–21*

April 11: *Acts 6:8–15; John 6:22–29*
April 12: *Acts 7:51—8:1a; John 6:30–35*
April 13: *Acts 8:1b–8; John 6:35–40*
April 14: *Acts 8:26–40; John 6:44–51*
April 15: *Acts 9:1–20; John 6:52–59*
April 16: *Acts 9:31–42; John 6:60–69*

April 18: Acts 11:1–18; John 10:1–10
April 19: Acts 11:19–26; John 10:22–30
April 20: Acts 12:24—13:5a; John 12:44–50
April 21: Acts 13:13–25; John 13:16–20
April 22: Acts 13:26–33; John 14:1–6
April 23: Acts 13:44–52; John 14:7–14
April 25: Feast of St. Mark, Evangelist
1 Peter 5:5b–14; Mark 16:15–20

April 26: *Acts 14:19–28; John 14:27–31a*
April 27: *Acts 15:1–6; John 15:1–8*
April 28: *Acts 15:7–21; John 15:9–11*
April 29: *Acts 15:22–31; John 15:12–17*
April 30: *Acts 16:1–10; John 15:18–21*

May 2: Acts 16:11–15; John 15:26—16:4a
May 3: Feast of Sts. Philip and James, Apostles
1 Corinthians 15:1–8; John 14:6–14
May 4: *Acts 17:15, 22—18:1; John 16:12–15*

May 5: Solemnity of the Ascension of the Lord [In some
regions, transferred to Seventh Sunday of Easter]
Acts 1:1–11; Ephesians 1:17–23 or Hebrews 9:24–28;
10:19–23; Luke 24:46–53
May 6: *Acts 18:9–18; John 16:20–23*
May 7: *Acts 18:23–28; John 16:23b–28*

May 9: Acts 19:1–8; John 16:29–33
May 10: Acts 20:17–27; John 17:1–11a
May 11: Acts 20:28–38; John 17:11b–19
May 12: Acts 22:30; 23:6–11; John 17:20–26
May 13: Acts 25:13b–21; John 21:15–19
May 14: Feast of St. Matthias, Apostle
Acts 1:15–17, 20–26; John 15:9–17

March 27, 2016 Easter Sunday: The Resurrection of the Lord

Reading I *Acts 10:34a; 37–43*

Peter proceeded to speak and said: "You know what has happened all over Judea, beginning in Galilee after the baptism that John preached, how God anointed Jesus of Nazareth with the Holy Spirit and power. He went about doing good and healing all those oppressed by the devil, for God was with him. We are witnesses of all that he did both in the country of the Jews and in Jerusalem. They put him to death by hanging him on a tree. This man God raised on the third day and granted that he be visible, not to all the people, but to us, the witnesses chosen by God in advance, who ate and drank with him after he rose from the dead. He commissioned us to preach to the people and testify that he is the one appointed by God as judge of the living and the dead. To him all the prophets bear witness, that everyone who believes in him will receive forgiveness of sins through his name."

Responsorial Psalm
Psalm 118:1–2, 16–17, 22–23 (24)

R. This is the day the Lord has made; let us
        rejoice and be glad.
or: Alleluia.

Give thanks to the Lord, for he is good,
  for his mercy endures forever.
Let the house of Israel say,
  "His mercy endures forever." R.

"The right hand of the Lord has struck
        with power;
  the right hand of the Lord is exalted.
  I shall not die, but live,
  and declare the works of the Lord." R.

The stone which the builders rejected
  has become the cornerstone.
By the Lord has this been done;
  it is wonderful in our eyes. R.

Reading II *Colossians 3:1–4*

Alternate: 1 Corinthians 5:6b–8

Brothers and sisters: If then you were raised with Christ, seek what is above, where Christ is seated at the right hand of God. Think of what is above, not of what is on earth. For you have died, and your life is hidden with Christ in God. When Christ your life appears, then you too will appear with him in glory.

Gospel *John 20:1–9*

Alternate readings: Luke 24:1–12; or at an afternoon or evening Mass: Luke 24:13–35

On the first day of the week, Mary of Magdala came to the tomb early in the morning, while it was still dark, and saw the stone removed from the tomb. So she ran and went to Simon Peter and to the other disciple whom Jesus loved, and told them, "They have taken the Lord from the tomb, and we don't know where they put him." So Peter and the other disciple went out and came to the tomb. They both ran, but the other disciple ran faster than Peter and arrived at the tomb first; he bent down and saw the burial cloths there, but did not go in. When Simon Peter arrived after him, he went into the tomb and saw the burial cloths there, and the cloth that had covered his head, not with the burial cloths but rolled up in a separate place. Then the other disciple also went in, the one who had arrived at the tomb first, and he saw and believed. For they did not yet understand the Scripture that he had to rise from the dead.

Practice of Hope

Hope is usually intermingled with fear, but hope can triumph. After the Crucifixion, the disciples fled for their lives. Now, even after an alarming report, Peter and John run headlong into the fray and find evidence for the greatest of all hopes. ✦ Choose one of your fears, something holding you back, and dash toward it. Perhaps you need to confront someone or confess something, or maybe you have always wanted to volunteer at a family shelter. ✦ Read St. John Paul's book, *Crossing the Threshold of Hope*. This is the man who told us, "Do not be afraid. . . . Put out into the deep and let down your nets for a catch." ✦ As the sun sets, review the day's blessings and troubles. Then remember, as the letter to the Colossians says, that now "your life is hidden with Christ in God" and that fear no longer makes sense.

Download more questions and activities for families, Christian initiation groups, and other adult groups at http://www.ltp.org/t-productsupplements.aspx.

Scripture Insights

Throughout Easter Time readings are taken from the New Testament. The post-Resurrection stories, the preaching of Paul, and the events in the first communities all celebrate the Paschal Mystery and explore its implication for the lives of believers.

In the First Reading from Acts, we hear Peter's basic evangelization message. We can sense the excitement as Peter recounts Jesus' mission from his baptism until his Resurrection. Then Peter announces that he and the Apostles are "witnesses chosen by God in advance," to preach this great news: first, that God has raised Jesus and appointed him "judge of the living and the dead," and second, that everyone who believes in the risen Christ will "receive forgiveness of sins through his name."

On this Easter morning we sing the refrain for Psalm 118: "This is the day the Lord has made: let us rejoice and be glad." We give joyful thanks, for the Lord's "mercy endures forever." The psalmist exclaims "I shall not die but live, and declare the works of the LORD."

At the request of the founder of the community, Paul writes to the Colossians to reaffirm foundational truths of the faith and counter false teachers. Paul does not know them personally, but he patiently explains what they have received in their Baptism: nothing less than dying and rising with Christ. They are not who they were; their lives have been "hidden with Christ in God," so now they must act out of their new lives and "seek what is above."

Jesus' first post-Resurrection appearance to the disciples happened "on the first day of the week," a fit time for something new to unfold. It is Sunday, the day that Christians celebrate the Resurrection of the Lord, and the story of the Resurrection begins with an empty tomb. The entire Christian tradition is based on this mysterious discovery—a mystery full enough for a lifetime of pondering.

✦ What in this Gospel story enlightens you this year?

✦ How do you witness to the Resurrection of Christ?

✦ What signs do you see that there is new life in the world around you?

April 3, 2016

READING I Acts 5:12–16

Many signs and wonders were done among the people at the hands of the apostles. They were all together in Solomon's portico. None of the others dared to join them, but the people esteemed them. Yet more than ever, believers in the Lord, great numbers of men and women, were added to them. Thus they even carried the sick out into the streets and laid them on cots and mats so that when Peter came by, at least his shadow might fall on one or another of them. A large number of people from the towns in the vicinity of Jerusalem also gathered, bringing the sick and those disturbed by unclean spirits, and they were all cured.

RESPONSORIAL PSALM
Psalm 118:2–4, 13–15, 22–24 (1)

R. Give thanks to the Lord, for he is good, his
　　　love is everlasting.
or: Alleluia.

Let the house of Israel say,
　　"His mercy endures forever."
Let the house of Aaron say,
　　"His mercy endures forever."
Let those who fear the LORD say,
　　"His mercy endures forever." R.

I was hard pressed and was falling,
　　but the LORD helped me.
My strength and my courage is the LORD,
　　and he has been my savior.
The joyful shout of victory
　　in the tents of the just. R.

The stone which the builders rejected
　　has become the cornerstone.
By the LORD has this been done;
　　it is wonderful in our eyes.
This is the day the LORD has made;
　　let us be glad and rejoice in it. R.

READING II
Revelation 1:9–11a, 12–13, 17–19

I, John, your brother, who share with you the distress, the kingdom, and the endurance we have in Jesus, found myself on the island called Patmos because I proclaimed God's word and gave testimony to Jesus. I was caught up in spirit on the Lord's day and heard behind me a voice as loud as a trumpet, which said, "Write on a scroll what you see." Then I turned to see whose voice it was that spoke to me, and when I turned, I saw seven gold lampstands and in the midst of the lampstands one like a son of man, wearing an ankle-length robe, with a gold sash around his chest.

When I caught sight of him, I fell down at his feet as though dead. He touched me with his right hand and said, "Do not be afraid. I am the first and the last, the one who lives. Once I was dead, but now I am alive forever and ever. I hold the keys to death and the netherworld. Write down, therefore, what you have seen, and what is happening, and what will happen afterwards."

GOSPEL John 20:19–31

On the evening of that first day of the week, when the doors were locked, where the disciples were, for fear of the Jews, Jesus came and stood in their midst and said to them, "Peace be with you." When he had said this, he showed them his hands and his side. The disciples rejoiced when they saw the Lord. Jesus said to them again, "Peace be with you. As the Father has sent me, so I send you." And when he had said this, he breathed on them and said to them, "Receive the Holy Spirit. Whose sins you forgive are forgiven them, and whose sins you retain are retained."

Thomas, called Didymus, one of the Twelve, was not with them when Jesus came. So the other disciples said to him, "We have seen the Lord." But he said to them, "Unless I see the mark of the nails in his hands and put my finger into the nailmarks and put my hand into his side, I will not believe."

Now a week later his disciples were again inside and Thomas was with them. Jesus came, although the doors were locked, and stood in their midst and said, "Peace be with you." Then he said to Thomas, "Put your finger here and see my hands, and bring your hand and put it into my side, and do not be unbelieving, but believe." Thomas answered and said to him, "My Lord and my God!" Jesus said to him, "Have you come to believe because you have seen me? Blessed are those who have not seen and have believed."

Now Jesus did many other signs in the presence of his disciples that are not written in this book. But these are written that you may come to believe that Jesus is the Christ, the Son of God, and that through this belief you may have life in his name.

Practice of Charity

Signs and wonders are done "at the hands of the apostles." The "one like a son of man" touches the author of Revelation with his right hand. The Risen Lord overcomes doubt by showing his wounded hands. We Christians have always been called to use our hands to further the Kingdom. ◆ Catholic Relief Services' Helping Hands ministry sponsors gatherings around the nation where volunteers pack food boxes for people in developing nations. In addition to feeding bodies, the Gospel-inspired handiwork evangelizes (http://helping hands.crs.org/about-us; 877-435-7277). ◆ We also use our hands in the liturgy: to make the Sign of the Cross, to pray, to give the sign of peace, and (for many) to receive communion. Each of these gestures conveys a prayer for the world, a stand in solidarity with the entire body of Christ. ◆ Read the poem attributed to St. Teresa of Avila, "Christ Has No Body," in which she writes, "Yours are the hands with which He is to bless his people."

Download more questions and activities for families, Christian initiation groups, and other adult groups at http://www.ltp.org/t-productsupplements.aspx.

Scripture Insights

The readings for the Sundays of Easter explore the Paschal Mystery—these dying and rising of Christ. Originally the texts were selected for the newly baptized, offering a follow-up catechesis after initiation. But it became clear that they provided continuing catechesis for everyone. Each year we more deeply embrace the astonishing grace of the Resurrection. The First Readings, from Acts, describe the life of the fledgling Christian community celebrating the mission and teaching of Jesus. The Second Readings are from Revelation. The Gospel accounts come mainly from John: some recount post-Resurrection appearances of Jesus; others are taken from Jesus' earthly ministry, but have implications for the disciples after Jesus is raised from the dead.

Today's First Reading describes life within the community of believers. Their numbers increased because of "signs and wonders" performed by the Apostles. Among those was the healing of the sick, showing that God was working through them as he had through Jesus. The Book of Revelation (Second Reading) is part of a particular Jewish and Christian literary genre called "apocalyptic." Such writings often include a vision of supernatural events concerning the end-time described in symbolic language. They are written to encourage the people to be hopeful, especially in times of persecution. The speaker, John, describes his vision of the "one like a son of man" who asks him to write this divine message.

The Gospel describes Jesus' commissioning of the disciples and then the conversion of Thomas. Thomas's doubt anticipates the readers' question: was Jesus' presence after the Resurrection physical or spiritual? John's account is not an answer but a proclamation that faith in the Risen Lord was the beginning of a new life among the disciples.

◆ How does your parish compare to the community in Acts?

◆ What "signs and wonders" do you see as evidence of the Lord's presence today?

◆ In what way do you empathize with the uncertainty Thomas feels?

71

READING I *Acts 5:27–32, 40b–41*

When the captain and the court officers had brought the apostles in and made them stand before the Sanhedrin, the high priest questioned them, "We gave you strict orders, did we not, to stop teaching in that name? Yet you have filled Jerusalem with your teaching and want to bring this man's blood upon us." But Peter and the apostles said in reply, "We must obey God rather than men. The God of our ancestors raised Jesus, though you had him killed by hanging him on a tree. God exalted him at his right hand as leader and savior to grant Israel repentance and forgiveness of sins. We are witnesses of these things, as is the Holy Spirit whom God has given to those who obey him."

The Sanhedrin ordered the apostles to stop speaking in the name of Jesus, and dismissed them. So they left the presence of the Sanhedrin, rejoicing that they had been found worthy to suffer dishonor for the sake of the name.

RESPONSORIAL PSALM
Psalm 30:2, 4, 5–6, 11–12, 13 (2a)

R. I will praise you, Lord, for you have rescued me.
or: Alleluia.

I will extol you, O LORD, for you drew me clear
    and did not let my enemies rejoice over me.
O LORD, you brought me up from the
            netherworld;
    you preserved me from among those going
            down into the pit. R.

Sing praise to the LORD, you his faithful ones,
    and give thanks to his holy name.
For his anger lasts but a moment;
    a lifetime, his good will.
At nightfall; weeping enters in,
    but with the dawn, rejoicing. R.

Hear, O LORD, and have pity on me;
    O LORD, be my helper.
You changed my mourning into dancing;
    O LORD, my God, forever will I give
            you thanks. R.

READING II *Revelation 5:11–14*

I, John, looked and heard the voices of many angels who surrounded the throne and the living creatures and the elders. They were countless in number, and they cried out in a loud voice:
    "Worthy is the Lamb that was slain
        to receive power and riches, wisdom
                and strength,
        honor and glory and blessing."
Then I heard every creature in heaven and on earth and under the earth and in the sea, everything in the universe, cry out:
    "To the one who sits on the
                throne and to the Lamb
        be blessing and honor, glory and might,
        forever and ever."
The four living creatures answered, "Amen," and the elders fell down and worshiped.

GOSPEL *John 21:1–19*

Shorter: John 21:1–14

At that time, Jesus revealed himself again to his disciples at the Sea of Tiberias. He revealed himself in this way. Together were Simon Peter, Thomas called Didymus, Nathanael from Cana in Galilee, Zebedee's sons, and two others of his disciples. Simon Peter said to them, "I am going fishing." They said to him, "We also will come with you." So they went out and got into the boat, but that night they caught nothing. When it was already dawn, Jesus was standing on the shore; but the disciples did not realize that it was Jesus. Jesus said to them, "Children, have you caught anything to eat?" They answered him, "No." So he said to them, "Cast the net over the right side of the boat and you will find something." So they cast it, and were not able to pull it in because of the number of fish. So the disciple whom Jesus loved said to Peter, "It is the Lord." When Simon Peter heard that it was the Lord, he tucked in his garment, for he was lightly clad, and jumped into the sea. The other disciples came in the boat, for they were not far from shore, only about a hundred yards, dragging the net with the fish. When they climbed out on shore, they saw a charcoal fire with fish on it and bread. Jesus said to them, "Bring some of the fish you just caught." So Simon Peter went over and dragged the net ashore full of one hundred fifty-three large fish. Even though there were so many, the net was not torn. Jesus said to them, "Come, have breakfast." And none of the disciples dared to ask him, "Who are you?" because they realized it was the Lord. Jesus came over and took the bread and gave it to them, and in like manner the fish. This was now the third time Jesus was revealed to his disciples after being raised from the dead.

When they had finished breakfast, Jesus said to Simon Peter, "Simon, son of John, do you love me more than these?" Simon Peter answered him, "Yes, Lord, you know that I love you." Jesus said to him, "Feed my lambs." He then said to Simon Peter a second time, "Simon, son of John, do you love me?" Simon Peter answered him, "Yes, Lord, you know that I love you." Jesus said to him, "Tend my sheep." Jesus said to him the third time, "Simon, son of John, do you love me?" Peter was distressed that Jesus had said to him a third time, "Do you love me?" and he said to him, "Lord, you know everything; you know that I love you." Jesus said to him, "Feed my sheep. Amen, amen, I say to you, when you were younger, you used to dress yourself and go where you wanted; but when you grow old, you will stretch out your hands, and someone else will dress you and lead you where you do not want to go." He said this signifying by what kind of death he would glorify God. And when he had said this, he said to him, "Follow me."

Practice of Faith

To be effective evangelizers, we need to be fed. Where do you find food for the work God asks of you? ◆ Book a retreat at a local retreat house; spend time in prayer and discernment. ◆ Seek guidance from a spiritual director to help you see where God is leading you. ◆ Pray for the sensitivity to notice who is seeking a conversation about faith, and be ready to listen to their story.

Download more questions and activities for families, Christian initiation groups, and other adult groups at http://www.ltp.org/t-productsupplements.aspx.

Scripture Insights

As Peter and the other Apostles stand before the Sanhedrin in the First Reading, we remember Jesus' condemnation by that group. The Apostles' preaching has been effective, and the Sanhedrin fears it will be blamed for Jesus' Crucifixion. Peter boldly asserts that the Apostles are not subject to orders of the court, but only to God, and their preaching is rooted in the tradition of Israel. Surprisingly, they are dismissed with a reprimand and leave "rejoicing that they had been found worthy to suffer dishonor" in Christ's name. Psalm 30 could have been the Apostles' song after their court appearance, for they felt the Lord had delivered them. Like the psalmist, they know the dangers behind and ahead, but their trust and gratitude are firm.

In the Second Reading, John stands in a great throne room, where countless angels surround the throne of the Lord of the cosmos. He hears "everything in the universe cry out" their praise and blessing "to the one who sits on the throne and to the Lamb." This powerful image of the entire universe bowing to the authority of the Father and the Son affirms for Christians of every age that ultimately justice will triumph.

John layers many meanings into his stories. As in other post-Resurrection appearances, the disciples don't recognize Jesus immediately. Still grieving and confused, they have returned to fishing, but Jesus calls them away from their nets once again. That moment of recognition is exciting—for the disciples and for us readers. The encounter must have felt so familiar—a meal, which included both food Jesus had prepared for them and some they provided from their catch. The conversation with Peter after the meal is a "call" story in which Peter must first pledge his love for the Lord before he is ready for ministry.

◆ What images of Eucharist do you find in the Gospel story?

◆ Why do you think Jesus repeats his question to Peter three times?

◆ What circumstances have made you reluctant to proclaim the Word of God?

READING I *Acts 13:14, 43–52*

Paul and Barnabas continued on from Perga and reached Antioch in Pisidia. On the sabbath they entered the synagogue and took their seats. Many Jews and worshipers who were converts to Judaism followed Paul and Barnabas, who spoke to them and urged them to remain faithful to the grace of God.

On the following sabbath almost the whole city gathered to hear the word of the Lord. When the Jews saw the crowds, they were filled with jealousy and with violent abuse contradicted what Paul said. Both Paul and Barnabas spoke out boldly and said, "It was necessary that the word of God be spoken to you first, but since you reject it and condemn yourselves as unworthy of eternal life, we now turn to the Gentiles. For so the Lord has commanded us, *I have made you a light to the Gentiles, that you may be an instrument of salvation to the ends of the earth.*"

The Gentiles were delighted when they heard this and glorified the word of the Lord. All who were destined for eternal life came to believe, and the word of the Lord continued to spread through the whole region. The Jews, however, incited the women of prominence who were worshipers and the leading men of the city, stirred up a persecution against Paul and Barnabas, and expelled them from their territory. So they shook the dust from their feet in protest against them, and went to Iconium. The disciples were filled with joy and the Holy Spirit.

RESPONSORIAL PSALM
Psalm 100:1–2, 3, 5 (3c)

R. We are his people, the sheep of his flock.
or: Alleluia.

Sing joyfully to the LORD, all you lands;
 serve the LORD with gladness;
 come before him with joyful song. R.

Know that the LORD is God;
 he made us, his we are,
 his people, the flock he tends. R.

The LORD is good:
 his kindness endures forever,
 and his faithfulness, to all generations. R.

READING II *Revelation 7:9, 14b–17*

I, John, had a vision of a great multitude, which no one could count, from every nation, race, people, and tongue. They stood before the throne and before the Lamb, wearing white robes and holding palm branches in their hands.

Then one of the elders said to me, "These are the ones who have survived the time of great distress; they have washed their robes and made them white in the blood of the Lamb.

"For this reason they stand before God's throne
 and worship him day and night in his temple.
 The one who sits on the throne
  will shelter them.
They will not hunger or thirst anymore,
 nor will the sun or any heat strike them.
For the Lamb who is in the center of the throne
 will shepherd them
and lead them to springs
  of life-giving water,
 and God will wipe away every tear from
  their eyes."

GOSPEL *John 10:27–30*

Jesus said: "My sheep hear my voice; I know them, and they follow me. I give them eternal life, and they shall never perish. No one can take them out of my hand. My Father, who has given them to me, is greater than all, and no one can take them out of the Father's hand. The Father and I are one."

Practice of Hope

The ones who "survived the time of great distress" stand before God's throne, to be led to springs of life-giving water. Amid family and at work, we face trials daily, some modest, some substantial. Often, we respond by being defensive or controlling. How can we instead, like those who heard Paul and Barnabas, "remain faithful to the grace of God" and trust in the care of the Good Shepherd? ◆ Ask a friend to accompany you on a "trust walk." Take turns with one blindfolded, the other leading the way. ◆ Read Fr. Henri Nouwen's book, *The Road to Daybreak: A Spiritual Journey* (ISBN 0-385-41607-5), which chronicles his life in a L'Arche community with people with disabilities. ◆ Pray John Henry Cardinal Newman's short poem, "Lead, Kindly Light," which says in part, "I loved to choose and see my path, but now lead thou me on!"

Download more questions and activities for families, Christian initiation groups, and other adult groups at http://www.ltp.org/t-productsupplements.aspx.

Scripture Insights

The First Reading from Acts describes a turning point in Paul's mission. When the members of the synagogue react angrily to his and Barnabas's preaching in Antioch, Paul decides that the Jews are unwilling to accept his message, and he announces that he will seek out the Gentiles instead. On hearing this, the Gentiles "were delighted." Many "came to believe, and the word of the Lord continued to spread." This account shows us both the power of the Word to attract people and the sad break between the Christian community and Judaism.

Having just heard how the "flock" of the Lord was taking shape in the early days of the faith, we can find today's Responsorial Psalm refrain fitting— and even more so when we consider the next two readings. These verses express joy and gratitude at being led and cared for by the Good Shepherd.

In the Second Reading we are once again standing with John in his heavenly throne room vision. Now he sees a great multitude in white robes and is told that they "have survived the time of great distress" and washed their robes "in the blood of the Lamb." They seem to be the victims of persecution who have been faithful to Christ, who are now safe, singing before the Lamb sitting on the throne.

This Sunday has often been referred to as "Good Shepherd Sunday" because the Gospel readings for Year A, B, and C are from chapter 10 of John's Gospel account, in which Jesus portrays himself as the Good Shepherd. Sheep do recognize the voice of the shepherd and follow his lead, so the image is apt for Jesus. Followers recognize his voice by attending to his Word, his teaching, and in doing so, they enter into an intimate relationship with him, just as he enjoys an intimate relationship with the Father.

◆ What do you make of Jesus as Lamb in one reading and Jesus as shepherd in another?

◆ What other characteristics of a shepherd does Jesus exemplify?

◆ In what ways is the image of the faithful as a flock of sheep helpful or unhelpful?

April 24, 2016 FIFTH SUNDAY OF EASTER

READING I *Acts 14:21–27*

After Paul and Barnabas had proclaimed the good news to that city and made a considerable number of disciples, they returned to Lystra and to Iconium and to Antioch. They strengthened the spirits of the disciples and exhorted them to persevere in the faith, saying, "It is necessary for us to undergo many hardships to enter the kingdom of God." They appointed elders for them in each church and, with prayer and fasting, commended them to the Lord in whom they had put their faith. Then they traveled through Pisidia and reached Pamphylia. After proclaiming the word at Perga they went down to Attalia. From there they sailed to Antioch, where they had been commended to the grace of God for the work they had now accomplished. And when they arrived, they called the church together and reported what God had done with them and how he had opened the door of faith to the Gentiles.

RESPONSORIAL PSALM
Psalm 145:8–9, 10–11, 12–13 (see 1)

R. I will praise your name for ever, my king and
        my God.
or: Alleluia.

The LORD is gracious and merciful,
    slow to anger and of great kindness.
The LORD is good to all
    and compassionate toward all his works. R.

Let all your works give you thanks, O LORD,
    and let your faithful ones bless you.
Let them discourse of the glory of your kingdom
    and speak of your might. R.

Let them make known your might to the
        children of Adam,
    and the glorious splendor of your kingdom.
Your kingdom is a kingdom for all ages,
    and your dominion endures through
        all generations. R.

READING II *Revelation 21:1–5a*

Then I, John, saw a new heaven and a new earth. The former heaven and the former earth had passed away, and the sea was no more. I also saw the holy city, a new Jerusalem, coming down out of heaven from God, prepared as a bride adorned for her husband. I heard a loud voice from the throne saying, "Behold, God's dwelling is with the human race. He will dwell with them and they will be his people and God himself will always be with them as their God. He will wipe every tear from their eyes, and there shall be no more death or mourning, wailing or pain, for the old order has passed away."

The One who sat on the throne said, "Behold, I make all things new."

GOSPEL *John 13:31–33a, 34–35*

When Judas had left them, Jesus said, "Now is the Son of Man glorified, and God is glorified in him. If God is glorified in him, God will also glorify him in himself, and God will glorify him at once. My children, I will be with you only a little while longer. I give you a new commandment: love one another. As I have loved you, so you also should love one another. This is how all will know that you are my disciples, if you have love for one another."

Practice of Charity

At the liturgy of Holy Thursday, we witnessed the washing of the feet. But our loving service to the world cannot be limited to that night, or to this Easter Time; it must become part of everyday life. "As I have loved you, so you also should love one another," Jesus tells his followers. That's a tall order we can fulfill only by God's grace. ◆ This week, perform one concrete act in which you love as Jesus loved. For example, listen compassionately to a coworker, neighbor, or family member you usually find difficult to relate to. Look for a new way to understand that person. ◆ Read chapter 15 of book 1 of *The Imitation of Christ* by Thomas à Kempis. (For free access to an online copy, search by title on the site of the Christian Classics Ethereal Library, http://www.ccel.org/search/books /?&order =score&advanced.) ◆ Meditate with an icon or other image of Jesus, asking that your will become more conformed to his.

Download more questions and activities for families, Christian initiation groups, and other adult groups at http://www.ltp.org/t-productsupplements.aspx.

Scripture Insights

The First Reading gives us another report of the successful missionary activity of Paul and Barnabas. As the number of believers continues to grow, Paul appoints "elders" to take care of them. Although we don't learn the elders' responsibilities, likely they assisted with the social and liturgical life of the believers. When Paul returns to Antioch he reports on the success of their journey, making clear that it was God who "opened the door of faith to the Gentiles."

Psalm 145 praises the wonders of God and declares complete devotion to "my king and my God." These phrases describing God are familiar: "gracious and merciful," "slow to anger and of great kindness," "good to all and compassionate." God cares deeply for all that God has created. God's love is "for all ages" and "all generations."

Today's reading from Revelation is frequently chosen for funeral liturgies. John employs several images to emphasize a new life with God: a new heaven and a new earth, the disappearance of the sea, (a biblical symbol of chaos), tears from past tribulations are wiped away, and even death and mourning are no more. John's vision gives hope to his readers, encouraging them to be strong in their faith because God has made all things new.

John's account of the Last Supper includes a lengthy teaching by Christ; we hear a brief but key part of it today. Once Judas has left, Jesus indicates that the time has come for him to fulfill his mission. It will glorify both himself and the Father; all things will be made new. The disciples will share in this glorification when they enact a new commandment: to love one another. This will require the same sacrificial love for others as Christ had for them, and it will become the defining feature in the identity of a disciple, including us.

◆ What references can you discover in the readings that emphasize the action of God on our behalf?

◆ What phrases in the reading from Revelation would give comfort to those who mourn?

◆ What does sacrificial love mean to you?

READING I *Acts 15:1–2, 22–29*

Some who had come down from Judea were instructing the brothers, "Unless you are circumcised according to the Mosaic practice, you cannot be saved." Because there arose no little dissension and debate by Paul and Barnabas with them, it was decided that Paul, Barnabas, and some of the others should go up to Jerusalem to the apostles and elders about this question.

The apostles and elders, in agreement with the whole church, decided to choose representatives and to send them to Antioch with Paul and Barnabas. The ones chosen were Judas, who was called Barsabbas, and Silas, leaders among the brothers. This is the letter delivered by them:

"The apostles and the elders, your brothers, to the brothers in Antioch, Syria, and Cilicia of Gentile origin: greetings. Since we have heard that some of our number who went out without any mandate from us have upset you with their teachings and disturbed your peace of mind, we have with one accord decided to choose representatives and to send them to you along with our beloved Barnabas and Paul, who have dedicated their lives to the name of our Lord Jesus Christ. So we are sending Judas and Silas who will also convey this same message by word of mouth: 'It is the decision of the Holy Spirit and of us not to place on you any burden beyond these necessities, namely, to abstain from meat sacrificed to idols, from blood, from meats of strangled animals, and from unlawful marriage. If you keep free of these, you will be doing what is right. Farewell.'"

RESPONSORIAL PSALM
Psalm 67:2–3, 5, 6, 8 (4)

R. O God, let all the nations praise you!
or: Alleluia.

May God have pity on us and bless us;
    may he let his face shine upon us.
So may your way be known upon earth;
    among all nations, your salvation. R.

May the nations be glad and exult
    because you rule the peoples in equity;
    the nations on the earth you guide. R.

May the peoples praise you, O God;
    may all the peoples praise you!
May God bless us,
    and may all the ends of the earth
            fear him! R.

READING II *Revelation 21:10–14, 22–23*

The angel took me in spirit to a great, high mountain and showed me the holy city Jerusalem coming down out of heaven from God. It gleamed with the splendor of God. Its radiance was like that of a precious stone, like jasper, clear as crystal. It had a massive, high wall, with twelve gates where twelve angels were stationed and on which names were inscribed, the names of the twelve tribes of the Israelites. There were three gates facing east, three north, three south, and three west. The wall of the city had twelve courses of stones as its foundation, on which were inscribed the twelve names of the twelve apostles of the Lamb.

I saw no temple in the city for its temple is the Lord God almighty and the Lamb. The city had no need of sun or moon to shine on it, for the glory of God gave it light, and its lamp was the Lamb.

GOSPEL *John 14:23–29*

Jesus said to his disciples: "Whoever loves me will keep my word, and my Father will love him, and we will come to him and make our dwelling with him. Whoever does not love me does not keep my words; yet the word you hear is not mine but that of the Father who sent me.

"I have told you this while I am with you. The Advocate, the Holy Spirit, whom the Father will send in my name, will teach you everything and remind you of all that I told you. Peace I leave with you; my peace I give to you. Not as the world gives do I give it to you. Do not let your hearts be troubled or afraid. You heard me tell you, 'I am going away and I will come back to you.' If you loved me, you would rejoice that I am going to the Father; for the Father is greater than I. And now I have told you this before it happens, so that when it happens you may believe."

Practice of Faith

Faith is more than an intellectual feat and adherence to rituals and actions. Deep faith begins in relationship with the person, Jesus Christ. "Whoever loves me will keep my word," Jesus told his disciples. He promised that Father, Son, and Spirit—a loving community—would always dwell with such a person. ◆ To develop your relationship with God, begin as you would with any friend—communicate frequently and openly. Spend time together. One Benedictine Sister uses driving time, imagining that Jesus is in the passenger seat. ◆ Read Pope Francis's electric homily from January 2014, in which he said priests must have a living relationship with Jesus. Though intended for clergy, it has a lot to say to all Christians. (http://w2.vatican.va/content/francesco/en/cotidie/2014/documents/papa-francesco-cotidie_20140111_priest.html) ◆ Every participation in liturgy or devotions is an opportunity to respond to God's unrestricted offer of loving relationship, rather than an effort to win God over.

Download more questions and activities for families, Christian initiation groups, and other adult groups at http://www.ltp.org/t-productsupplements.aspx.

Scripture Insights

Today's reading from Acts describes an important event in the early Church. Paul, who had made many converts among the Gentiles, had a dispute with Peter, the head of the Church in Jerusalem. When initiating Gentiles, Paul did not require them to be circumcised, but the Jewish converts believed that circumcision was a prerequisite for being Christian. This passage describes how the issue was settled, although it leaves out the interesting speeches that led to the decision. (See Acts 15:6–21.) The leaders in Jerusalem come to agree with Paul and send him a letter. The "apostles and elders" in Jerusalem write the letter; however, they specify that the decision has come from the Holy Spirit.

John's vision is a spectacular description of the Holy City of Jerusalem. In apocalyptic literature the number twelve represents fullness or completeness, and it appears six times in the text. Two other elements emphasize the wonder and glory of the vision. First, there is "no temple in the city," because now God is the Temple, the epitome of all worship and glory. This relates to Jesus' prediction that if the Temple were destroyed he would rebuild it in three days. The second element of God's glory is the absence of the sun and moon. The natural light of creation is no longer needed; it is the glory and splendor of God that sheds eternal light.

Today's Gospel is part of Jesus' "farewell discourse." He instructs the disciples that to remember him is to love him. Their remembering is not simply a calling to mind of his Word but a real and active life of love. Jesus assures them that they will receive the help of the Spirit that the Father will send in his name. His parting words are a blessing, "my peace I give to you" and an assurance that they need not let their "hearts be troubled or afraid."

◆ What signs of something new do you find in the readings?

◆ How can we keep our hearts from being "troubled or afraid"?

◆ When has the Holy Spirit helped you make a decision?

READING I *Acts 1:1–11*

In the first book, Theophilus, I dealt with all that Jesus did and taught until the day he was taken up, after giving instructions through the Holy Spirit to the apostles whom he had chosen. He presented himself alive to them by many proofs after he had suffered, appearing to them during forty days and speaking about the kingdom of God. While meeting with them, he enjoined them not to depart from Jerusalem, but to wait for "the promise of the Father about which you have heard me speak; for John baptized with water, but in a few days you will be baptized with the Holy Spirit."

When they had gathered together they asked him, "Lord, are you at this time going to restore the kingdom to Israel?" He answered them, "It is not for you to know the times or seasons that the Father has established by his own authority. But you will receive power when the Holy Spirit comes upon you, and you will be my witnesses in Jerusalem, throughout Judea and Samaria, and to the ends of the earth." When he had said this, as they were looking on, he was lifted up, and a cloud took him from their sight. While they were looking intently at the sky as he was going, suddenly two men dressed in white garments stood beside them. They said, "Men of Galilee, why are you standing there looking at the sky? This Jesus who has been taken up from you into heaven will return in the same way as you have seen him going into heaven."

RESPONSORIAL PSALM
Psalm 47:2–3, 6–7, 8–9 (6)

R. God mounts his throne to shouts of joy:
  a blare of trumpets for the Lord.
or: Alleluia.

All you peoples, clap your hands,
  shout to God with cries of gladness,
For the LORD, the Most High, the awesome,
  is the great king over all the earth.   R.

God mounts his throne amid shouts of joy;
  the LORD, amid trumpet blasts.
Sing praise to God, sing praise;
  sing praise to our king, sing praise.   R.

For king of all the earth is God;
  sing hymns of praise.
God reigns over the nations,
  God sits upon his holy throne.   R.

READING II *Hebrews 9:24–28; 10:19–23*

Alternate reading: Ephesians 1:17–23

Christ did not enter into a sanctuary made by hands, a copy of the true one, but heaven itself, that he might now appear before God on our behalf. Not that he might offer himself repeatedly, as the high priest enters each year into the sanctuary with blood that is not his own; if that were so, he would have had to suffer repeatedly from the foundation of the world. But now once for all he has appeared at the end of the ages to take away sin by his sacrifice. Just as it is appointed that men and women die once, and after this the judgment, so also Christ, offered once to take away the sins of many, will appear a second time, not to take away sin but to bring salvation to those who eagerly await him.

Therefore, brothers and sisters, since through the blood of Jesus we have confidence of entrance into the sanctuary by the new and living way he opened for us through the veil, that is, his flesh, and since we have "a great priest over the house of God," let us approach with a sincere heart and in absolute trust, with our hearts sprinkled clean from an evil conscience and our bodies washed in pure water. Let us hold unwaveringly to our confession that gives us hope, for he who made the promise is trustworthy.

GOSPEL *Luke 24:46–53*

Jesus said to his disciples: "Thus it is written that the Christ would suffer and rise from the dead on the third day and that repentance, for the forgiveness of sins, would be preached in his name to all the nations, beginning from Jerusalem. You are witnesses of these things. And behold I am sending the promise of my Father upon you; but stay in the city until you are clothed with power from on high."

Then he led them out as far as Bethany, raised his hands, and blessed them. As he blessed them he parted from them and was taken up to heaven. They did him homage and then returned to Jerusalem with great joy, and they were continually in the temple praising God.

Practice of Faith

When a mentor leaves, we feel rudderless. But it's then that we step forward to speak and act with authority. Like the Apostles after Jesus ascended, we are called to give voice to belief and serve in the world—with the aid of the Holy Spirit. ◆ The Apostles praised God constantly. Whenever you sense that someone is discouraged let that person know how you see God working in the world today. Use social media to advocate for just causes, such as immigration reform or services for pregnant women. ◆ Read Jesuit Father Greg Boyle's *Tattoos on the Heart* (http://www.homeboyindustries.org/shop-homeboy/view/tattoos-on-the-heart-english-paperback/ or call (323) 526-1254 for information) to see how the Holy Spirit works where you'd least expect: in this case a Los Angeles district troubled by gangs. ◆ Go to the top of a knoll or hill (or to an upper story of a tall building) so you can look over your city or neighborhood. Pray for the strength to continue Jesus' work in that place.

Download more questions and activities for families, Christian initiation groups, and other adult groups at http://www.ltp.org/t-productsupplements.aspx.

Scripture Insights

Luke is regarded as the author of the Acts of the Apostles as well as his Gospel account. Both in today's reading from the beginning of Acts and in the Gospel from the end of Luke's account, the author describes the Ascension of Jesus. For Luke, the Ascension is a bridge between the life of Christ and the life of the Church as it begins to bear witness to the Resurrection of the Lord. In Acts, Luke portrays Jesus telling the Apostles that they will be baptized in the Holy Spirit, and with that power they will bear witness to the Lord "to the ends of the earth."

Today's psalm provides the perfect refrain for the occasion: "God mounts his throne to shouts of joy." The psalmist describes an enthronement scene: with trumpet blasts and hymns of praise, people acclaim their God and King ruling over the nations.

For Jews, the Temple was the place where heaven and earth connected through the sacrifices offered there. The author of Hebrews distinguishes between the physical Temple and the spiritual dwelling of God, into which Christ has entered as the one who's single sacrificial offering need not be repeated as are those in the earthly Temple. Jesus' offering has taken away all sin and given believers "a new and living way" to follow Christ to the Father.

In the Gospel, Jesus' final instructions to the disciples recall his Passion. Previously eyewitnesses of his Death and Resurrection, they are now sent as witnesses in another way, by their lives. Before then they will be "clothed with power from on high" when the Holy Spirit comes. Jesus blesses them and is taken up to heaven. The disciples return to Jerusalem "with great joy," a contrast to the mood they experienced after Jesus' Crucifixion. This time they understand.

◆ What is "the promise of my Father" that Jesus refers to in the Gospel?

◆ What connections do you find between the Resurrection and the Ascension in the First Reading?

◆ What approaches to Christian witness come most easily to you?

May 8, 2016 SEVENTH SUNDAY OF EASTER

READING I *Acts 7:55–60*

Stephen, filled with the Holy Spirit, looked up intently to heaven and saw the glory of God and Jesus standing at the right hand of God, and Stephen said, "Behold, I see the heavens opened and the Son of Man standing at the right hand of God." But they cried out in a loud voice, covered their ears, and rushed upon him together. They threw him out of the city, and began to stone him. The witnesses laid down their cloaks at the feet of a young man named Saul. As they were stoning Stephen, he called out, "Lord Jesus, receive my spirit." Then he fell to his knees and cried out in a loud voice, "Lord, do not hold this sin against them"; and when he said this, he fell asleep.

RESPONSORIAL PSALM
Psalm 97:1–2, 6–7, 9 (1a, 9a)

R. The Lord is king, the most high over all
    the earth.
or: Alleluia.

The LORD is king; let the earth rejoice;
    let the many islands be glad.
Justice and judgment are the foundation of
        his throne.   R.

The heavens proclaim his justice,
    and all peoples see his glory.
All gods are prostrate before him.   R.

You, O LORD, are the Most High over all the earth,
    exalted far above all gods.   R.

READING II
Revelation 22:12–14, 16–17, 20

I, John, heard a voice saying to me: "Behold, I am coming soon. I bring with me the recompense I will give to each according to his deeds. I am the Alpha and the Omega, the first and the last, the beginning and the end."

Blessed are they who wash their robes so as to have the right to the tree of life and enter the city through its gates.

"I, Jesus, sent my angel to give you this testimony for the churches. I am the root and offspring of David, the bright morning star."

The Spirit and the bride say, "Come." Let the hearer say, "Come." Let the one who thirsts come forward, and the one who wants it receive the gift of life-giving water.

The one who gives this testimony says, "Yes, I am coming soon." Amen! Come, Lord Jesus!

GOSPEL *John 17:20–26*

Lifting up his eyes to heaven, Jesus prayed, saying: "Holy Father, I pray not only for them, but also for those who will believe in me through their word, so that they may all be one, as you, Father, are in me and I in you, that they also may be in us, that the world may believe that you sent me. And I have given them the glory you gave me, so that they may be one, as we are one, I in them and you in me, that they may be brought to perfection as one, that the world may know that you sent me, and that you loved them even as you loved me. Father, they are your gift to me. I wish that where I am they also may be with me, that they may see my glory that you gave me, because you loved me before the foundation of the world. Righteous Father, the world also does not know you, but I know you, and they know that you sent me. I made known to them your name and I will make it known, that the love with which you loved me may be in them and I in them."

Practice of Hope

Jesus yearns for unity on many levels, including between God and humanity and among humans through time. Two millennia later, religion enters into violent strife, though socioeconomic factors are the main causes. We dare to hope for justice, healing, and common understanding, seeing faith as a path to cooperation. ◆ Read the Second Vatican Council's brief declaration on relations to non-Christians, which urges us to forget the past, work for mutual understanding and together promote social justice. (http://www.vatican.va/archive /hist_councils/ii_vatican_council/documents/vat -ii_decl_19651028_nostra-aetate_en.html) ◆ Many cities and towns have interfaith groups that focus on the common good and social service. Visit such an organization's website, attend a meeting, or join one of the ministries that speaks to your heart. ◆ Call a mosque, synagogue, or other place of worship and respectfully ask for a tour. Try to include a moment of quiet prayer for harmony among faiths, aware that unity does not mean uniformity.

Download more questions and activities for families, Christian initiation groups, and other adult groups at http://www.ltp.org/t-productsupplements.aspx.

Scripture Insights

The First Reading recalls the martyrdom of Stephen, a young disciple whose feast day is December 26. Notice the parallels between Stephen's death and that of Christ. His crime is blasphemy, and the execution takes place outside the walls of the city. In his final words he entrusts his spirit to the Lord and asks for forgiveness of those who stone him. His steadfast faith was a bold example for the first Christians.

In John's Gospel we find several famous "I am" statements by Jesus. In today's passage from Revelation, John adds others, spoken by the risen Lord. The first three are similar: "Alpha and Omega" (the first and last letter of the alphabet), "the first and the last," and "the beginning and the end." The other is "the root and offspring of David." In Revelation, the risen Lord is the Lord over all time and all things. Those "who wash their robes," that is, prepare themselves and remain faithful, are worthy to be in the presence of the risen one. This preparation may refer to baptism, it may be symbolic of a life of goodness, or it may refer to martyrdom. Moreover, they will have access to the tree of life, (in the Garden of Eden, meaning they will never die).

In the reading from John's account of the Gospel, Jesus' prayer for unity expresses a carefully thought-out identity of Jesus. He prays for his disciples, earnestly desiring that they come to know the same intimate union with him that he has with the Father. This union springs from the love of God for Jesus and his love for those the Father has given him. The love of the disciples will be a sign to the world that Jesus has come from the Father and will in turn bring glory to God.

◆ Toward the end of the reading from Revelation, what do you make of the multiple uses of the word, "come"?

◆ What modern-day Christian martyrs do you know of?

◆ How does Jesus' prayer for unity give you a sense of your own intimacy with the Lord when you pray?

READING I *Acts 2:1–11*

When the time for Pentecost was fulfilled, they were all in one place together. And suddenly there came from the sky a noise like a strong driving wind, and it filled the entire house in which they were. Then there appeared to them tongues as of fire, which parted and came to rest on each one of them. And they were all filled with the Holy Spirit and began to speak in different tongues, as the Spirit enabled them to proclaim.

Now there were devout Jews from every nation under heaven staying in Jerusalem. At this sound, they gathered in a large crowd, but they were confused because each one heard them speaking in his own language. They were astounded, and in amazement they asked, "Are not all these people who are speaking Galileans? Then how does each of us hear them in his native language? We are Parthians, Medes, and Elamites, inhabitants of Mesopotamia, Judea and Cappadocia, Pontus and Asia, Phrygia and Pamphylia, Egypt and the districts of Libya near Cyrene, as well as travelers from Rome, both Jews and converts to Judaism, Cretans and Arabs, yet we hear them speaking in our own tongues of the mighty acts of God."

RESPONSORIAL PSALM *Psalm 104:1, 24, 29–30, 31, 34 (see 30)*

R. Lord, send out your Spirit, and renew the face
      of the earth.
or: Alleluia.

Bless the LORD, O my soul!
  O LORD, my God, you are great indeed!
How manifold are your works, O LORD!
  The earth is full of your creatures. R.

If you take away their breath, they perish
  and return to their dust.
When you send forth your spirit, they are created,
  and you renew the face of the earth. R.

May the glory of the LORD endure forever;
  may the LORD be glad in his works!
Pleasing to him be my theme;
  I will be glad in the LORD. R.

READING II *Romans 8:8–17*

Alternate reading: 1 Corinthians 12:3b–7, 12–13

Brothers and sisters: Those who are in the flesh cannot please God. But you are not in the flesh; on the contrary, you are in the spirit, if only the Spirit of God dwells in you. Whoever does not have the Spirit of Christ does not belong to him. But if Christ is in you, although the body is dead because of sin, the spirit is alive because of righteousness. If the Spirit of the one who raised Jesus from the dead dwells in you, the one who raised Christ from the dead will give life to your mortal bodies also, through his Spirit that dwells in you. Consequently, brothers and sisters, we are not debtors to the flesh, to live according to the flesh. For if you live according to the flesh, you will die, but if by the Spirit you put to death the deeds of the body, you will live.

For those who are led by the Spirit of God are sons of God. For you did not receive a spirit of slavery to fall back into fear, but you received a spirit of adoption, through whom we cry, "Abba, Father!" The Spirit himself bears witness with our spirit that we are children of God, and if children, then heirs, heirs of God and joint heirs with Christ, if only we suffer with him so that we may also be glorified with him.

GOSPEL *John 14:15–16, 23b–26*

Alternate reading: John 20:19–23

Jesus said to his disciples: "If you love me, you will keep my commandments. And I will ask the Father, and he will give you another Advocate to be with you always.

"Whoever loves me will keep my word, and my Father will love him, and we will come to him and make our dwelling with him. Those who do not love me do not keep my words; yet the word you hear is not mine but that of the Father who sent me.

"I have told you this while I am with you. The Advocate, the Holy Spirit whom the Father will send in my name, will teach you everything and remind you of all that I told you."

Practice of Charity

"Breathe deep!" That's common advice at Providence Center for Medically Fragile Children in Portland, Oregon. Youngsters with profound disabilities receive round-the-clock care there, including respiratory therapy. The psalm we hear on Pentecost tells us that without God's breath, we perish, but with God's breath, we are created anew. At Providence, residents also take in great gulps of sustaining love from visiting Catholic school students. ◆ To learn more about the center, go to http://oregon.providence.org/our-services/c/center-for-medically-fragile-children/. To support its work, you may mail a donation to 830 NE 47th Ave., Portland, OR 97213. ◆ Read the United States Conference of Catholic Bishops' statement, "Welcome and Justice for Persons with Disabilities" (http://www.ncpd.org/views-news-policy/policy/church/bishops/welcome-and-justice) or call (202) 529-2933 to order a copy. ◆ Next time you settle down at home to pray, begin by taking deep, slow breaths. Imagine you are inhaling the life God has offered you and exhaling everything else.

Download more questions and activities for families, Christian initiation groups, and other adult groups at http://www.ltp.org/t-productsupplements.aspx.

Scripture Insights

Easter Time ends with the celebration of Pentecost. For fifty days the Church has been immersed in the mystery of new life with the risen Lord, a mystery that draws us into the relationship of Jesus and the Father. In the Resurrection, Jesus breaks the bonds of human limitations and promises that we too will be raised. In the Ascension, the Father receives the beloved Son into the divine realm, and with the sending of the Spirit, we become a dwelling place of the Advocate, who reminds us of all the Lord has told us. The coming of the Spirit is the birthday of the Church.

Luke describes this divine intervention in human affairs with the sound of wind and tongues of fire—divine energy that consumes and amazes the gathered assembly. The impact of the Spirit is destined to shape the Kingdom of God through the efforts of all those renewed by the Spirit—including us.

Paul tells the Romans that their very identity comes from the Spirit dwelling within them. They can no longer live "according to the flesh." The Spirit has made them adopted children of God. As "joint heirs with Christ" they are called to be witnesses by the power of the Spirit in their very lives.

In the Gospel according to John, Jesus himself delivers the Holy Spirit to the Apostles alone in the upper room, breathing on them and commissioning them. Clearly, the Spirit comes in many ways.

The Spirit of Pentecost is not confined by language, place of origin, gender, or social status; it is a universal gift that reminds us to put flesh, bones, hands, and feet on the teachings of Christ. It calls us to the mighty works of God, speaking them ourselves and seeing them in others. The gift of the Spirit is our source of life, not only for fifty days, but every day.

◆ What does the image of fire say about the work of the Spirit?

◆ What evidence in the Church points to the work of the Spirit?

◆ What does it mean to you to live according to the Spirit?

Ordinary Time, Summer

Prayer before Reading the Word

Wise and merciful God,
grant us a heart
thirsting for your truth,
longing for your presence,
and ready to hear you in the word of your Son.
Grant us the wisdom of your Spirit,
the understanding bestowed on
        the true disciples,
that we may carry the cross each day
and follow after your Son, our Lord Jesus Christ,
who lives and reigns with you
in the unity of the Holy Spirit,
one God, for ever and ever. Amen.

Prayer after Reading the Word

Your word resounds in your Church, O God,
as a fountain of wisdom and a rule of life;
make us, O God, faithful disciples of
        that wisdom,
whose Teacher and Master is Christ
and whose chair of learning is the Cross.
Schooled in this unique wisdom,
may we be prepared to conquer our fears
        and temptations,
to take up our cross daily
and to follow Jesus toward true life.
We ask this through our Lord Jesus Christ,
        your Son,
who lives and reigns with you
in the unity of the Holy Spirit,
one God, for ever and ever. Amen.

Weekday Readings

May 16: *James 3:13–18; Mark 9:14–29*
May 17: *James 4:1–10; Mark 9:30–37*
May 18: *James 4:13–17; Mark 9:38–40*
May 19: *James 5:1–6; Mark 9:41–50*
May 20: *James 5:9–12; Mark 10:1–12*
May 21: *James 5:13–20; Mark 10:13–16*

May 23: *1 Peter 1:3–9; Mark 10:17–27*
May 24: *1 Peter 1:10–16; Mark 10:28–31*
May 25: *1 Peter 1:18–25; Mark 10:32–45*
May 26: *1 Peter 2:2–5, 9–12; Mark 10:46–52*
May 27: *1 Peter 4:7–13; Mark 11:11–26*
May 28: *Jude 17, 20b–25; Mark 11:27–33*

May 30: *2 Peter 1:2–7; Mark 12:1–12*
May 31: Feast of the Visitation of the Blessed Virgin Mary
   Zephaniah 3:14–18a or Romans 12:9–16; Luke 1:39–56
June 1: *2 Timothy 1:1–3, 6–12; Mark 12:18–27*
June 2: *2 Timothy 2:8–15; Mark 12:28–34*
June 3: Solemnity of the Most Sacred Heart of Jesus
   Ezekiel 34:11–16: Romans 5:5b–11; Luke 15:3–7
June 4: *2 Timothy 4:1–8; Luke 2:41–51*

June 6: *1 Kings 17:1–6; Matthew 5:1–12*
June 7: *1 Kings 17:7–16; Matthew 5:13–16*
June 8: *1 Kings 18:20–39; Matthew 5:17–19*
June 9: *1 Kings 18:41–46; Matthew 5:20–26*
June 10: *1 Kings 19:9a, 11–16; Matthew 5:27–32*
June 11: *Acts 11:21b–26; 13:1–3; Matthew 5:33–37*

June 13: *1 Kings 21:1–16; Matthew 5:38–42*
June 14: *1 Kings 21:17–29; Matthew 5:43–48*
June 15: *2 Kings 2:1, 6–14; Matthew 6:1–6, 16–18*
June 16: *Sirach 48:1–14; Matthew 6:7–15*
June 17: *2 Kings 11:1–4, 9–18, 20; Matthew 6:19–23*
June 18: *2 Chronicles 24:17–25; Matthew 6:24–34*

June 20: *2 Kings 17:5–8, 13–15a, 18; Matthew 7:1–5*
June 21: *2 Kings 19:9b–11, 14–21, 31–35a, 36;*
   Matthew 7:6, 12–14
June 22: *2 Kings 22:8–13; 23:1–3; Matthew 7:15–20*
June 23: *2 Kings 24:8–17; Matthew 7:21–29*
June 24: Solemnity of the Nativity of St. John the Baptist
   Isaiah 49:1–6; Acts 13:22–26; Luke 1:57–66, 80
June 25: *Lamentations 2:2, 10–14, 18–19; Matthew 8:5–17*

June 27: *Amos 2:6–10, 13–16; Matthew 8:18–22*
June 28: *Amos 3:1–8; 4:11–12; Matthew 8:23–27*
June 29: Solemnity of Sts. Peter and Paul, Apostles
   Acts 12:1–11; 2 Timothy 4:6–8, 17–18; Matthew 16:13–19
June 30: *Amos 7:10–17; Matthew 9:1–8*
July 1: *Amos 8:4–6, 9–12; Matthew 9:9–13*
July 2: *Amos 9:11–15; Matthew 9:14–17*

July 4: *Hosea 2:16, 17b–18, 21–22; Matthew 9:18–26 or, for*
   Independence Day, any readings from the Lectionary for
   Ritual Masses (vol. IV), the Mass "For the Country or a
   City," nos. 882–886, or "For Peace and Justice," nos. 887–891
July 5: *Hosea 8:4–7, 11–13; Matthew 9:32–38*
July 6: *Hosea 10:1–3, 7–8, 12; Matthew 10:1–7*
July 7: *Hosea 11:1–4, 8c–9; Matthew 10:7–15*

July 8: *Hosea 14:2–10; Matthew 10:16–23*
July 9: *Isaiah 6:1–8; Matthew 10:24–33*

July 11: *Isaiah 1:10–17; Matthew 10:34—11:1*
July 12: *Isaiah 7:1–9; Matthew 11:20–24*
July 13: *Isaiah 10:5–7, 13b–16; Matthew 11:25–27*
July 14: *Isaiah 6:7–9, 12, 16–19; Matthew 11:28–30*
July 15: *Isaiah 38:1–6, 21–22, 7–8; Matthew 12:1–8*
July 16: *Micah 2:1–5; Matthew 12:14–21*

July 18: *Micah 6:1–4, 6–8; Matthew 12:38–42*
July 19: *Micah 7:14–15, 18–20; Matthew 12:46–50*
July 20: *Jeremiah 1:1, 4–10; Matthew 13:1–9*
July 21: *Jeremiah 2:1–3, 7–8, 12–13; Matthew 13:10–17*
July 22: *Jeremiah 3:14–17; John 20:1–2, 11–8*
July 23: *Jeremiah 7:1–11; Matthew 13:24–30*

July 25: Feast of St. James, Apostle
   2 Corinthians 4:7–15; Matthew 20:20–28
July 26: *Jeremiah 14:17–22; Matthew 13:36–43*
July 27: *Jeremiah 15:10, 16–21; Matthew 13:44–46*
July 28: *Jeremiah 18:1–6; Matthew 13:47–53*
July 29: *Jeremiah 26:1–9; John 11:19–27 or Luke 10:38–42*
July 30: *Jeremiah 26:11–16, 24; Matthew 14:1–12*

August 1: *Jeremiah 28:1–17; Matthew 14:13–21*
August 2: *Jeremiah 30:1–2, 12–15, 18–22;*
   Matthew 14:22–36 or 15:1–2, 10–14
August 3: *Jeremiah 31:1–7; Matthew 15:21–28*
August 4: *Jeremiah 31:31–34; Matthew 16:13–23*
August 5: *Nahum 2:1, 3; 3:1–3, 6–7; Matthew 16:24–28*
August 6: Feast of the Transfiguration of the Lord
   Daniel 7:9–10, 13–14; 2 Peter 1:16–19; Luke 9:28b–36

August 8: *Ezekiel 1:2–5, 24–28c; Matthew 17:22–27*
August 9: *Ezekiel 2:8—3:4; Matthew 18:1–5, 10, 12–14*
August 10: Feast of St. Lawrence, Deacon and Martyr
   2 Corinthians 9:6–10; John 12:24–26
August 11: *Ezekiel 12:1–12/Mt 18:21—19:1*
August 12: *Ezekiel 16:1–15, 60, 63 or 16:59–63;*
   Matthew 19:3–12
August 13: *Ezekiel 18:1–10, 13b, 30–32; Matthew 19:13–15*

August 15 Solemnity of the Assumption
   of the Blessed Virgin Mary
   Revelation 11:19a; 12:1–6a, 10ab;
   1 Corinthians 15:20–27; Luke 1:39–56
August 16: *Ezekiel 28:1–10; Matthew 19:23–30*
August 17: *Ezekiel 34:1–11; Matthew 20:1–16*
August 18: *Ezekiel 36:23–28; Matthew 22:1–14*
August 19: *Ezekiel 37:1–14; Matthew 22:34–40*
August 20: *Ezekiel 43:1–7a; Matthew 23:1–12*

August 22: *2 Thessalonians 1:1–5, 11–12; Matthew 23:13–22*
August 23: *2 Thessalonians 2:1–3a, 14–17; Matthew 23:23–26*
August 24: Feast of St. Bartholomew, Apostle
   Revelation 21:9b–14; John 1:45–51
August 25: *1 Corinthians 1:1–9; Matthew 24:42–51*
August 26: *1 Corinthians 1:17–25; Matthew 25:1–13*
August 27: *1 Corinthians 1:26–31; Matthew 25:14–30*

READING I *Proverbs 8:22–31*

Thus says the wisdom of God:
"The LORD possessed me, the beginning
      of his ways,
   the forerunner of his prodigies of long ago;
from of old I was poured forth,
   at the first, before the earth.
When there were no depths I was brought forth,
   when there were no fountains or springs
         of water;
before the mountains were settled into place,
   before the hills, I was brought forth;
while as yet the earth and fields were not made,
   nor the first clods of the world.

"When the Lord established the heavens
      I was there,
   when he marked out the vault over the face of
      the deep;
when he made firm the skies above,
   when he fixed fast the foundations of
      the earth;
when he set for the sea its limit,
   so that the waters should not transgress
      his command;
then was I beside him as his craftsman,
   and I was his delight day by day,
playing before him all the while,
   playing on the surface of his earth;
   and I found delight in the human race."

RESPONSORIAL PSALM
Psalm 8:4–5, 6–7, 8–9 (2a)

R. O Lord, our God, how wonderful your name
      in all the earth!

When I behold your heavens, the work of
         your fingers,
   the moon and the stars which you set
         in place—
what is man that you should be mindful of him,
   or the son of man that you should care
         for him? R.

You have made him little less than the angels,
   and crowned him with glory and honor.
You have given him rule over the works of
         your hands,
   putting all things under his feet. R.

All sheep and oxen,
   yes, and the beasts of the field,
the birds of the air, the fishes of the sea,
   and whatever swims the paths
         of the seas. R.

READING II *Romans 5:1–5*

Brothers and sisters: Therefore, since we have been justified by faith, we have peace with God through our Lord Jesus Christ, through whom we have gained access by faith to this grace in which we stand, and we boast in hope of the glory of God. Not only that, but we even boast of our afflictions, knowing that affliction produces endurance, and endurance, proven character, and proven character, hope, and hope does not disappoint, because the love of God has been poured out into our hearts through the Holy Spirit that has been given to us.

GOSPEL *John 16:12–15*

Jesus said to his disciples: "I have much more to tell you, but you cannot bear it now. But when he comes, the Spirit of truth, he will guide you to all truth. He will not speak on his own, but he will speak what he hears, and will declare to you the things that are coming. He will glorify me, because he will take from what is mine and declare it to you. Everything that the Father has is mine; for this reason I told you that he will take from what is mine and declare it to you."

Practice of Faith

We resume Ordinary Time with the Solemnity of the Most Holy Trinity, a celebration of the way God has revealed Godself to us: three Persons in one—Father, Son, and Holy Spirit. In becoming human, Jesus invited everyone to participate in the loving communion that the Father, Son, and Holy Spirit share. We respond to this invitation each time we bless ourselves with the Sign of the Cross. ◆ During the next few weeks, try to be more mindful as you make the Sign of the Cross. In marking our bodies and speaking the words, "In the name of the Father . . . ," we physically and spiritually incorporate ourselves into communion with the Trinity. ◆ After reading the First Reading, pray the psalm aloud, slowly, picturing wisdom working with God at the creation. ◆ Christianity is famous for its visual symbolism of threes that evokes the Trinity. It appears especially vividly in stained glass. Conduct an online image search using the search term "Trinity stained glass window." Browse the depictions and notice their colorful variety. Which do you think are particularly expressive of the Trinity, and why?

Download more questions and activities for families, Christian initiation groups, and other adult groups at http://www.ltp.org/t-productsupplements.aspx.

Scripture Insights

The Most Holy Trinity is a central mystery of our faith, and in today's readings we can see the Three Persons relating to humanity. Our Trinitarian God is passionately relational. This is not a distant, abstract God, but a God whose divine energy acts within the lives of all creatures, a God who has chosen to be in divine friendship with us, who views humans as cocreators of a world of justice and truth.

The beautiful poetry of Proverbs presents the wisdom of God as a companion to God, existing before creation, a craftsperson who assists with creation, and in whom God delights. Scripture scholars see wisdom as a foreshadowing of the Second Person of the Trinity, the Logos or Christ. But at this stage the author of Proverbs simply suggests that God enjoys a rich inner life.

In teaching the Christians in Rome that they have been justified by faith, Paul suggests the cooperative way that the Three Persons interact to bring about human salvation. Since the Romans have been justified by faith in Christ Jesus, they are empowered to live in the love of God, and that love of God has been poured into their hearts through the Holy Spirit.

Jesus' instruction to the disciples in the Gospel also alludes to the collective work of the Trinity: the Spirit will guide and teach them out of the store of truth shared mutually by the Father and Son: "Everything that the Father has is mine," and the disciples (we) will receive it when the Spirit declares it to us. The same collaboration of the Three Persons was at work in our Baptisms.

So the mystery of the Trinity is more than a prayer formula, as beloved and familiar as it is ("In the name of the Father . . ."). It is a life of relationship with God and with each other.

◆ Which of today's readings gave you a new insight into the Trinity?

◆ When have you experienced the Three Persons working together in your life?

◆ What Person of the Trinity do you most easily associate with in your prayer life?

READING I *Genesis 14:18–20*

In those days, Melchizedek, king of Salem, brought out bread and wine, and being a priest of God Most High, he blessed Abram with these words: / "Blessed be Abram by God Most High, / the creator of heaven and earth; / and blessed be God Most High, / who delivered your foes into your hand." / Then Abram gave him a tenth of everything.

RESPONSORIAL PSALM
Psalm 110:1, 2, 3, 4 (4b)

R. You are a priest for ever, in the line
of Melchizedek.

The Lord said to my Lord: "Sit at my right hand
till I make your enemies your footstool."   R.

The scepter of your power the Lord will stretch
forth from Zion:
"Rule in the midst of your enemies."   R.

"Yours is princely power in the day of your birth,
in holy splendor;
before the daystar, like the dew,
I have begotten you."   R.

The Lord has sworn, and he will not repent:
"You are a priest forever, according to the
order of Melchizedek."   R.

READING II *1 Corinthians 11:23–26*

Brothers and sisters: I received from the Lord what I also handed on to you, that the Lord Jesus, on the night he was handed over, took bread, and, after he had given thanks, broke it and said, "This is my body that is for you. Do this in remembrance of me." In the same way also the cup, after supper, saying, "This cup is the new covenant in my blood. Do this, as often as you drink it, in remembrance of me." For as often as you eat this bread and drink the cup, you proclaim the death of the Lord until he comes.

GOSPEL *Luke 9:11b–17*

Jesus spoke to the crowds about the kingdom of God, and he healed those who needed to be cured. As the day was drawing to a close, the Twelve approached him and said, "Dismiss the crowd so that they can go to the surrounding villages and farms and find lodging and provisions; for we are in a deserted place here." He said to them, "Give them some food yourselves." They replied, "Five loaves and two fish are all we have, unless we ourselves go and buy food for all these people." Now the men there numbered about five thousand. Then he said to his disciples, "Have them sit down in groups of about fifty." They did so and made them all sit down. Then taking the five loaves and the two fish, and looking up to heaven, he said the blessing over them, broke them, and gave them to the disciples to set before the crowd. They all ate and were satisfied. And when the leftover fragments were picked up, they filled twelve wicker baskets.

Practice of Faith

Today we celebrate a second solemnity, the Most Holy Body and Blood of Christ, sometimes called *Corpus Christi* (Latin for "Body of Christ"). Several traditional practices help us meditate on the ways Christ makes himself present through his Body and Blood. Find out what your parish is doing this year and participate. ◆ Many parishes organize a procession with the Blessed Sacrament after Mass, taking the Blessed Sacrament (placed in a monstrance) out into their neighborhood. Making the Body of Christ visible in the everyday world helps us, and our neighbors, realize that the risen Christ is always present in every aspect of our lives. Often parishes link the procession to Exposition of the Holy Eucharist, in which the Blessed Sacrament, in a monstrance, is placed on the altar for a period of adoration, sometimes accompanied by Scripture reading and song, sometimes by deep, prayerful silence. ◆ Serving Holy Communion at Mass and bringing Holy Communion to the sick and homebound of our communities is one of the many ways we are the Body of Christ for others. Prayerfully consider if God is calling you to serve as an Extraordinary Minister of Holy Communion in your parish.

Download more questions and activities for families, Christian initiation groups, and other adult groups at http://www.ltp.org/t-productsupplements.aspx.

Scripture Insights

On this Solemnity of the Body and Blood of Christ, the readings are connected by themes of blessing, thanksgiving, and memorial, offering insights for Eucharistic reflection. In the First Reading from Genesis, Melchizedek, "a priest of God Most High," offers a blessing prayer with two related meanings. He pronounces Abram to be blessed by God and then he blesses or offers thanksgiving to God who helped Abram win his battle. The interplay of blessing and thanksgiving is at the heart of the Eucharistic liturgy.

In the Second Reading, having just criticized the Corinthians for their disregard of others at the Lord's Supper, Paul passes on the inheritance: a retelling of Christ's words and actions on that very occasion. He recalls for the Corinthians Christ's own self-sacrifice and his charge that disciples repeat this ritual in memory of him.

Luke's account of the feeding of the five thousand is rich with imagery and Eucharistic overtones. The miracle of feeding so many with so little sends some searching for a logical explanation. But that exercise distracts us from the heart of the story: an astonishing expression of God's generosity acting through Jesus. Jesus' action is another gesture of compassion in his ministry, and a continuation of the providence of God in the history of God's people.

Notice the transformation of the disciples in this story. At first they suggest the people should fend for themselves, but Jesus draws them to cooperate with his mission. They distribute the food. What God has made possible through Jesus, Jesus extends through the disciples. The compassionate love of the Father is the work of those whom Jesus sends forth into the midst of human need. This is the tradition that has been handed on to us who celebrate the Lord's Supper today.

◆ How would you explain what Jesus teaches the disciples?

◆ Who handed the traditions of your faith on to you?

◆ How do you feed others with the gift of the Eucharist?

READING I *1 Kings 17:17–24*

Elijah went to Zarephath of Sidon to the house of a widow. The son of the mistress of the house fell sick, and his sickness grew more severe until he stopped breathing. So she said to Elijah, "Why have you done this to me, O man of God? Have you come to me to call attention to my guilt and to kill my son?" Elijah said to her, "Give me your son." Taking him from her lap, he carried the son to the upper room where he was staying, and put him on his bed. Elijah called out to the LORD: "O LORD, my God, will you afflict even the widow with whom I am staying by killing her son?" Then he stretched himself out upon the child three times and called out to the LORD: "O LORD, my God, let the life breath return to the body of this child." The LORD heard the prayer of Elijah; the life breath returned to the child's body and he revived. Taking the child, Elijah brought him down into the house from the upper room and gave him to his mother. Elijah said to her, "See! Your son is alive." The woman replied to Elijah, "Now indeed I know that you are a man of God. The word of the LORD comes truly from your mouth."

RESPONSORIAL PSALM
Psalm 30:2, 4, 5–6, 11, 12, 13 (2a)

R. I will praise you, Lord, for you have
    rescued me.

I will extol you, O LORD, for you drew me clear
    and did not let my enemies rejoice over me.
O LORD, you brought me up from the
    nether world;
    you preserved me from among those going
      down into the pit. R.

Sing praise to the LORD, you his faithful ones,
    and give thanks to his holy name.
For his anger lasts but a moment;
    a lifetime, his good will.
At nightfall, weeping enters in,
    but with the dawn, rejoicing. R.

Hear, O LORD, and have pity on me;
    O LORD, be my helper.

You changed my mourning into dancing;
    O LORD, my God, forever will I give
      you thanks. R.

READING II *Galatians 1:11–19*

I want you to know, brothers and sisters, that the gospel preached by me is not of human origin. For I did not receive it from a human being, nor was I taught it, but it came through a revelation of Jesus Christ.

For you heard of my former way of life in Judaism, how I persecuted the church of God beyond measure and tried to destroy it, and progressed in Judaism beyond many of my contemporaries among my race, since I was even more a zealot for my ancestral traditions. But when God, who from my mother's womb had set me apart and called me through his grace, was pleased to reveal his Son to me, so that I might proclaim him to the Gentiles, I did not immediately consult flesh and blood, nor did I go up to Jerusalem to those who were apostles before me; rather, I went into Arabia and then returned to Damascus.

Then after three years I went up to Jerusalem to confer with Cephas and remained with him for fifteen days. But I did not see any other of the apostles, only James the brother of the Lord.

GOSPEL *Luke 7:11–17*

Jesus journeyed to a city called Nain, and his disciples and a large crowd accompanied him. As he drew near to the gate of the city, a man who had died was being carried out, the only son of his mother, and she was a widow. A large crowd from the city was with her. When the Lord saw her, he was moved with pity for her and said to her, "Do not weep." He stepped forward and touched the coffin; at this the bearers halted, and he said, "Young man, I tell you, arise!" The dead man sat up and began to speak, and Jesus gave him to his mother. Fear seized them all, and they glorified God, exclaiming, "A great prophet has arisen in our midst," and "God has visited his people." This report about him spread through the whole of Judea and in all the surrounding region.

Practice of Charity

We may know someone who has lost a child. What can we say or do? Part of carrying on Jesus' healing ministry is simple presence, staying with the grieving person without offering fixes and without expecting any specific "results." ◆ To learn about a longtime ministry to grieving parents, go to www.compassionatefriends.org or call (877) 969-0010. The organization offers support and resources, putting grieving parents in touch with one another and informing those who want to support them about what is most helpful. ◆ If you know someone who has lost a child, offer a listening, compassionate ear. ◆ Pray for parents whose children have died, seeking special intercession of St. Felicity of Rome, patron of parents who have lost children. She and her seven children were martyred in the second century.

Download more questions and activities for families, Christian initiation groups, and other adult groups at http://www.ltp.org/t-productsupplements.aspx.

Scripture Insights

One of the most difficult situations in a priest's ministry is presiding at a child's funeral. The grief of parents is intense and heart breaking. Today's readings show us two widows, two sons, and two restorations of life.

In ancient, patriarchal societies widows were vulnerable and powerless. They found themselves on the edges, struggling to survive and bereft of social standing. Jesus and Elijah were surely aware of this. In restoring life to the sons, they restored emotional and physical life to the mothers as well.

The Gospel account tells us that when Jesus saw the widow, a stranger to him, "he was moved with pity for her." Immediately, he crosses the line of his own social tradition, for touching a dead body would render him unclean in the eyes of the religious community. Jesus' action underlines the very heart of his ministry: to bring compassion to others, no matter their social standing. The Kingdom of God and the love of the Father have no boundaries.

Elijah and Jesus are aware that their power to give life comes from God. Elijah calls on God to "let the life breath return to the body of this child." The bystanders in the Gospel proclaim the source of Jesus' intervention: "God has visited his people." Paul tells the Galatians that his call to ministry came from God "who from my mother's womb had set me apart." As do Elijah and Jesus, Paul understands that the good he does is really the grace of God flowing thorough him.

We who listen to these texts may identify with the widows as we take up the refrain of the Responsorial Psalm and make the verses our own prayer—praising God for a miraculous rescue. We are also disciples, empowered and encouraged to follow the lead of the divine compassion that wells up in us, pressing us to comfort the brokenhearted.

◆ What connections do you see between Elijah and Jesus?

◆ What spiritual comfort or insight do you find in these two stories?

◆ What have you learned from offering solace to those who grieve?

READING I *2 Samuel 12:7–10, 13*

Nathan said to David: "Thus says the LORD God of Israel: 'I anointed you king of Israel. I rescued you from the hand of Saul. I gave you your lord's house and your lord's wives for your own. I gave you the house of Israel and of Judah. And if this were not enough, I could count up for you still more. Why have you spurned the LORD and done evil in his sight? You have cut down Uriah the Hittite with the sword; you took his wife as your own, and him you killed with the sword of the Ammonites. Now, therefore, the sword shall never depart from your house, because you have despised me and have taken the wife of Uriah to be your wife.'" Then David said to Nathan, "I have sinned against the LORD." Nathan answered David: "The LORD on his part has forgiven your sin: you shall not die."

RESPONSORIAL PSALM
Psalm 32:1–2, 5, 7, 11 (see 5c)

R. Lord, forgive the wrong I have done.

Blessed is the one whose fault is taken away,
    whose sin is covered.
Blessed the man to whom the LORD imputes
        not guilt,
    in whose spirit there is no guile. R.

I acknowledged my sin to you,
    my guilt I covered not.
I said, "I confess my faults to the LORD,"
    and you took away the guilt of my sin. R.

You are my shelter; from distress you will
        preserve me;
    with glad cries of freedom you will ring
        me round. R.

Be glad in the LORD and rejoice, you just;
    exult, all you upright of heart. R.

READING II *Galatians 2:16, 19–21*

Brothers and sisters: We who know that a person is not justified by works of the law but through faith in Jesus Christ, even we have believed in Christ Jesus that we may be justified by faith in Christ and not by works of the law, because by works of the law no one will be justified. For through the law I died to the law, that I might live for God. I have been crucified with Christ; yet I live, no longer I, but Christ lives in me; insofar as I now live in the flesh, I live by faith in the Son of God who has loved me and given himself up for me. I do not nullify the grace of God; for if justification comes through the law, then Christ died for nothing.

GOSPEL *Luke 7:36—8:3*

Shorter: Luke 7:36–50

A Pharisee invited Jesus to dine with him, and he entered the Pharisee's house and reclined at table. Now there was a sinful woman in the city who learned that he was at table in the house of the Pharisee. Bringing an alabaster flask of ointment, she stood behind him at his feet weeping and began to bathe his feet with her tears. Then she wiped them with her hair, kissed them, and anointed them with the ointment. When the Pharisee who had invited him saw this he said to himself, "If this man were a prophet, he would know who and what sort of woman this is who is touching him, that she is a sinner." Jesus said to him in reply, "Simon, I have something to say to you." "Tell me, teacher," he said. "Two people were in debt to a certain creditor; one owed five hundred day's wages and the other owed fifty. Since they were unable to repay the debt, he forgave it for both. Which of them will love him more?" Simon said in reply, "The one, I suppose, whose larger debt was forgiven." He said to him, "You have judged rightly."

Then he turned to the woman and said to Simon, "Do you see this woman? When I entered your house, you did not give me water for my feet, but she has bathed them with her tears and wiped them with her hair. You did not give me a kiss, but she has not ceased kissing my feet since the time I entered. You did not anoint my head with oil, but she anointed my feet with ointment. So I tell you, her many sins have been forgiven because she has shown great love. But the one to whom little is forgiven, loves little." He said to her, "Your sins are forgiven." The others at table said to themselves, "Who is this who even forgives sins?" But he said to the woman, "Your faith has saved you; go in peace."

Afterward he journeyed from one town and village to another, preaching and proclaiming the good news of the kingdom of God. Accompanying him were the Twelve and some women who had been cured of evil spirits and infirmities, Mary, called Magdalene, from whom seven demons had gone out, Joanna, the wife of Herod's steward Chuza, Susanna, and many others who provided for them out of their resources.

Practice of Hope

The drama of sin often plays out in our own homes. Our misdeeds may not reach the level of King David's, but domestic dishonesty and greed harm the household's relationships and dampen our hope. The only way to repair the rift is forthright acknowledgement of sin, followed by forgiveness. ◆ Think of something you've done that hurt your spouse, child, parent, or sibling. Though you may not bear the sole blame, be the one to begin healing by offering these simple words: "I was wrong. Please forgive me." ◆ Worldwide Marriage Encounter has been helping couples and families for decades by teaching communication skills, especially for occasions when someone feels hurt. Go to www.wwme.org or call (800)795-LOVE to learn more and find out about a Marriage Encounter weekend retreat in your area. ◆ As a family, consider using the Church's beautiful evening prayer before or after dinner. Find one version online at http://www.universalis.com/vespers.htm.

Download more questions and activities for families, Christian initiation groups, and other adult groups at http://www.ltp.org/t-productsupplements.aspx.

Scripture Insights

The First Reading and Gospel present people who have faced their sins, who are deeply sorry, and who receive forgiveness. King David, so beloved by God, who had been living a righteous life, suddenly committed grave, shocking sins. Earlier in chapter 12, Nathan, the prophet, told David a parable that opened his mind. Today's reading begins with Nathan speaking for God, confronting David directly. Now David understands fully and is horrified by what he has done. But as Nathan reveals, God has forgiven David.

The Responsorial Psalm seems to express the emotional stages of sorrow for sin, confession, receiving forgiveness, giving thanks, and rejoicing. We find those emotions echoed in the behavior of the "sinful woman" in the Gospel. She has recognized her sins and seeks out Jesus, perhaps sensing that his compassion can heal her guilt and sorrow. Her posture, at his feet, expresses her utter sincerity and lack of defensiveness. By contrast, Simon is silently judging her—and Jesus as well—pleased with his righteousness. Like Nathan, Jesus tells Simon a parable to break through his defenses. But the key agent of healing is the generous forgiveness that God grants.

Paul explains that since forgiveness (or justification) cannot be earned by "works of the law," (the specialty of the Pharisee in the Gospel), Paul lives "by faith in the Son of God who has loved me and given himself up for me." It is the love of God, and not compliance with the Law, that ultimately saves us and invites our loving response—witness the cured women providing for Jesus "out of their resources."

The desire to love greatly comes from the unconditional love of the Lord expressed in forgiveness of our sins. Forgiveness leads to more loving, a response rooted in the love and compassion of the Lord. So when we eat at the Lord's Table we are called to love others as much as the Lord loves us.

◆ Which reading touched you or gave insight?

◆ How have you experienced forgiveness leading to greater love?

◆ What do you think Jesus means by "your faith has saved you"?

June 19, 2016 TWELFTH SUNDAY IN ORDINARY TIME

READING I *Zechariah 12:10–11; 13:1*

Thus says the LORD:

I will pour out on the house of David and on the inhabitants of Jerusalem a spirit of grace and petition; and they shall look on him whom they have pierced, and they shall mourn for him as one mourns for an only son, and they shall grieve over him as one grieves over a firstborn.

On that day the mourning in Jerusalem shall be as great as the mourning of Hadadrimmon in the plain of Megiddo.

On that day there shall be open to the house of David and to the inhabitants of Jerusalem, a fountain to purify from sin and uncleanness.

RESPONSORIAL PSALM
Psalm 63:2, 3–4, 5–6, 8–9 (2b)

R. My soul is thirsting for you, O Lord my God.

O God, you are my God whom I seek;
　for you my flesh pines and my soul thirsts
　　like the earth, parched, lifeless and
　　　　without water. R.

Thus have I gazed toward you in the sanctuary
　to see your power and your glory,
for your kindness is a greater good than life;
　my lips shall glorify you. R.

Thus will I bless you while I live;
　lifting up my hands, I will call upon
　　　　your name.
As with the riches of a banquet shall my soul
　　　　be satisfied,
　and with exultant lips my mouth shall
　　　　praise you. R.

You are my help,
　and in the shadow of your wings I shout
　　　　for joy.
My soul clings fast to you;
　your right hand upholds me. R.

READING II *Galatians 3:26–29*

Brothers and sisters:

Through faith you are all children of God in Christ Jesus. For all of you who were baptized into Christ have clothed yourselves with Christ. There is neither Jew nor Greek, there is neither slave nor free person, there is not male and female; for you are all one in Christ Jesus. And if you belong to Christ, then you are Abraham's descendant, heirs according to the promise.

GOSPEL *Luke 9:18–24*

Once when Jesus was praying in solitude, and the disciples were with him, he asked them, "Who do the crowds say that I am?" They said in reply, "John the Baptist; others, Elijah; still others, 'One of the ancient prophets has arisen.'" Then he said to them, "But who do you say that I am?" Peter said in reply, "The Christ of God." He rebuked them and directed them not to tell this to anyone.

He said, "The Son of Man must suffer greatly and be rejected by the elders, the chief priests, and the scribes, and be killed and on the third day be raised." Then he said to all, "If anyone wishes to come after me, he must deny himself and take up his cross daily and follow me. For whoever wishes to save his life will lose it, but whoever loses his life for my sake will save it."

Practice of Faith

It's easy to believe we control our lives. We can be entertained on demand, get plastic surgery and create online personas on Facebook. But our real identity, says St. Paul, is as dependent children of God. The psalmist envisions us being held in the divine hand. Life affirms the lessons of Scripture: disappointment, poverty, illness, or death awaken us to the folly of so-called autonomy. It's at low points when we can finally see that Jesus is our savior. ◆ Addicts in recovery have long been surrendering to a Higher Power. Suggest that your parish host addiction support groups. ◆ Read section 53 of *Lumen Gentium* (http://www.vatican .va/archive/hist_councils/ii_vatican_council /documents/vat-ii_const_19641121_lumen -gentium_en.html) from the Second Vatican Council. It explains Mary as a model of the kind of surrender needed in discipleship. ◆ Pray the Suscipe of St. Ignatius of Loyola, a prayer that begins, "Take, Lord, and receive all my liberty . . ." (http://www.bc.edu/bc_org/prs/stign/prayers .html).

Download more questions and activities for families, Christian initiation groups, and other adult groups at http://www.ltp.org/t-productsupplements.aspx.

Scripture Insights

Luke often describes Jesus in prayer, staying close to the Father, seeking to know the Father's will, and discerning the focus of his ministry. Today's Gospel begins with Jesus "praying in solitude" just before he opens a probing conversation with the disciples, a conversation that takes the disciples into frightening new territory.

Zechariah's prophecy in the First Reading has already sounded a minor key. It describes a scene that almost seems a prediction of the aftermath of Jesus' Passion. Such redemptive suffering and death is far from the minds of the disciples when Jesus begins his conversation about the future.

The disciples report that the crowds see Jesus as a prophet. But Jesus is also the Messiah—a challenge to the crowds, religious leaders, and his own disciples. Many expected the Messiah to over throw the political oppressors of Israel. Jesus understands his mission differently; he wants to know if the disciples have come to that awareness. Peter responds correctly, but Jesus proceeds to describe exactly what that will mean in the days ahead. Jesus' Death and Resurrection are hard for the disciples to fathom, and harder still to accept is the news that in following Jesus, they too will be asked to endure their own cross.

Paul writes about a different consequence of belonging to Christ. If we are "baptized into Christ," (and we know Paul sees baptism as dying and rising with Christ) all separating identities will fall away. The categories to which disciples cling in earthly life (the political overthrow of oppression or our very identities) will be upended.

Our cross may not be the literal suffering and death that Jesus endured; it is found in many ways throughout life when we deny our own comfort and place ourselves at the service of others. Jesus shows us that in the face of such challenges, prayer will be our lifeline: "My soul is thirsting for you, O Lord my God."

◆ How did you come to understand that you share in Jesus' Passion?

◆ What do you consider to be your cross in life?

◆ How does prayer sustain you?

READING I *1 Kings 19:16b, 19–21*

The LORD said to Elijah: "You shall anoint Elisha, son of Shaphat of Abel-meholah, as prophet to succeed you."

Elijah set out and came upon Elisha, son of Shaphat, as he was plowing with twelve yoke of oxen; he was following the twelfth. Elijah went over to him and threw his cloak over him. Elisha left the oxen, ran after Elijah, and said, "Please, let me kiss my father and mother goodbye, and I will follow you." Elijah answered, "Go back! Have I done anything to you?" Elisha left him, and taking the yoke of oxen, slaughtered them; he used the plowing equipment for fuel to boil their flesh, and gave it to his people to eat. Then Elisha left and followed Elijah as his attendant.

RESPONSORIAL PSALM *Psalm 16:1–2, 5, 7–8, 9–10, 11 (see 5a)*

R. You are my inheritance, O Lord.

Keep me, O God, for in you I take refuge;
    I say to the LORD, "My Lord are you."
O LORD, my allotted portion and my cup,
    you it is who hold fast my lot.   R.

I bless the LORD who counsels me;
    even in the night my heart exhorts me.
I set the LORD ever before me;
        with him at my right hand, I shall not be
            disturbed.   R.

Therefore my heart is glad and my soul rejoices;
    my body, too, abides in confidence,
because you will not abandon my soul to the
            netherworld,
        nor will you suffer your faithful one to
            undergo corruption.   R.

You will show me the path to life,
    fullness of joys in your presence,
        the delights at your right hand forever.   R.

READING II *Galatians 5:1, 13–18*

Brothers and sisters: For freedom Christ set us free; so stand firm and do not submit again to the yoke of slavery.

For you were called for freedom, brothers and sisters. But do not use this freedom as an opportunity for the flesh; rather, serve one another through love. For the whole law is fulfilled in one statement, namely, *You shall love your neighbor as yourself.* But if you go on biting and devouring one another, beware that you are not consumed by one another.

I say, then: live by the Spirit and you will certainly not gratify the desire of the flesh. For the flesh has desires against the Spirit, and the Spirit against the flesh; these are opposed to each other, so that you may not do what you want. But if you are guided by the Spirit, you are not under the law.

GOSPEL *Luke 9:51–62*

When the days for Jesus' being taken up were fulfilled, he resolutely determined to journey to Jerusalem, and he sent messengers ahead of him. On the way they entered a Samaritan village to prepare for his reception there, but they would not welcome him because the destination of his journey was Jerusalem. When the disciples James and John saw this they asked, "Lord, do you want us to call down fire from heaven to consume them?" Jesus turned and rebuked them, and they journeyed to another village.

As they were proceeding on their journey someone said to him, "I will follow you wherever you go." Jesus answered him, "Foxes have dens and birds of the sky have nests, but the Son of Man has nowhere to rest his head."

And to another he said, "Follow me." But he replied, "Lord, let me go first and bury my father." But he answered him, "Let the dead bury their dead. But you, go and proclaim the kingdom of God." And another said, "I will follow you, Lord, but first let me say farewell to my family at home." To him Jesus said, "No one who sets a hand to the plow and looks to what was left behind is fit for the kingdom of God."

Practice of Charity

We sometimes wander from one civic cause to another. Discouraged by lack of results, even devoted advocates of social justice can take a mercurial path, never forming deep bonds. This will change when we discover that we are working not only for specific earthly outcomes, but for the truth of the cause and for harmony in human relationships—those that characterize the Kingdom of God. Keeping the hand to the plow means staying steadfast, not necessarily looking for successful resolutions. ◆ Make a list of your charitable or social justice activities. Ask if you are focused on material ends alone or on Kingdom-oriented value. ◆ Read Trappist monk Fr. Thomas Merton's *Letter to a Young Activist* (http://bintana.tripod.com/ref /letter.htm). It applies even to those who are no longer young. ◆ Pray the Lord's Prayer, focusing for an extended time on the line, "thy Kingdom come, thy will be done."

Download more questions and activities for families, Christian initiation groups, and other adult groups at http://www.ltp.org/t-productsupplements.aspx.

Scripture Insights

Many passages in the Gospel make us affirmed in our discipleship. Just as Jesus treated his first followers with affection and understanding, we believe he regards us in the same way. His teaching about the love and mercy of the Father must have given them courage and strengthened their decision to follow him. We look forward to some affirmation as we try to live our mission as his disciples. Today's Gospel may not be one of those passages!

Jesus is on his way to Jerusalem, and we know what awaits him there. The conversation between Jesus and the three would-be followers is a reality check for those who are already disciples, those who want to be, and for us. The seeming harshness of Jesus' brief responses cannot be taken literally, nor can they be taken lightly.

To the first, Jesus responds that he has no place or home; he has a destination that will involve suffering and death. The inquirer is left to decide whether he or she will go that far. To the second person who must first return home to bury his father, Jesus implies that a bigger family should be his first concern. The third person wants to wait until he bids farewell to his family. Jesus says that once a disciple has accepted the call and put his hand to the plow, other details must be put aside.

The call of Elisha that comes from God through Elijah demands the same hard choices. Elisha's dramatic slaughtering his oxen indicates his choice to accept the mantle (the cloak) of Elijah, leaving his former way of life and following the will of the Lord.

For Jesus, the call to do the work of the Father is an urgent and critical decision; it means accepting the mission of the Kingdom without condition or hesitation. Jesus offers this choice to all of us; not just once but many times.

◆ With which of the inquirers in the Gospel do you identify?

◆ What decisions do you need to make in order to follow the Lord every day?

◆ How do you understand Paul's advice to "live by the Spirit"?

READING I *Isaiah 66:10–14c*

Thus says the LORD:
Rejoice with Jerusalem and be glad because
  of her,
 all you who love her;
exult, exult with her,
 all you who were mourning over her!
Oh, that you may suck fully
 of the milk of her comfort,
that you may nurse with delight
 at her abundant breasts!
 For thus says the LORD:
Lo, I will spread prosperity over Jerusalem
  like a river,
 and the wealth of the nations
   like an overflowing torrent.
As nurslings, you shall be carried in her arms,
 and fondled in her lap;
as a mother comforts her child,
 so will I comfort you;
 in Jerusalem you shall find your comfort.

When you see this, your heart shall rejoice
 and your bodies flourish like the grass;
the LORD's power shall be known to
  his servants.

RESPONSORIAL PSALM
Psalm 66:1–3, 4–5, 6–7, 16, 20 (1)

R. Let all the earth cry out to God with joy.

Shout joyfully to God, all the earth;
 sing praise to the glory of his name;
 proclaim his glorious praise.
Say to God, "How tremendous are
  your deeds!" R.

"Let all on earth worship and sing praise to you,
 sing praise to your name!"
Come and see the works of God,
 his tremendous deeds among the children
  of Adam. R.

He changed the sea into dry land;
 through the river they passed on foot;
 therefore let us rejoice in him.
He rules by his might forever. R.

Hear now, all you who fear God,
 while I declare what he has done for me.
Blessed be God, who refused me not
 my prayer or his kindness! R.

READING II *Galatians 6:14–18*

Brothers and sisters: May I never boast except in the cross of our Lord Jesus Christ, through which the world has been crucified to me, and I to the world. For neither does circumcision mean anything, nor does uncircumcision, but only a new creation. Peace and mercy be to all who follow this rule and to the Israel of God.

From now on, let no one make troubles for me; for I bear the marks of Jesus on my body.

The grace of our Lord Jesus Christ be with your spirit, brothers and sisters. Amen.

GOSPEL *Luke 10:1–12, 17–20*

Shorter: Luke 10:1–9

At that time the Lord appointed seventy-two others whom he sent ahead of him in pairs to every town and place he intended to visit. He said to them, "The harvest is abundant but the laborers are few; so ask the master of the harvest to send out laborers for his harvest. Go on your way; behold, I am sending you like lambs among wolves. Carry no money bag, no sack, no sandals; and greet no one along the way. Into whatever house you enter, first say, 'Peace to this household.' If a peaceful person lives there, your peace will rest on him; but if not, it will return to you. Stay in the same house and eat and drink what is offered to you, for the laborer deserves his payment. Do not move about from one house to another. Whatever town you enter and they welcome you, eat what is set before you, cure the sick in it and say to them, 'The kingdom of God is at hand for you.' Whatever town you enter and they do not receive you, go out into the streets and say, 'The dust of your town that clings to our feet, even that we shake off against you.' Yet know this: the kingdom of God is at hand. I tell you, it will be more tolerable for Sodom on that day than for that town."

The seventy-two returned rejoicing, and said, "Lord, even the demons are subject to us because of your name." Jesus said, "I have observed Satan fall like lightning from the sky. Behold, I have given you the power to 'tread upon serpents' and scorpions and upon the full force of the enemy and nothing will harm you. Nevertheless, do not rejoice because the spirits are subject to you, but rejoice because your names are written in heaven."

Practice of Faith

The words "Mass" and "mission" have the same Latin root. Worship leads us to live out faith in everyday life. When the priest says "The Mass is ended," consider that a beginning of action. The mission of the earliest disciples, and of the Israelites before them, was to speak about the wonderful things God had done in their lives. Personal witness is still the most powerful evangelization. ◆ Think of one person you know who seems open to talking about deep matters but who is not part of your church. Find the right time to talk about how you believe God is involved in your life. ◆ Read the introduction (paragraphs 1–9) of the United States Conference of Catholic Bishops' document on evangelization, *Go and Make Disciples* (www. usccb.org/beliefs-and-teachings/how-we-teach /evangelization/go-and-make-disciples or call 877-978-0757 to request a copy). The bishops say we all have a compelling story of faith to share. ◆ Pray the bishops' New Evangelization Prayer (www.usccb. org/prayer-and-worship/prayers-and-devotions /prayers/new-evangelization-prayer.cfm).

Download more questions and activities for families, Christian initiation groups, and other adult groups at http://www.ltp.org/t-productsupplements.aspx.

Scripture Insights

When Jesus sends the disciples to "every town and place he intended to visit" they became both migrants and missionaries. In some places they were unwelcome and their message not well received. We can identify. Often our individual efforts to bring the Word of God to bear on a situation, a relationship, or a course of action can seem fruitless. And yet Jesus sends the disciples ahead of him. At other times disciples follow, and in a sense we always follow him. In another sense, he comes after us, gathering up the results of our labor to present to the Father.

In spite of the challenges of the disciples' mission ("I am sending you like lambs among wolves") the tone of today's readings is joy: "exult, exult. . . all you who were mourning over [Jerusalem]," says Isaiah. As Jesus imbued his disciples with everything they needed for their mission, God, Isaiah shows us, is the prime mover in his time as well: "I will spread prosperity over Jerusalem like a river . . . the LORD's power shall be known to his servants."

Paul, too, says all that he does is rooted in the grace of God. He can boast of nothing except the power of the Lord working through him. We have received the same mandate as the disciples: to go into the whole world to preach the Good News. Today's Responsorial Psalm would make a perfect song for evangelizers: "Let all the earth cry out to God with joy" and "Hear now . . . while I declare what he has done for me." We don't need any luggage to do this. Whenever we have helped another person in their faith journey, it wasn't what we owned that made a difference. It was what we believed in, how we loved, and the way we were present that was transforming.

◆ What aspects of the call to discipleship do you see in each reading?

◆ What elements of the Gospel text give you courage in your ministry?

◆ Is there any luggage that you could leave behind on your journey of faith?

READING I *Deuteronomy 30:10–14*

Moses said to the people: "If only you would heed the voice of the LORD, your God, and keep his commandments and statutes that are written in this book of the law, when you return to the LORD, your God, with all your heart and all your soul.

"For this command that I enjoin on you today is not too mysterious and remote for you. It is not up in the sky, that you should say, 'Who will go up in the sky to get it for us and tell us of it, that we may carry it out?' Nor is it across the sea, that you should say, 'Who will cross the sea to get it for us and tell us of it, that we may carry it out?' No, it is something very near to you, already in your mouths and in your hearts; you have only to carry it out."

RESPONSORIAL PSALM *Psalm 69:14, 17, 30–31, 33–34, 36, 37 (see 33)*

Alternate reading: Psalm 19:8, 9, 10, 11 (9a)

R. Turn to the Lord in your need, and you
will live.

I pray to you, O LORD,
for the time of your favor, O God!
In your great kindness answer me
with your constant help.
Answer me, O LORD, for bounteous is
your kindness;
in your great mercy turn toward me. R.

I am afflicted and in pain;
let your saving help, O God, protect me.
I will praise the name of God in song,
and I will glorify him
with thanksgiving. R.

"See, you lowly ones, and be glad;
you who seek God, may your hearts revive!
For the LORD hears the poor,
and his own who are in bonds
he spurns not." R.

For God will save Zion
and rebuild the cities of Judah.
The descendants of his servants shall inherit it,
and those who love his name shall inhabit it.

READING II *Colossians 1:15–20*

Christ Jesus is the image of the invisible God,
the firstborn of all creation.
For in him were created all things
in heaven and on earth,
the visible and the invisible,
whether thrones or dominions or
principalities or powers;
all things were created through him and
for him.
He is before all things,
and in him all things hold together.
He is the head of the body, the church.
He is the beginning, the firstborn from the dead,
that in all things he himself might
be preeminent.
For in him all the fullness was pleased to dwell,
and through him to reconcile
all things for him,
making peace by the blood of his cross
through him, whether those on earth or those
in heaven.

GOSPEL *Luke 10:25–37*

There was a scholar of the law who stood up to test him and said, "Teacher, what must I do to inherit eternal life?" Jesus said to him, "What is written in the law? How do you read it?" He said in reply,
"*You shall love the Lord, your God,*
with all your heart,
with all your being,
with all your strength,
and with all your mind,
and your neighbor as yourself."
He replied to him, "You have answered correctly; do this and you will live."

But because he wished to justify himself, he said to Jesus, "And who is my neighbor?" Jesus replied, "A man fell victim to robbers as he went down from Jerusalem to Jericho. They stripped and beat him and went off leaving him half-dead. A priest happened to be going down that road, but when he saw him, he passed by on the opposite side. Likewise a Levite came to the place, and when he saw him, he passed by on the opposite side. But a

Samaritan traveler who came upon him was moved with compassion at the sight. He approached the victim, poured oil and wine over his wounds and bandaged them. Then he lifted him up on his own animal, took him to an inn, and cared for him. The next day he took out two silver coins and gave them to the innkeeper with the instruction, 'Take care of him. If you spend more than what I have given you, I shall repay you on my way back.' Which of these three, in your opinion, was neighbor to the robbers' victim?" He answered, "The one who treated him with mercy." Jesus said to him, "Go and do likewise."

Practice of Hope

Often, we hope for flashy divine action in the world. But usually, God works subtly in the everyday events of life. Our task is to respond openly and lovingly to what God sets before us. We cannot walk past unaware. ◆ Next time you meet a person who is homeless or mentally ill, try to welcome the encounter as a gift from God. If possible, ask to listen to the person's story, offering human dignity instead of spare change. If the only safe course is prayer, do that. ◆ Watch the 2005 film *Millions*, rated PG. Quirky but reverent, it shows a boy who is conscious of how God operates in the world's odd circumstances. ◆ At the end of the day, before you get sleepy, write in your journal about the ways God was present to you over the past 24 hours. That is a version of a longtime Catholic prayer form, the examen.

Download more questions and activities for families, Christian initiation groups, and other adult groups at http://www.ltp.org/t-productsupplements.aspx.

Scripture Insights

The familiar parable of the Good Samaritan always catches our attention and leads us to examine our conscience. The "scholar of the law" is testing Jesus, hoping to expose a flaw. But Jesus uses the opportunity to teach a lesson the scholar does not anticipate. When Jesus invites him to share his interpretation, he quotes the great summary of the law in Deuteronomy 6:4. Later in that chapter, Moses will point out what we hear in the First Reading—that the law is not complex or remote. In other words, one should not need a "scholar of the law" to understand it, because it is "already in your mouths and in your hearts." It is a matter of the heart, not the intellect.

In Jesus' parable, those capable and obligated to help (the priest and the Levite) pass by the helpless victim. The Samaritan, who is not obligated to give assistance, does. The point of the encounter in Jesus' parable is the difference between knowing and doing. Knowing the law is one thing; actually living it is another. The compassion of the Samaritan is not rooted in the law or social conventions; it is simply an act of human decency that responds to the situation from the heart.

Perhaps the priest and Levite were paralyzed by trying to rationalize the situation—mentally looking for a loophole in the law to exempt themselves. The Samaritan, by contrast, had an inner source for his action. Jesus connects it with the love of God found in the commandment quoted by the scholar, the love already in the outcast Samaritan's heart. Jesus redistributes the weight of the law, emphasizing love over knowledge.

A modern-day paraphrase might be that the love of God and love of neighbor is our spiritual DNA. It's what defines us as disciples. The scholar receives an answer to his question. We don't know what the scholar did after that; we do know what we must do.

◆ What part of the law did the scholar not understand?

◆ When have you been a Good Samaritan?

◆ What hinders us from living the commandment of love of God?

READING I *Genesis 18:1–10a*

The LORD appeared to Abraham by the terebinth of Mamre, as he sat in the entrance of his tent, while the day was growing hot. Looking up, Abraham saw three men standing nearby. When he saw them, he ran from the entrance of the tent to greet them; and bowing to the ground, he said: "Sir, if I may ask you this favor, please do not go on past your servant. Let some water be brought, that you may bathe your feet, and then rest yourselves under the tree. Now that you have come this close to your servant, let me bring you a little food, that you may refresh yourselves; and afterward you may go on your way." The men replied, "Very well, do as you have said."

Abraham hastened into the tent and told Sarah, "Quick, three measures of fine flour! Knead it and make rolls." He ran to the herd, picked out a tender, choice steer, and gave it to a servant, who quickly prepared it. Then Abraham got some curds and milk, as well as the steer that had been prepared, and set these before the three men; and he waited on them under the tree while they ate.

They asked Abraham, "Where is your wife Sarah?" He replied, "There in the tent." One of them said, "I will surely return to you about this time next year, and Sarah will then have a son."

RESPONSORIAL PSALM
Psalm 15:2–3, 3–4, 5 (1a)

R. He who does justice will live in the presence
of the Lord.

One who walks blamelessly and does justice;
who thinks the truth in his heart
and slanders not with his tongue.   R.

Who harms not his fellow man,
nor takes up a reproach against his neighbor;
by whom the reprobate is despised,
while he honors those who fear the LORD.   R.

Who lends not his money at usury
and accepts no bribe against the innocent.
One who does these things
shall never be disturbed.   R.

READING II *Colossians 1:24–28*

Brothers and sisters: Now I rejoice in my sufferings for your sake, and in my flesh I am filling up what is lacking in the afflictions of Christ on behalf of his body, which is the church, of which I am a minister in accordance with God's stewardship given to me to bring to completion for you the word of God, the mystery hidden from ages and from generations past. But now it has been manifested to his holy ones, to whom God chose to make known the riches of the glory of this mystery among the Gentiles; it is Christ in you, the hope for glory. It is he whom we proclaim, admonishing everyone and teaching everyone with all wisdom, that we may present everyone perfect in Christ.

GOSPEL *Luke 10:38–42*

Jesus entered a village where a woman whose name was Martha welcomed him. She had a sister named Mary who sat beside the Lord at his feet listening to him speak. Martha, burdened with much serving, came to him and said, "Lord, do you not care that my sister has left me by myself to do the serving? Tell her to help me." The Lord said to her in reply, "Martha, Martha, you are anxious and worried about many things. There is need of only one thing. Mary has chosen the better part and it will not be taken from her."

Practice of Charity

Liturgy begins before we sing the opening song. The way we greet each other, and especially the quality of our welcome to newcomers, establishes our worship as a preview of God's Kingdom. Hospitality can bring us into the presence of the holy. ◆ Prayerfully consider becoming a greeter at your parish. If you are an introvert, you have an irreplaceable role, too, perhaps in designing the strategy of welcome as part of a parish hospitality committee. ◆ Read the Rule of St. Benedict, chapter 53, "On the Reception of Guests," (www.osb.org /rb/text/rbeaad1.html or order a copy from Paraclete Press, 800-451-5006). The monks are champions of hospitality. They are taught to revere guests, especially the poor and pilgrims, because Christ "is received in their persons." ◆ Imagine yourself as a character in the story of Martha and Mary. Pray to see the value in what each woman did.

Download more questions and activities for families, Christian initiation groups, and other adult groups at http://www.ltp.org/t-productsupplements.aspx.

Scripture Insights

Some preachers have given Martha a bad rap. She is portrayed as the complainer and Mary as the good sister who honors Jesus by sitting and listening to him. Other commentators say that when Luke wrote his Gospel for the early Church he was responding to their search for the meaning of discipleship. Was it found in service or in contemplation?

Ample evidence in the letters of Paul and in Acts of the Apostles points to many forms of ministry in the early Church: ministries of leadership and teaching; ministries at the Lord's table; ministries of social care, especially for the poor, the widows, and orphans; and ministries within the liturgy, such as preachers and evangelizers. This passage would support the role of men and women in both forms of ministry: prayerful support of the message of the Lord as well as engagement in the needs of the community.

The question raised for both men and women is what to do in response to the call of the Lord. Mary and Martha could represent both aspects of discipleship. It is not a matter of which is more important, but how they complement each other.

Jesus seeks to change Martha's way of thinking. Her gestures of hospitality are good things to do, but she has become anxious and her gestures of service risk becoming a burden and not a source of joy.

We usually connect gestures of Christian hospitality with joy. Abraham is delighted as he hurries to extend hospitality to his visitors. He offers an effusive welcome and waits on them while they eat.

There are two elements in ministry: to listen attentively and to act lovingly. Like Mary we listen to the teaching of the Lord; like Martha we also serve. The true disciple is the one who can serve without forgetting to listen, and who can listen without forgetting to serve.

◆ What gestures or words of hospitality do you find in the readings?

◆ Do you identify with Mary or Martha?

◆ In what sense are we welcoming the Lord when we offer hospitality?

READING I *Genesis 18:20–32*

In those days, the LORD said: "The outcry against Sodom and Gomorrah is so great, and their sin so grave, that I must go down and see whether or not their actions fully correspond to the cry against them that comes to me. I mean to find out."

While Abraham's visitors walked on farther toward Sodom, the LORD remained standing before Abraham. Then Abraham drew nearer and said: "Will you sweep away the innocent with the guilty? Suppose there were fifty innocent people in the city; would you wipe out the place, rather than spare it for the sake of the fifty innocent people within it? Far be it from you to do such a thing, to make the innocent die with the guilty so that the innocent and the guilty would be treated alike! Should not the judge of all the world act with justice?" The LORD replied, "If I find fifty innocent people in the city of Sodom, I will spare the whole place for their sake." Abraham spoke up again: "See how I am presuming to speak to my LORD, though I am but dust and ashes! What if there are five less than fifty innocent people? Will you destroy the whole city because of those five?" He answered, "I will not destroy it, if I find forty-five there." But Abraham persisted, saying "What if only forty are found there?" He replied, "I will forbear doing it for the sake of the forty." Then Abraham said, "Let not my Lord grow impatient if I go on. What if only thirty are found there?" He replied, "I will forbear doing it if I can find but thirty there." Still Abraham went on, "Since I have thus dared to speak to my Lord, what if there are no more than twenty?" The LORD answered, "I will not destroy it, for the sake of the twenty." But he still persisted: "Please, let not my Lord grow angry if I speak up this last time. What if there are at least ten there?" He replied, "For the sake of those ten, I will not destroy it."

RESPONSORIAL PSALM
Psalm 138:1–2, 2–3, 6–7, 7–8 (3a)

R. Lord, on the day I called for help, you
      answered me.

I will give thanks to you, O LORD, with all
      my heart,
  for you have heard the words of my mouth;
  in the presence of the angels
      I will sing your praise;
I will worship at your holy temple
  and give thanks to your name.   R.

Because of your kindness and your truth;
  for you have made great above all things
  your name and your promise.
When I called you answered me;
  you built up strength within me.   R.

The LORD is exalted, yet the lowly he sees,
  and the proud he knows from afar.
Though I walk amid distress, you preserve me;
  against the anger of my enemies you raise
      your hand.   R.

Your right hand saves me.
  The LORD will complete what he has done
      for me;
your kindness, O LORD, endures forever;
  forsake not the work of your hands.

READING II *Colossians 2:12–14*

Brothers and sisters: You were buried with him in baptism, in which you were also raised with him through faith in the power of God, who raised him from the dead. And even when you were dead in transgressions and the uncircumcision of your flesh, he brought you to life along with him, having forgiven us all our transgressions; obliterating the bond against us, with its legal claims, which was opposed to us, he also removed it from our midst, nailing it to the cross.

GOSPEL *Luke 11:1–13*

Jesus was praying in a certain place, and when he had finished, one of his disciples said to him, "Lord, teach us to pray just as John taught his disciples." He said to them, "When you pray, say:

Father, hallowed be your name,
your kingdom come.
Give us each day our daily bread
and forgive us our sins
for we ourselves forgive everyone in debt to us,
and do not subject us to the final test."

And he said to them, "Suppose one of you has a friend to whom he goes at midnight and says, 'Friend, lend me three loaves of bread, for a friend of mine has arrived at my house from a journey and I have nothing to offer him,' and he says in reply from within, 'Do not bother me; the door has already been locked and my children and I are already in bed. I cannot get up to give you anything.' I tell you, if he does not get up to give the visitor the loaves because of their friendship, he will get up to give him whatever he needs because of his persistence.

"And I tell you, ask and you will receive; seek and you will find; knock and the door will be opened to you. For everyone who asks, receives; and the one who seeks, finds; and to the one who knocks, the door will be opened. What father among you would hand his son a snake when he asks for a fish? Or hand him a scorpion when he asks for an egg? If you then, who are wicked, know how to give good gifts to your children, how much more will the Father in heaven give the Holy Spirit to those who ask him?"

Practice of Hope

Watch the film version of *Fiddler on the Roof*. Pay attention to Tevye's frank relationship with God. ◆ List three things you hope for. Ask God for them, but pray that God's will be done in all things. ◆ Food banks run short in summer. Be part of God's plan to provide daily bread to a family.

Download more questions and activities for families, Christian initiation groups, and other adult groups at http://www.ltp.org/t-productsupplements.aspx.

Scripture Insights

Today's readings explore the dynamics of prayer. When the disciples ask Jesus to teach them to pray as he prays, they want to know what comes from his heart when he goes off by himself to pray. They know the traditional Jewish prayers, like the psalms, but they want to learn the prayer that comes from his heart as he prays before the Father. Learning the Son's prayer will help them learn and live into the disposition of his heart.

First he tells them, turn to God in humility: "Father, hallowed be your name." Begin from the place that knows you are not in control, that you are vulnerable and need God. Then he teaches them the prayer that we know as the Our Father. It is often called the all-purpose Christian prayer that we know by heart from our earliest years. In that prayer we discover a wonderful insight: it is not a prayer asking God for something that God may or may not be willing to give. God gave us his Son Jesus; would God withhold anything we seek?

Abraham asks God six times to spare the people of the town; each time God relents and agrees to be merciful. He seems to welcome the requests because he wants to be merciful. In the Gospel the sleeping friend will eventually respond to his friend's request for bread, not only because he is able to, but because of the friend's persistent trust. And the father will not give his son a scorpion but an egg, not only because he can, but because he desires to do so.

The point of Jesus' stories is that the Father is willing and waiting to give! Learning to pray the prayer of Jesus is learning the art of reception. We seem to have mastered the prayers of supplication and intercession; we need also to learn how to receive what God so deeply and lovingly desires to bestow upon us.

◆ Why do you think Jesus prayed? What clues do you find in the Scripture? How do his reasons relate to your reasons for prayer?

◆ What words of the Our Father are most meaningful for you at this time?

◆ How is praying an act of faith and trust for you?

READING I *Ecclesiastes 1:2; 2:21–23*

Vanity of vanities, says Qoheleth,
    vanity of vanities! All things are vanity!
    Here is one who has labored with wisdom and knowledge and skill, and yet to another who has not labored over it, he must leave property. This also is vanity and a great misfortune. For what profit comes to man from all the toil and anxiety of heart with which he has labored under the sun? All his days sorrow and grief are his occupation; even at night his mind is not at rest. This also is vanity.

RESPONSORIAL PSALM *Psalm 90:3–4, 5–6, 12–13, 14, 17 (8)*

R. If today you hear his voice, harden not
        your hearts.

You turn man back to dust,
    saying, "Return, O children of men."
For a thousand years in your sight
    are as yesterday, now that it is past,
    or as a watch of the night.   R.

You make an end of them in their sleep;
    the next morning they are like
        the changing grass,
which at dawn springs up anew,
    but by evening wilts and fades.   R.

Teach us to number our days aright,
    that we may gain wisdom of heart.
Return, O LORD! How long?
    Have pity on your servants!   R.

Fill us at daybreak with your kindness,
    that we may shout for joy
        and gladness all our days.
And may the gracious care of the LORD our God
        be ours;
    prosper the work of our hands for us!
    Prosper the work of our hands!   R.

READING II *Colossians 3:1–5, 9–11*

Brothers and sisters: If you were raised with Christ, seek what is above, where Christ is seated at the right hand of God. Think of what is above, not of what is on earth. For you have died, and your life is hidden with Christ in God. When Christ your life appears, then you too will appear with him in glory.

Put to death, then, the parts of you that are earthly: immorality, impurity, passion, evil desire, and the greed that is idolatry. Stop lying to one another, since you have taken off the old self with its practices and have put on the new self, which is being renewed, for knowledge, in the image of its creator. Here there is not Greek and Jew, circumcision and uncircumcision, barbarian, Scythian, slave, free; but Christ is all and in all.

GOSPEL *Luke 12:13–21*

Someone in the crowd said to Jesus, "Teacher, tell my brother to share the inheritance with me." He replied to him, "Friend, who appointed me as your judge and arbitrator?" Then he said to the crowd, "Take care to guard against all greed, for though one may be rich, one's life does not consist of possessions."

Then he told them a parable. "There was a rich man whose land produced a bountiful harvest. He asked himself, 'What shall I do, for I do not have space to store my harvest?' And he said, 'This is what I shall do: I shall tear down my barns and build larger ones. There I shall store all my grain and other goods and I shall say to myself, "Now as for you, you have so many good things stored up for many years, rest, eat, drink, be merry!"' But God said to him, 'You fool, this night your life will be demanded of you; and the things you have prepared, to whom will they belong?' Thus will it be for all who store up treasure for themselves but are not rich in what matters to God."

Practice of Faith

A recent luxury car commercial pushes conspicuous consumerism as the American way, even poking fun at less prosperous societies. But it's as clear now as it was in Jesus' time: the more we own, the more potential barriers we have in our relationship with God. If we have too many belongings, we suffer for it. ◆ Take a survey of your possessions. Do one thing to reduce what you own. For example, give away clothes or shoes, donate a car, or cut your cable channels. ◆ Learn about the Chicago-based Ignatian Spirituality Program (www.ispretreats .org or 312-226-9184). The mostly volunteer-run organization provides free retreats for people recovering from addiction to alcohol, drugs, and other things that displaced God and human relationships from the center of their lives. The retreats seek to help addicts regain their priorities and find their true selves. ◆ Reflect on what displaces God from your life.

Download more questions and activities for families, Christian initiation groups, and other adult groups at http://www.ltp.org/t-productsupplements.aspx.

Scripture Insights

Scripture often addresses the tension between the priorities of our earthly life and the priorities of the spiritual life. The author of Ecclesiastes seeks wisdom on this human predicament. The word *vanity,* repeated six times in this short passage, means "that which is transitory or lacking in substance." No wonder, then, that the pursuit of things for their own sake is pointless. Instead of bringing joy it causes "anxiety of heart," even "sorrow and grief."

The Gospel parable offers wisdom to help disciples discern what is valuable in the labors of life. The farmer is successful and happy. But the parable reveals a crucial flaw in his thinking: the enormous harvest is his and he should keep all of it, taking it easy and making merry. He becomes fixated on building bigger barns to store his produce. Even acknowledging that he worked very hard, still the harvest wasn't entirely his doing. The land could be an image of God who always provides more than expected.

As the farmer reflects on his good fortune he uses the pronoun "I" six times, and sets up the tension between greed and gift, mine and ours, selfishness and selflessness.

Jesus does not condemn possessions, though he often speaks of them as an obstacle to the Kingdom, advising people to sell their goods, give the money to the poor, and follow him. He challenges the notion that life is found in building bigger barns (or closets). At some point things actually own us. Paul makes a similar point about spiritual matters. We are to put aside "what is on earth" in order to focus on a life in Christ.

The challenge placed before us by each of the readings is found in the words of Jesus: "one's life does not consist of possessions" but to be rich in everything that "matters to God."

◆ How would you explain Jesus' thinking on the accumulation of possessions?

◆ Do you sometimes feel like the farmer, needing more space for stuff?

◆ Why are we so reluctant to separate ourselves from material things?

READING I *Wisdom 18:6–9*

The night of the passover was known
    beforehand to our fathers,
  that, with sure knowledge of the oaths in
    which they put their faith,
  they might have courage.
Your people awaited the salvation of the just
  and the destruction of their foes.
For when you punished our adversaries,
  in this you glorified us whom you
    had summoned.
For in secret the holy children of the good were
  offering sacrifice
  and putting into effect with one accord the
    divine institution.

RESPONSORIAL PSALM
Psalm 33:1, 12, 18–19, 20–22 (12b)

R. Blessed the people the Lord has chosen to
    be his own.

Exult, you just, in the LORD;
  praise from the upright is fitting.
Blessed the nation whose God is the LORD,
  the people he has chosen for his own
    inheritance. R.

See, the eyes of the LORD are upon those who
    fear him,
  upon those who hope for his kindness,
to deliver them from death
  and preserve them in spite of famine. R.

Our soul waits for the LORD,
  who is our help and our shield.
May your kindness, O LORD, be upon us
  who have put our hope in you. R.

READING II *Hebrews 11:1–2, 8–12*

Longer: Hebrews 11:1–2, 8–19

Brothers and sisters: Faith is the realization of
what is hoped for and evidence of things not seen.
Because of it the ancients were well attested.

    By faith Abraham obeyed when he was called
to go out to a place that he was to receive as an
inheritance; he went out, not knowing where he
was to go. By faith he sojourned in the promised
land as in a foreign country, dwelling in tents with
Isaac and Jacob, heirs of the same promise; for he
was looking forward to the city with foundations,
whose architect and maker is God. By faith he
received power to generate, even though he was past
the normal age—and Sarah herself was sterile—for
he thought that the one who had made the promise was trustworthy. So it was that there came
forth from one man, himself as good as dead,
descendants as numerous as the stars in the sky
and as countless as the sands on the seashore.

GOSPEL *Luke 12:32–48*

Shorter: Luke 12:35–40

Jesus said to his disciples: "Do not be afraid any
longer, little flock, for your Father is pleased to give
you the kingdom. Sell your belongings and give
alms. Provide money bags for yourselves that do
not wear out, an inexhaustible treasure in heaven
that no thief can reach nor moth destroy. For where
your treasure is, there also will your heart be.

    "Gird your loins and light your lamps and be
like servants who await their master's return from
a wedding, ready to open immediately when he
comes and knocks. Blessed are those servants
whom the master finds vigilant on his arrival.
Amen, I say to you, he will gird himself, have them
recline at table, and proceed to wait on them. And
should he come in the second or third watch and
find them prepared in this way, blessed are those
servants. Be sure of this: if the master of the house
had known the hour when the thief was coming,
he would not have let his house be broken into.
You also must be prepared, for at an hour you do
not expect, the Son of Man will come."

    Then Peter said, "Lord, is this parable meant
for us or for everyone?" And the Lord replied,
"Who, then, is the faithful and prudent steward
whom the master will put in charge of his servants
to distribute the food allowance at the proper
time? Blessed is that servant whom his master on
arrival finds doing so. Truly, I say to you, the master will put the servant in charge of all his property. But if that servant says to himself, 'My master

is delayed in coming,' and begins to beat the menservants and the maidservants, to eat and drink and get drunk, then that servant's master will come on an unexpected day and at an unknown hour and will punish the servant severely and assign him a place with the unfaithful. That servant who knew his master's will but did not make preparations nor act in accord with his will shall be beaten severely; and the servant who was ignorant of his master's will but acted in a way deserving of a severe beating shall be beaten only lightly. Much will be required of the person entrusted with much, and still more will be demanded of the person entrusted with more."

Practice of Hope

As summer winds down, we anticipate autumn with hope, but often with anxiety. Students wonder if they'll be popular, if they'll make the team, or if classes will overwhelm them. Adults foresee project-laden months on the job. For retirees, the coming winter may seem daunting. ◆ Jesus told his followers to cast aside fear because fear is not useful in the Kingdom. List two situations you dread, plus strategies for overcoming fear. How can your courage help build up the Kingdom? ◆ Read section 5 of St. John Paul's 1978 papal inauguration homily, in which he urges Catholics to welcome Christ into their lives without fear: http://www.vatican.va/holy_father/john_paul_ii/homilies/1978/documents/hf_jp-ii_hom_19781022_inizio-pontificato_en.html or call 877-978-0757 (United States Conference of Catholic Bishops Publications) to order a copy. ◆ Hope and courage resulted in Abraham and Sarah's descendants, numerous as the stars. Pray about what your "descendants" might be. What legacy will your hope and courage create?

Download more questions and activities for families, Christian initiation groups, and other adult groups at http://www.ltp.org/t-productsupplements.aspx.

Scripture Insights

We live in a society in which plans, schedules, appointments, and agendas consume our time, not only the present as it unfolds, but our future. Often such attention to plans is necessary to help us negotiate our life. But in our life of faith there is always the element of the unplanned, the possibilities that we have not scheduled, the pathways on which the Lord leads us, and the grace that comes to us unsolicited but always promised.

The story of Abraham is one of great faith, of trust in the promise of God. In the Second Reading, the descriptive words of the author of Hebrews might give many of us great anxiety: "he went out, not knowing where he was to go"! Yet he traveled to the promised land because he believed the promise of God. The pregnancy of Sarah was itself a sign that God would be faithful, even in the most surprising way.

Today's Gospel could seem more appropriate to Advent, but placed near the halfway point in Jesus' public ministry, it is an urgent instruction to the disciples to be prepared for their own task of preaching the Good News of the Kingdom of God. Their plans for this future ministry are to rely more on their spiritual treasure than any material resource. Jesus asks them to be as vigilant as the servant who prepares for the return of the master of the household. And this vigilance is not merely *waiting* around for the master, it is time spent *doing* the will of the master.

Like the servant and the first disciples, we do not know when the Lord will return to take us to the Father, but we are ever vigilant in our ministry of preaching the Word of God in the meantime. With the faith of Abraham we are ready to accept and engage the grace that God gives us to be faithful servants.

◆ What is a "prudent" servant expected to do?

◆ How does the example of Abraham inspire you to move forward?

◆ What issues in your life challenge your faith that God's grace will be with you for whatever comes?

111

READING I *Jeremiah 38:4–6, 8–10*

In those days, the princes said to the king: "Jeremiah ought to be put to death; he is demoralizing the soldiers who are left in this city, and all the people, by speaking such things to them; he is not interested in the welfare of our people, but in their ruin." King Zedekiah answered: "He is in your power"; for the king could do nothing with them. And so they took Jeremiah and threw him into the cistern of Prince Malchiah, which was in the quarters of the guard, letting him down with ropes. There was no water in the cistern, only mud, and Jeremiah sank into the mud.

Ebed-melech, a court official, went there from the palace and said to him: "My lord king, these men have been at fault in all they have done to the prophet Jeremiah, casting him into the cistern. He will die of famine on the spot, for there is no more food in the city." Then the king ordered Ebed-melech the Cushite to take three men along with him, and draw the prophet Jeremiah out of the cistern before he should die.

RESPONSORIAL PSALM
Psalm 40:2, 3, 4, 18 (14b)

R. Lord, come to my aid!

I have waited, waited for the LORD,
   and he stooped toward me.   R.

The LORD heard my cry.
He drew me out of the pit of destruction,
   out of the mud of the swamp;
he set my feet upon a crag;
   he made firm my steps.   R

And he put a new song into my mouth,
   a hymn to our God.
Many shall look on in awe
   and trust in the Lord.   R.

Though I am afflicted and poor,
   yet the Lord thinks of me.
You are my help and my deliverer;
   O my God, hold not back!   R.

READING II *Hebrews 12:1–4*

Brothers and sisters: Since we are surrounded by so great a cloud of witnesses, let us rid ourselves of every burden and sin that clings to us and persevere in running the race that lies before us while keeping our eyes fixed on Jesus, the leader and perfecter of faith. For the sake of the joy that lay before him he endured the cross, despising its shame, and has taken his seat at the right of the throne of God. Consider how he endured such opposition from sinners, in order that you may not grow weary and lose heart. In your struggle against sin you have not yet resisted to the point of shedding blood.

GOSPEL *Luke 12:49–53*

Jesus said to his disciples: "I have come to set the earth on fire, and how I wish it were already blazing! There is a baptism with which I must be baptized, and how great is my anguish until it is accomplished! Do you think that I have come to establish peace on the earth? No, I tell you, but rather division. From now on a household of five will be divided, three against two and two against three; a father will be divided against his son and a son against his father, a mother against her daughter and a daughter against her mother, a mother-in-law against her daughter-in-law and a daughter-in-law against her mother-in-law."

Practice of Hope

We Christians sometimes feel we should always be agreeable. But often we are called to utter uncomfortable truths, like a prophet or Jesus himself. ◆ Whether it's defending unborn life, calling for economic justice in our neighborhoods, or being critical of fighting a war, our faith sometimes calls us to rock the boat. Write a letter to your local newspaper, expressing what you know is true about an issue on which you feel called to act. ◆ But before proclaiming, become well educated about your cause. Visit the website of the United States Conference of Catholic Bishops, www.usccb.org. Type the issue of concern into the search box and read through the selections. You can order documents by calling 877 978 0757. ◆ Life can be hard for truth tellers. They must trust God's plan when times get tough. Maintain hope that God will guide you to the truth and help you in times of trouble.

Download more questions and activities for families, Christian initiation groups, and other adult groups at http://www.ltp.org/t-productsupplements.aspx.

Scripture Insights

In Scripture, fire is a powerful image. The pillar of fire led the Israelites to freedom; the tongues of fire hovered over the disciples at Pentecost; the disciples of Emmaus reported that their hearts were on fire after eating with the risen Lord.

Spiritual writers speak of a fire of love, of a passion for the work of the Gospel burning within the hearts of the faithful.

Today's Gospel portrays Jesus at his most vehement and unsettling. He says that he has come to set the world on fire. For him the world is the people of God and the fire is the energy of his mission. John the Baptist had proclaimed that one was coming after him who would baptize with the Holy Spirit and fire, inflaming his disciples. Jesus speaks of a baptism that he has accepted (his suffering and Death) and implies that those who hear his teaching will need the same energy for the mission that he has.

The author of Hebrews speaks of Christ's whole-hearted dedication to the mission, a level of conviction that eventually led him to the Cross. This is the example placed before those who follow Jesus "while keeping [their] eyes fixed" on him.

Jesus acknowledges that his message will likely bring division between those who accept it and those who do not. The issues of justice and acceptance and equality were often contentious in his time; and they often cause division in our own day.

It is not always easy to proclaim the Gospel. Prophets are hard to come by and those who step forward are often mistreated; Jeremiah, in the First Reading, was passionate in speaking God's words of warning and condemnation as the country crumbled, and was often attacked for it.

By virtue of our own Baptism, we already share in Jesus' mission. Maybe the attitude of the disciple is to be ever ready to catch on fire with Jesus' love.

◆ What similarities do you see between Jeremiah and Jesus?

◆ What particular teaching of Jesus gives you a fire for discipleship?

◆ Have you ever known of a time when the Word of God caused division?

August 21, 2016 Twenty-First Sunday in Ordinary Time

Reading I *Isaiah 66:18–21*

Thus says the Lord: I know their works and their thoughts, and I come to gather nations of every language; they shall come and see my glory. I will set a sign among them; from them I will send fugitives to the nations: to Tarshish, Put and Lud, Mosoch, Tubal and Javan, to the distant coastlands that have never heard of my fame, or seen my glory; and they shall proclaim my glory among the nations. They shall bring all your brothers and sisters from all the nations as an offering to the Lord, on horses and in chariots, in carts, upon mules and dromedaries, to Jerusalem, my holy mountain, says the Lord, just as the Israelites bring their offering to the house of the Lord in clean vessels. Some of these I will take as priests and Levites, says the Lord.

Responsorial Psalm
Psalm 117:1, 2 (Mark 16:15)

R. Go out to all the world and tell the
       Good News.
or: Alleluia.

Praise the Lord, all you nations;
   glorify him, all you peoples! R.

For steadfast is his kindness toward us,
   and the fidelity of the Lord endures
            forever. R.

Reading II *Hebrews 12:5–7, 11–13*

Brothers and sisters: You have forgotten the exhortation addressed to you as children: "My son, do not disdain the discipline of the Lord or lose heart when reproved by him; for whom the Lord loves, he disciplines; he scourges every son he acknowledges." Endure your trials as "discipline"; God treats you as sons. For what "son" is there whom his father does not discipline? At the time, all discipline seems a cause not for joy but for pain, yet later it brings the peaceful fruit of righteousness to those who are trained by it.

So strengthen your drooping hands and your weak knees. Make straight paths for your feet, that what is lame may not be disjointed but healed.

Gospel *Luke 13:22–30*

Jesus passed through towns and villages, teaching as he went and making his way to Jerusalem. Someone asked him, "Lord, will only a few people be saved?" He answered them, "Strive to enter through the narrow gate, for many, I tell you, will attempt to enter but will not be strong enough. After the master of the house has arisen and locked the door, then will you stand outside knocking and saying, 'Lord, open the door for us.' He will say to you in reply, 'I do not know where you are from.' And you will say, 'We ate and drank in your company and you taught in our streets.' Then he will say to you, 'I do not know where you are from. Depart from me, all you evildoers!' And there will be wailing and grinding of teeth when you see Abraham, Isaac, and Jacob and all the prophets in the kingdom of God and you yourselves cast out. And people will come from the east and the west and from the north and the south and will recline at table in the kingdom of God. For behold, some are last who will be first, and some are first who will be last."

Practice of Charity

Being a member of any group—a church or a nation—can lead to good things. Belonging gives us identity and calls us to be selfless and devoted to mission. On the other hand, strong affiliation can leave us insular or haughty, which runs counter to the Kingdom of God. ◆ Study the Church's position on immigration reform at www.usccb.org/issues-and-action/human-life-and-dignity/immigration/churchteachingonimmigrationreform.cfm or call 877-978-0757 to obtain a copy of any of the statements by the United States Conference of Catholic Bishops. The bishops call for family reunification and earned legalization for those who have crossed the border without authorization. ◆ After study and reflection, contact your federal lawmaker and explain the kind of immigration reform you want to see. ◆ Attend a Mass held in Spanish or Vietnamese in your neighborhood, which will perhaps inspire you to pray with some immigrants. Ponder Pope Francis' words that he wants all Catholics and Christians to think of each other first as brother or sister.

Download more questions and activities for families, Christian initiation groups, and other adult groups at http://www.ltp.org/t-productsupplements.aspx.

Scripture Insights

If there is one common characteristic associated with entrance into the Kingdom of God in references by the great Hebrew prophets and the teachings of Jesus, it is its unpredictability. In the First Reading from Isaiah and in the Gospel, the surprise of the Kingdom of God is the difference between who is included and who could be excluded.

Isaiah describes the gathering of "nations of every language" who come to see the glory of the Lord. But the nations named are not part of the Chosen People of Israel. They represent pagan peoples who have not heard of the "fame" of the Lord; yet they are destined to proclaim the glory of the Lord. The salvation of God will be universal; it will not belong to one nation or people but be offered to everyone.

The teaching of Jesus in the Gospel echoes this new understanding. Those who thought they would be allowed into the home of the master because they had some casual acquaintance with him will be disappointed when others may enter and they are turned away. Being part of the master's household requires more than a social relationship. Although the invitation to the Kingdom of God is freely given, our response to such a gift cannot be a smugness that we deserved it and others did not. In other teachings Jesus will give many examples of how his followers ought to live in response to the promise of the Father's favor.

The author of Hebrews speaks of paying attention to "the discipline of the Lord." The word *discipline* does not mean "punishment," but rather "wise instruction"—even "healing." Just as a son or daughter pays attention to a parent's discipline, so the follower of Christ attends to his teachings in order to attain the "peaceful fruit of righteousness."

◆ How do you understand the phrase, "some are last who will be first, and some are first who will be last?"

◆ Whom do you think Christians sometimes exclude from the Kingdom of God?

◆ How could your parish be more inclusive?

August 28, 2016 — Twenty-Second Sunday in Ordinary Time

READING I *Sirach 3:17–18, 20, 28–29*

My child, conduct your affairs with humility,
  and you will be loved more than a giver
      of gifts.
Humble yourself the more, the greater you are,
  and you will find favor with God.
What is too sublime for you, seek not,
  into things beyond your strength search not.
The mind of a sage appreciates proverbs,
  and an attentive ear is the joy of the wise.
Water quenches a flaming fire,
  and alms atone for sins.

RESPONSORIAL PSALM
Psalm 68:4–5, 6–7, 10–11 (see 11b)

R. God, in your goodness, you have made
      a home for the poor.

The just rejoice and exult before God;
  they are glad and rejoice.
Sing to God, chant praise to his name;
  whose name is the LORD. R.

The father of orphans and the defender
      of widows
  is God in his holy dwelling.
God gives a home to the forsaken;
  he leads forth prisoners to prosperity. R.

A bountiful rain you showered down, O God,
      upon your inheritance;
  you restored the land when it languished;
your flock settled in it;
  in your goodness, O God, you provided it for
      the needy. R.

READING II
Hebrews 12:18–19, 22–24a

Brothers and sisters: You have not approached that which could be touched and a blazing fire and gloomy darkness and storm and a trumpet blast and a voice speaking words such that those who heard begged that no message be further addressed to them. No, you have approached Mount Zion and the city of the living God, the heavenly Jerusalem, and countless angels in festal gathering, and the assembly of the firstborn enrolled in heaven, and God the judge of all, and the spirits of the just made perfect, and Jesus, the mediator of a new covenant, and the sprinkled blood that speaks more eloquently than that of Abel.

GOSPEL *Luke 14:1, 7–14*

On a sabbath Jesus went to dine at the home of one of the leading Pharisees, and the people there were observing him carefully.

He told a parable to those who had been invited, noticing how they were choosing the places of honor at the table. "When you are invited by someone to a wedding banquet, do not recline at table in the place of honor. A more distinguished guest than you may have been invited by him, and the host who invited both of you may approach you and say, 'Give your place to this man,' and then you would proceed with embarrassment to take the lowest place. Rather, when you are invited, go and take the lowest place so that when the host comes to you he may say, 'My friend, move up to a higher position.' Then you will enjoy the esteem of your companions at the table. For every one who exalts himself will be humbled, but the one who humbles himself will be exalted." Then he said to the host who invited him, "When you hold a lunch or a dinner, do not invite your friends or your brothers or your relatives or your wealthy neighbors, in case they may invite you back and you have repayment. Rather, when you hold a banquet, invite the poor, the crippled, the lame, the blind; blessed indeed will you be because of their inability to repay you. For you will be repaid at the resurrection of the righteous."

Practice of Charity

"I like to stay behind the scenes."

"Not one for the limelight."

Across the nation, salt-of-the earth people labor quietly in charitable causes. They fill food boxes for needy families or organize auctions for schools. Whatever they do, they avoid personal glory and so follow the Gospel in a particularly effective way. ◆ Contact your local St. Vincent de Paul conference to join or make a donation. St. Vincent de Paul is full of humble workers, whether in the pantry or in the office tallying regional food distribution. For more information, go to www.svdpusa.org or call 314-576-3993 ◆ Read section 93 of Pope Francis' *Joy of the Gospel*, in which he cautions Catholics against spiritual worldliness and advises them to see God's glory. (http://w2.vatican.va/content/francesco/en/apost _exhortations/documents/papa-francesco _esortazione-ap_20131124_evangelii-gaudium .html) ◆ St. Vincent de Paul, 1581–1660, once said, "Humility is nothing but truth, and pride is nothing but lying." Use this idea as a basis for prayer.

Download more questions and activities for families, Christian initiation groups, and other adult groups at http://www.ltp.org/t-productsupplements.aspx.

Scripture Insights

Humility has always been an essential attitude in the spiritual life. Taming our human tendencies toward self-importance can be a challenge. The author of Sirach teaches that humility brings more honor than gift giving. And, the important person who is humble will find favor with God. Being humble is accepting the truth that one's state and status in life come from God, not from a person's own initiative.

The psalmist extols the graciousness of God who showers goodness on the needy and gives a home to those whom others have forsaken. Clearly such recipients of God's favor are not able to repay God; nor are they obligated to do so. The providence of God is pure gift.

In the Gospel parable, Jesus continues to affirm the place of humility in the life of those who would enter the Kingdom of God. Once again Jesus is a guest at a meal, observing people closely. When the moment is right, he tells a parable that could sound like advice on etiquette (how to avoid embarrassment at a dinner party), but it is rooted in a teaching about humility. To those who have been trying to find places of honor at the table, he advises taking the lowest place, for "every one who exalts himself will be humbled, but the one who humbles himself will be exalted." The implied teaching is that the banquet of the Kingdom is open to all; God's grace is inclusive, not exclusive. The one who is humble enough to recognize that always receives the best place, no matter where it is.

The parable also includes important advice for the host. If the ones invited to the banquet are able to return the favor in kind, then where is the virtue of generosity? The virtuous host invites those who cannot repay; therein lays his or her reward. In this way they become imitators of the Lord whose goodness to others is lauded in the psalm.

◆ How does the parable apply to our celebration of Eucharist?

◆ What gestures of humility do you find difficult in your ministry?

◆ What keeps you humble in your life as a disciple?

Prayer before
Reading the Word

God of the covenant,
whose promises can never fail,
in every age you place your words
on the lips of the prophets.
We children of this age come to you in faith,
longing to be transformed in Christ
as children of the Resurrection.

Give us humility of heart.
Let us cling to your Word
in Moses, the prophets, and the Gospel.
Let each new day be for us
a time to testify to the Gospel.

We ask this through our Lord
        Jesus Christ, your Son,
who lives and reigns with you
in the unity of the Holy Spirit,
one God, for ever and ever. Amen.

Prayer after
Reading the Word

O God, author of life and resurrection,
before whom even the dead are alive,
grant that the Word of your Son,
sown in our hearts,
may blossom and bear fruit in every good work,
so that both in life and in death
our hearts may be strengthened
by eternal comfort and good hope.

We ask this through our Lord
        Jesus Christ, your Son,
who lives and reigns with you
in the unity of the Holy Spirit,
one God, for ever and ever. Amen.

August 29: *1 Corinthians 2:1–5; Mark 6:17–29*
August 30: *1 Corinthians 2:10b–16; Luke 4:31–37*
August 31: *1 Corinthians 3:1–9; Luke 4:38–44*
September 1: *1 Corinthians 3:18–23; Luke 5:1–11*
September 2: *1 Corinthians 4:1–5; Luke 5:33–39*
September 3: *1 Corinthians 4:6b–15; Luke 6:1–5*

September 5: *1 Corinthians 5:1–8; Luke 6:6–11*
September 6: *1 Corinthians 6:1–11; Luke 6:12–19*
September 7: *1 Corinthians 7:25–31; Luke 6:20–26*
**September 8: Feast of the Nativity of the Blessed
    Virgin Mary**
**Micah 5:1–4a or Romans 8:28–30; Matthew 1:1–16, 18–23
    or 1:18–23**
September 9: *1 Corinthians 9:16–19, 22b–27; Luke 6:39–42*
September 10: *1 Corinthians 10:14–22; Luke 6:43–49*

September 12: *1 Corinthians 11:17–26, 33; Luke 7:1–10*
September 13: *1 Corinthians 12:12–14, 27–31a; Luke 7:11–17*
**September 14: Feast of the Exaltation of the Holy Cross
    Numbers 21:4b–9; Philippians 2:6–11; John 3:13–17**
September 15: *1 Corinthians 15:1–11; John 19:25–27 or
    Luke 2:33–35*
September 16: *1 Corinthians 15:12–20; Luke 8:1–3*
September 17: *1 Corinthians 15:35–37, 42–49; Luke 8:4–15*

September 19: Proverbs 3:27–34; Luke 8:16–18
September 20: Proverbs 21:1–6, 10–13; Luke 8:19–21
**September 21: Feast of St. Matthew, Apostle and Evangelist
    Ephesians 4:1–7, 11–13; Matthew 9:9–13**
September 22: *Ecclesiastes 1:2–11; Luke 9:7–9*
September 23: *Ecclesiastes 3:1–11; Luke 9:18–22*
September 24: *Ecclesiastes 11:9—12:8; Luke 9:43b–45*

September 26: *Job 1:6–22; Luke 9:46–50*
September 27: *Job 3:1–3, 11–17, 20–23; Luke 9:51–56*
September 28: *Job 9:1–12, 14–16; Luke 9:57–62*
**September 29: Feast of Sts. Michael, Gabriel and
    Raphael, Archangels**
Daniel 7:9–10, 13–14 or Revelation 12:7–12a; John 1:47–51
September 30: Job 38:1, 12–21; 40:3–5; Luke 10:13–16
October 1: Job 42:1–3, 5–6, 12–17; Luke 10:17–24

October 3: *Galatians 1:6–12; Luke 10:25–37*
October 4: *Galatians 1:13–24; Luke 10:38–42*
October 5: *Galatians 2:1–2, 7–14; Luke 11:1–4*
October 6: *Galatians 3:1–5; Luke 11:5–13*
October 7: *Galatians 3:7–14; Luke 11:15–26*
October 8: *Galatians 3:22–29; Luke 11:27–28*

October 10: *Galatians 4:22–24, 26–27, 31—5:1; Luke 11:29–32*
October 11: *Galatians 5:1–6; Luke 11:37–41*
October 12: *Galatians 5:18–25; Luke 11:42–46*
October 13: *Ephesians 1:1–10; Luke 11:47–54*
October 14: *Ephesians 1:11–14; Luke 12:1–7*
October 15: *Ephesians 1:15–23; Luke 12:8–12*

October 17: *Ephesians 2:1–10; Luke 12:13–21*
**October 18: Feast of St. Luke, Evangelist
    2 Timothy 4:10–17b; Luke 10:1–9**
October 19: *Ephesians 3:2–12; Luke 12:39–48*
October 20: *Ephesians 3:14–21; Luke 12:49–53*
October 21: *Ephesians 4:1–6; Luke 12:54–59*
October 22: *Ephesians 4:7–16; Luke 13:1–9*

October 24: *Ephesians 4:32—5:8; Luke 13:10–17*
October 25: *Ephesians 5:21–33 or 5:2a, 25–32; Luke 13:18–21*
October 26: *Ephesians 6:1–9; Luke 13:22–30*
October 27: *Ephesians 6:10–20; Luke 13:31–35*
**October 28: Feast of Sts. Simon and Jude, Apostles
    Ephesians 2:19–22; Luke 6:12–16**
October 29: *Philippians 1:18b–26; Luke 14:1, 7–11*

October 31: *Philippians 2:1–4; Luke 14:12–14*
**November 1: Solemnity of All Saints
    Revelation 7:2–4, 9–14; 1 John 3:1–3; Matthew 5:1–12a**
**November 2: Commemoration of All the Faithful Departed
    (All Souls' Day)
    Wisdom 3:1–9; Romans 5:5–11 or Romans 6:3–9;
    John 6:37–40**
November 3: *Philippians 3:3–8a; Luke 15:1–10*
November 4: *Philippians 3:17—4:1; Luke 16:1–8*
November 5: *Philippians 4:10–19; Luke 16:9–15*

November 7: *Titus 1:1–9; Luke 17:1–6*
November 8: *Titus 2:1–8, 11–14; Luke 17:7–10*
**November 9: Feast of the Dedication of the Lateran Basilica
    Ezekiel 47:1–2, 8–9, 12; 1 Corinthians 3:9c–11, 16–17;
    John 2:13–22**
November 10: *Philemon 7–20; Luke 17:20–25*
November 11: *2 John 4–9; Luke 17:26–37*
November 12: *3 John 5–8; Luke 18:1–8*

November 14: *Revelation 1:1–4; 2:1–5; Luke 18:35–43*
November 15: *Revelation 3:1–6, 14–22; Luke 19:1–10*
November 16: *Revelation 4:1–11; Luke 19:11–28*
November 17: *Revelation 5:1–10; Luke 19:41–44*
November 18: *Revelation 10:8–11; Luke 19:45–48*
**or, for the Memorial of the Dedication of the Basilicas of
    Sts. Peter and Paul, Apostles,**
Acts 28:11–16, 30–31; Matthew 14:22–33
November 19: *Revelation 11:4–12; Luke 20:27–40*

November 21: *Revelation 14:1–3, 4b–5; Luke 21:1–4*
November 22: *Revelation 14:14–19; Luke 21:5–11*
November 23: *Revelation 15:1–4; Luke 21:12–19*
November 24: *Revelation 18:1–2, 21–23; 19:1–3, 9a;
    Luke 21:20–28,*
**or, for Thanksgiving Day, any readings from the
    Lectionary for Ritual Masses (vol. IV), the Mass "In
    Thanksgiving to God," nos. 943–947 (see esp. Sirach
    50:22–24; 1 Corinthians 1:3–9; Luke 17:11–19)**
November 25: *Revelation 20:1–4, 11—21:2; Luke 21:29–33*
November 26: *Revelation 22:1–7; Luke 21:34–36*

READING I *Wisdom 9:13–18b*

Who can know God's counsel,
   or who can conceive what the LORD intends?
For the deliberations of mortals are timid,
   and unsure are our plans.
For the corruptible body burdens the soul
   and the earthen shelter weighs down the mind
         that has many concerns.
And scarce do we guess the things on earth,
   and what is within our grasp
         we find with difficulty;
but when things are in heaven,
         who can search them out?
Or who ever knew your counsel, except you
         had given wisdom
   and sent your holy spirit from on high?
And thus were the paths of those
         on earth made straight.

RESPONSORIAL PSALM
Psalm 90:3–4, 5–6, 12–13, 14, 17 (1)

R. In every age, O Lord,
         you have been our refuge.

You turn man back to dust,
   saying, "Return, O children of men."
For a thousand years in your sight
   are as yesterday, now that it is past,
   or as a watch of the night.   R.

You make an end of them in their sleep;
   the next morning they are
         like the changing grass,
which at dawn springs up anew,
   but by evening wilts and fades.   R.

Teach us to number our days aright,
   that we may gain wisdom of heart.
Return, O LORD! How long?
   Have pity on your servants!   R.

Fill us at daybreak with your kindness,
   that we may shout for joy and gladness
         all our days.

And may the gracious care of the LORD our God
         be ours;
   prosper the work of our hands for us!
   Prosper the work of our hands! R.

READING II *Philemon 9–10, 12–17*

I, Paul, an old man, and now also a prisoner for Christ Jesus, urge you on behalf of my child Onesimus, whose father I have become in my imprisonment; I am sending him, that is, my own heart, back to you. I should have liked to retain him for myself, so that he might serve me on your behalf in my imprisonment for the gospel, but I did not want to do anything without your consent, so that the good you do might not be forced but voluntary. Perhaps this is why he was away from you for a while, that you might have him back forever, no longer as a slave but more than a slave, a brother, beloved especially to me, but even more so to you, as a man and in the Lord. So if you regard me as a partner, welcome him as you would me.

GOSPEL *Luke 14:25–33*

Great crowds were traveling with Jesus, and he turned and addressed them, "If anyone comes to me without hating his father and mother, wife and children, brothers and sisters, and even his own life, he cannot be my disciple. Whoever does not carry his own cross and come after me cannot be my disciple. Which of you wishing to construct a tower does not first sit down and calculate the cost to see if there is enough for its completion? Otherwise, after laying the foundation and finding himself unable to finish the work the onlookers should laugh at him and say, 'This one began to build but did not have the resources to finish.' Or what king marching into battle would not first sit down and decide whether with ten thousand troops he can successfully oppose another king advancing upon him with twenty thousand troops? But if not, while he is still far away, he will send a delegation to ask for peace terms. In the same way, anyone of you who does not renounce all his possessions cannot be my disciple."

Practice of Faith

What blocks you from the Reign of God? Career? Bank account? Housework? Are you so mesmerized by family drama that you neglect spiritual obligations and the needs of others? Every one of us faces obstacles to discipleship. ◆ We cannot desert family or job, but we can incorporate prayerfulness and charity into both. Pray for five minutes before work and before you see your family in the evening. We have well-founded faith that the Holy Spirit makes a difference in day-to-day matters. ◆ Read the section "Called to Justice in Everyday Life," in the United States Conference of Catholic Bishops' pastoral letter, "Everyday Christianity: To Hunger and Thirst for Justice." (www.usccb.org /beliefs-and-teachings/what-we-believe/catholic -social-teaching/everyday-christianity-to-hunger -and-thirst-for-justice.cfm) ◆ In a journal, write about times when you've lost perspective on your role in the world; for example, when you've felt like a failure or sensed despair. Ask the Holy Spirit to help you understand how this pain might be converted to strengthen your discipleship.

Download more questions and activities for families, Christian initiation groups, and other adult groups at http://www.ltp.org/t-productsupplements.aspx.

Scripture Insights

Wisdom can be an elusive element in making human choices. Each of today's readings offers perspective on wisdom. The author of the Book of Wisdom begs the question, "Who can know God's counsel [wisdom] or who can conceive what the LORD intends?" The answer is, of course, no one. In fact, the author states, even humans are not sure of their own plans, let alone those of God. But God chooses to bestow wisdom on people and it is this divine gift that allows "those on earth" to choose wisely.

The wisdom in Jesus' teaching is twofold. First, those choosing to follow Jesus need practical wisdom. They will have to leave behind whatever distractions would hinder them from accepting the mission he desires for them. They will need to discern what it will take for them to "finish the work" of discipleship, as workers need to do when completing a construction project.

The second wisdom is a deeper sense of commitment, a choice that will mean following Jesus as their first priority in life and relationships. The word *hating* that appears in the translation should not be understood in the same sense that we associate with despising another. Jesus never advocated hatred, always love. He impresses upon his listeners that following him is a radical choice, and will take great spiritual courage.

In his letter, Paul writes about Gospel wisdom. He appeals to Philemon, the owner of Onesimus the slave, in the spirit of brotherhood that comes from the shared mission they have in Christ Jesus. He implores Philemon to put aside his former way of relating to Onesimus, as an owner, and to accept him as he would accept Paul, in a spirit of partnership. The wisdom of God comes to us both as gift and as responsibility.

◆ How is humility, as expressed in the First Reading, an aspect of wisdom?

◆ What helps you to choose wisely in matters of faith?

◆ How daunting is it to hear Jesus describe discipleship in such stark terms? Are we up to it?

READING I *Exodus 32:7–11, 13–14*

The LORD said to Moses, "Go down at once to your people, whom you brought out of the land of Egypt, for they have become depraved. They have soon turned aside from the way I pointed out to them, making for themselves a molten calf and worshiping it, sacrificing to it and crying out, 'This is your God, O Israel, who brought you out of the land of Egypt!' I see how stiff-necked this people is," continued the LORD to Moses. "Let me alone, then, that my wrath may blaze up against them to consume them. Then I will make of you a great nation."

But Moses implored the LORD, his God, saying, "Why, O LORD, should your wrath blaze up against your own people, whom you brought out of the land of Egypt with such great power and with so strong a hand? Remember your servants Abraham, Isaac, and Israel, and how you swore to them by your own self, saying, 'I will make your descendants as numerous as the stars in the sky; and all this land that I promised, I will give your descendants as their perpetual heritage.'" So the LORD relented in the punishment he had threatened to inflict on his people.

READING II *1 Timothy 1:12–17*

Beloved: I am grateful to him who has strengthened me, Christ Jesus our Lord, because he considered me trustworthy in appointing me to the ministry. I was once a blasphemer and a persecutor and arrogant, but I have been mercifully treated because I acted out of ignorance in my unbelief. Indeed, the grace of our Lord has been abundant, along with the faith and love that are in Christ Jesus. This saying is trustworthy and deserves full acceptance: Christ Jesus came into the world to save sinners. Of these I am the foremost. But for that reason I was mercifully treated, so that in me, as the foremost, Christ Jesus might display all his patience as an example for those who would come to believe in him for everlasting life. To the king of ages, incorruptible, invisible, the only God, honor and glory forever and ever. Amen.

GOSPEL *Luke 15:1–32*

Shorter: Luke 15:1–10

Tax collectors and sinners were all drawing near to listen to Jesus, but the Pharisees and scribes began to complain, saying, "This man welcomes sinners and eats with them." So to them he addressed this parable. "What man among you having a hundred sheep and losing one of them would not leave the ninety-nine in the desert and go after the lost one until he finds it? And when he does find it, he sets it on his shoulders with great joy and, upon his arrival home, he calls together his friends and neighbors and says to them, 'Rejoice with me because I have found my lost sheep.' I tell you, in just the same way there will be more joy in heaven over one sinner who repents than over ninety-nine righteous people who have no need of repentance.

"Or what woman having ten coins and losing one would not light a lamp and sweep the house, searching carefully until she finds it? And when she does find it, she calls together her friends and neighbors and says to them, 'Rejoice with me because I have found the coin that I lost.' In just the same way, I tell you, there will be rejoicing among the angels of God over one sinner who repents."

Then he said, "A man had two sons, and the younger son said to his father, 'Father give me the share of your estate that should come to me.' So the father divided the property between them. After a few days, the younger son collected all his belongings and set off to a distant country where he squandered his inheritance on a life of dissipation. When he had freely spent everything, a severe famine struck that country, and he found himself in dire need. So he hired himself out to one of the local citizens who sent him to his farm to tend the swine. And he longed to eat his fill of the pods on which the swine fed, but nobody gave him any. Coming to his senses he thought, 'How many of my father's hired workers have more than enough food to eat, but here am I, dying from hunger. I shall get up and go to my father and I shall say to him, "Father, I have sinned against heaven and against you. I no longer deserve to be called your son; treat me as you would treat one of your hired workers."' So he got up and went back to his father. While he was still a long way off, his father caught sight of him, and was filled with compassion. He ran to his son, embraced him and kissed him. His son said to him, 'Father, I have sinned against heaven and against you; I no longer deserve to be called your son.' But his father ordered his servants, 'Quickly bring the finest robe and put it on him; put a ring on his finger and sandals on his feet. Take the fattened calf and slaughter it. Then let us celebrate with a feast, because this son of mine was dead, and has come to life again; he was lost, and has been found.' Then the celebration began. Now the older son had been out in the field and, on his way back, as he neared the house, he heard the sound of music and dancing. He called one of the servants and asked what this might mean. The servant said to him, 'Your brother has returned and your father has slaughtered the fattened calf because he has him back safe and sound.' He became angry, and when he refused to enter the house, his father came out and pleaded with him. He said to his father in reply, 'Look, all these years I served you and not once did I disobey your orders; yet you never gave me even a young goat to feast on with my friends. But when your son returns, who swallowed up your property with prostitutes, for him you slaughter the fattened calf.' He said to him, 'My son, you are here with me always; everything I have is yours. But now we must celebrate and rejoice, because your brother was dead and has come to life again; he was lost and has been found.'"

Scripture Insights

Today's readings reflect on the unconditional and astonishing mercy of God. The conversation between God and Moses is especially engaging. Who would blame God for being angry and disappointed with the Israelites for their incredible acts of brazen infidelity? Moses calls on God to remember the covenant, and in response to the supplication of Moses, God relents.

The mercy that Paul experiences is personal. He readily confesses that his life as a "blasphemer and persecutor" is deserving of punishment, but the grace of God "has been abundant" and he has been "mercifully treated" by the Lord. Paul believes that the love and patience of Christ that he has received were intended to give encouragement to others, that they, too, will receive mercy.

The fifteenth chapter of Luke's Gospel account is the familiar collection of the three parables of forgiveness. The parables of the lost sheep, the lost coin, and the memorable story of the prodigal son are rich in meaning. Each reveals something about the nature of God, and the circumstances in the stories shape the lesson. For example, we know that neither the sheep nor the coin was responsible for getting lost. The joy of the shepherd and woman is without condition and certainly without any blame being assigned to the sheep or the coin. But the younger son makes a deliberate and selfish choice. This makes it all the more remarkable that even though the boy wasted his inheritance, his father waits for him and celebrates his return. The response of the older brother is different, and gives us a chance to reflect on times we may have felt resentment toward sinners who receive mercy. The closing lines of the parable should give all of us the courage to seek the loving mercy of the Father, no matter how lost we might feel in our spiritual journey. The embrace of the Father is never withheld.

◆ Which one of the three parables gives you hope?

◆ When have you felt so lost that you doubted the love of God?

◆ How have you celebrated the mercy of the Father deep in your heart?

READING I *Amos 8:4–7*

Hear this, you who trample upon the needy
  and destroy the poor of the land!
"When will the new moon be over," you ask,
  "that we may sell our grain,
  and the sabbath, that we may display
    the wheat?
We will diminish the ephah,
  add to the shekel,
  and fix our scales for cheating!
We will buy the lowly for silver,
  and the poor for a pair of sandals;
  even the refuse of the wheat we will sell!"
The LORD has sworn by the pride of Jacob:
  Never will I forget a thing they have done!

RESPONSORIAL PSALM
Psalm 113:1–2, 4–6, 7–8 *(see 1a, 7b)*

R. Praise the Lord, who lifts up the poor.
or: Alleluia.

Praise, you servants of the LORD,
  praise the name of the LORD.
Blessed be the name of the LORD
  both now and forever. R.

High above all nations is the LORD;
  above the heavens is his glory.
Who is like the LORD, our God,
      who is enthroned on high
  and looks upon the heavens
      and the earth below? R.

He raises up the lowly from the dust;
  from the dunghill he lifts up the poor
to seat them with princes,
  with the princes of his own people. R.

READING II *1 Timothy 2:1–8*

Beloved: First of all, I ask that supplications, prayers, petitions and thanksgivings be offered for everyone, for kings and for all in authority, that we may lead a quiet and tranquil life in all devotion and dignity. This is good and pleasing to God our savior, who wills everyone to be saved and to come to knowledge of the truth.

For there is one God.
There is also one mediator between God
      and men,
  the man Christ Jesus,
  who gave himself as ransom for all.

This was the testimony at the proper time. For this I was appointed preacher and apostle—I am speaking the truth, I am not lying—, teacher of the Gentiles in faith and truth.

It is my wish, then, that in every place the men should pray, lifting up holy hands, without anger or argument.

GOSPEL *Luke 16:1–13*

Shorter: Luke 16:10–13

Jesus said to his disciples, "A rich man had a steward who was reported to him for squandering his property. He summoned him and said, 'What is this I hear about you? Prepare a full account of your stewardship, because you can no longer be my steward.' The steward said to himself, 'What shall I do, now that my master is taking the position of steward away from me? I am not strong enough to dig and I am ashamed to beg. I know what I shall do so that, when I am removed from the stewardship, they may welcome me into their homes.' He called in his master's debtors one by one. To the first he said, 'How much do you owe my master?' He replied, 'One hundred measures of olive oil.' He said to him, 'Here is your promissory note. Sit down and quickly write one for fifty.' Then to another the steward said, 'And you, how much do you owe?' He replied, 'One hundred kors of wheat.' The steward said to him, 'Here is your promissory note; write one for eighty.' And the master commended that dishonest steward for acting prudently.

"For the children of this world are more prudent in dealing with their own generation than are the children of light. I tell you, make friends for yourselves with dishonest wealth, so that when it fails, you will be welcomed into eternal dwellings. The person who is trustworthy in very small matters is also trustworthy in great ones; and the person who is dishonest in very small matters is also dishonest in great ones. If, therefore, you are not trustworthy with dishonest wealth, who will trust you with true wealth? If you are not trustworthy with what belongs to another, who will give you what is yours? No servant can serve two masters. He will either hate one and love the other, or be devoted to one and despise the other. You cannot serve both God and mammon."

Practice of Charity

At its heart, today's Gospel commands each one of us to strive to be persons of Gospel integrity. People of Gospel integrity are honest, trustworthy, and act out of their core beliefs. In the spirit of St. Francis of Assisi, people of Gospel integrity preach the Gospel at all times through their daily choices and behaviors. ◆ People of Gospel integrity understand that they are stewards (caretakers) of material possessions, not owners. They readily share what they have with those they know to be in need. Take inventory of your charitable contributions thus far this year. Does your giving reflect generous stewardship? ◆ A person of Gospel integrity seeks to support merchants who reflect Gospel values. Do you know where the food you buy comes from and if the workers who prepared it were paid a fair wage? Take inventory of how you shop and your awareness of the fair trade principles used to produce the products you frequently buy. ◆ People of Gospel integrity understand the value of their time. Take inventory of how you spend your time over the course of a week. Do you spend the most amount of time with the people you hold most dear in your life? What adjustments can you make?

Download more questions and activities for families, Christian initiation groups, and other adult groups at http://www.ltp.org/t-productsupplements.aspx.

Scripture Insights

Today's readings raise the complex issue of our attitudes toward our material resources and our spiritual well-being. How much do we need for ourselves and how well do we share with those who have less?

The prophet Amos was a vehement defender of the poor. In the First Reading he characterizes the merchants as relentless deceivers, bent on destroying the poor for their own profit. Speaking for the LORD, he says "Never will I forget a thing they have done!"

In the Gospel, the dishonest steward has squandered his master's property and is fired. He solves the problem of his future livelihood by drastically lessening the debts of those who owe the master. Stewards in Palestine at this time were free to make money on the side by charging and pocketing high interest rates, so when the steward slashes the debts, he is most likely forfeiting his own profits and not the master's, knowing that the debtors will treat him well in the future. In doing this he is praised by the master—not for his dishonesty, but for his prudence in arranging for others to be indebted to him. This is the way of the world.

The parable has another teaching. The "children of light" are those who are trustworthy in the first place and do not need to resort to the ways of the world to be just stewards of the riches with which they have been entrusted. As children of the light they are to serve God and not material wealth. Children of the light would be those who heed Paul's exhortation to turn to God in prayer as a way to know the will of God. The positive lesson from the dishonest steward is the value of good relationships with others. With that in mind we do well to assess our relationship with material things to see which one is more important for our spiritual health.

◆ Why does Paul ask for prayers "for everyone"?

◆ How do you see yourself as a steward of the goods of the Lord?

◆ How does your parish share resources with those in need?

READING I *Amos 6:1a, 4–7*

Thus says the LORD, God of hosts:
Woe to the complacent in Zion!
Lying upon beds of ivory,
    stretched comfortably on their couches,
they eat lambs taken from the flock,
    and calves from the stall!
Improvising to the music of the harp,
    like David, they devise their
            own accompaniment.
They drink wine from bowls
    and anoint themselves with the best oils;
    yet they are not made ill
            by the collapse of Joseph!
Therefore, now they shall be
            the first to go into exile,
    and their wanton revelry shall be done
            away with.

RESPONSORIAL PSALM
Psalm 146:7, 8–9, 9–10 (1b)

R. Praise the Lord, my soul!
or: Alleluia.

Blessed is he who keeps faith forever,
    secures justice for the oppressed,
    gives food to the hungry.
The LORD sets captives free. R.

The LORD gives sight to the blind;
    the LORD raises up those
            who were bowed down.
The LORD loves the just;
    the LORD protects strangers. R.

The fatherless and the widow he sustains,
    but the way of the wicked he thwarts.
The LORD shall reign forever;
    your God, O Zion, through
            all generations. Alleluia. R.

READING II *1 Timothy 6:11–16*

But you, man of God, pursue righteousness, devotion, faith, love, patience, and gentleness. Compete well for the faith. Lay hold of eternal life, to which you were called when you made the noble confession in the presence of many witnesses. I charge you before God, who gives life to all things, and before Christ Jesus, who gave testimony under Pontius Pilate for the noble confession, to keep the commandment without stain or reproach until the appearance of our Lord Jesus Christ that the blessed and only ruler will make manifest at the proper time, the King of kings and Lord of lords, who alone has immortality, who dwells in unapproachable light, and whom no human being has seen or can see. To him be honor and eternal power. Amen.

GOSPEL *Luke 16:19–31*

Jesus said to the Pharisees: "There was a rich man who dressed in purple garments and fine linen and dined sumptuously each day. And lying at his door was a poor man named Lazarus, covered with sores, who would gladly have eaten his fill of the scraps that fell from the rich man's table. Dogs even used to come and lick his sores. When the poor man died, he was carried away by angels to the bosom of Abraham. The rich man also died and was buried, and from the netherworld, where he was in torment, he raised his eyes and saw Abraham far off and Lazarus at his side. And he cried out, 'Father Abraham, have pity on me. Send Lazarus to dip the tip of his finger in water and cool my tongue, for I am suffering torment in these flames.' Abraham replied, 'My child, remember that you received what was good during your lifetime while Lazarus likewise received what was bad; but now he is comforted here, whereas you are tormented. Moreover, between us and you a great chasm is established to prevent anyone from crossing who might wish to go from our side to yours or from your side to ours.' He said, 'Then I beg you, father, send him to my father's house, for I have five brothers, so that he may warn them, lest they too come to this place of torment.' But Abraham replied, 'They have Moses and the prophets. Let them listen to them.' He said, 'Oh no, father Abraham, but if someone from the dead goes to them, they will repent.' Then Abraham said, 'If they will not listen to Moses and the prophets, neither will they be persuaded if someone should rise from the dead.'"

Practice of Charity

The parable in today's Gospel reminds each of us to take the teachings of our faith seriously and to practice them sincerely during this lifetime. The rich man's callous disregard of Lazarus seems shocking, but in what ways are the economic systems and social expectations of our society also insensitive? ◆ The Society of St. Vincent de Paul seeks to help end poverty through systemic change, offering person-to-person assistance to those in need at a local level. To learn more and find a local council, visit www.svdpusa.org. ◆ The Church remembers St. Vincent de Paul on September 27. He was known as the "Apostle of Charity" and the "Father of the Poor." Read and learn about his life and ministry this week: http://www.newadvent.org/cathen/15434c.htm. ◆ The rich man missed the message while living his comfortable life, but we can take heed. We can grow in knowledge and understanding of our faith in many ways. STEP at the University of Notre Dame offers over fifty outstanding adult faith formation courses delivered in an online, inexpensive format. Visit step.nd.edu to read about the topics offered and register.

Download more questions and activities for families, Christian initiation groups, and other adult groups at http://www.ltp.org/t-productsupplements.aspx.

Scripture Insights

Luke's Gospel parable and the passage from Amos vividly address the issues of just access to resources and active concern for the needy. The rich man seems oblivious to the suffering of Lazarus, and similarly, the prophet Amos calls the rich "complacent" because they lack concern for others—even as their kingdom is falling to invaders who will send the people into exile.

The conversation between the condemned rich man and Father Abraham is particularly intriguing—displaying the gall of the rich man, even now wanting the humble Lazarus to do his bidding, and Abraham's firm insistence that the man's brothers will be just as deaf to Lazarus' warnings as they have been to Scripture. Here Luke has planted a foreshadowing of the rejection of Christ even after his Resurrection from the dead.

Some of this story's power comes from symbolic language: the door of the rich man's house, outside of which Lazarus is lying, marks a boundary between plenty and poverty that is similar to the boundary between the netherworld and the bosom of Abraham. The rich man could not open his door and there can be no passage between the saved and the damned. Amos' characterization of the rich through the objects they use conveys the same message: the "beds of ivory," and the use of the "best oils," suggest a lavish, carefree lifestyle.

The very sharp point of the stories is the sin of uncaring complacency that works against justice—in spite of a long tradition that teaches the opposite. Wealth is relative. Even those who do not consider themselves wealthy still live in more comfort than many others, and may also be uncaring or complacent. Every community of faith is charged with finding ways to extend its resources to those in need. In recent writings Pope Francis takes up this message, calling for more energetic action for justice motivated by mercy and compassion for the poor and marginalized of society.

◆ Who is "Lazarus" in our world today?

◆ What examples of complacency do you see around you?

◆ In what ways do you share resources with others?

READING I *Habakkuk 1:2–3; 2:2–4*

How long, O LORD? I cry for help
  but you do not listen!
I cry out to you, "Violence!"
  but you do not intervene.
Why do you let me see ruin;
  why must I look at misery?
Destruction and violence are before me;
  there is strife, and clamorous discord.
Then the LORD answered me and said:
  Write down the vision clearly upon the tablets,
  so that one can read it readily.
For the vision still has its time,
  presses on to fulfillment,
        and will not disappoint;
if it delays, wait for it,
  it will surely come, it will not be late.
The rash one has no integrity;
  but the just one, because of
        his faith, shall live.

RESPONSORIAL PSALM
Psalm 95:1–2, 6–7, 8–9 (8)

R. If today you hear his voice, harden not
        your hearts.

Come, let us sing joyfully to the LORD;
  let us acclaim the Rock of our salvation.
Let us come into his presence with thanksgiving;
  let us joyfully sing psalms to him.   R.

Come, let us bow down in worship;
  let us kneel before the LORD who made us.
For he is our God,
  and we are the people he shepherds, the flock
        he guides.   R.

Oh, that today you would hear his voice:
  "Harden not your hearts as at Meribah,
  as in the day of Massah in the desert,
where your fathers tempted me;
  they tested me though they had seen
        my works."   R.

READING II *2 Timothy 1:6–8, 13–14*

Beloved: I remind you, to stir into flame the gift of God that you have through the imposition of my hands. For God did not give us a spirit of cowardice but rather of power and love and self-control. So do not be ashamed of your testimony to our Lord, nor of me, a prisoner for his sake; but bear your share of hardship for the gospel with the strength that comes from God.

Take as your norm the sound words that you heard from me, in the faith and love that are in Christ Jesus. Guard this rich trust with the help of the Holy Spirit that dwells within us.

GOSPEL *Luke 17:5–10*

The apostles said to the Lord, "Increase our faith." The Lord replied, "If you have faith the size of a mustard seed, you would say to this mulberry tree, 'Be uprooted and planted in the sea,' and it would obey you.

"Who among you would say to your servant who has just come in from plowing or tending sheep in the field, 'Come here immediately and take your place at table'? Would he not rather say to him, 'Prepare something for me to eat. Put on your apron and wait on me while I eat and drink. You may eat and drink when I am finished'? Is he grateful to that servant because he did what was commanded? So should it be with you. When you have done all you have been commanded, say, 'We are unprofitable servants; we have done what we were obliged to do.'"

Practice of Hope

On October 4 the Church celebrates the Memorial of St. Francis of Assisi. Francis' astounding story of conversion to faith around the year 1206 is an inspiration for all of us. He became a sign of Gospel integrity, literally discarding all his wealth and possessions and seeking to rebuild the faith of the Church of his time on the foundation of the Word of God. ◆ St. Francis is the patron saint of animals and the environment. Many parishes offer a blessing of household animals in honor of St. Francis or plan other actions of stewardship of the environment. Join your parish's efforts or plan an initiative of your own. ◆ The Franciscan Friars are a religious order dedicated to carrying on the inspiration of St. Francis. Learn more about their mission and ministries as well as the life of St. Francis at www.hnp.org. ◆ On the day of his election as Pope, March 13, 2013, Jorge Mario Bergoglio chose the name Pope Francis. Read his messages to the Church and follow his ministry at http://www.vatican.va/holy_father//francesco/index.htm.

Download more questions and activities for families, Christian initiation groups, and other adult groups at http://www.ltp.org/t-productsupplements.aspx.

Scripture Insights

The cry of the prophet and the pleading of the disciples often echo in our own prayer before the Lord: "increase our faith." In the verses before today's Gospel begins, Luke describes Jesus teaching the disciples that misleading the "little ones" (the poor or marginalized) is a grievous sin with a gruesome punishment. In addition, one must be ready to forgive as often as pardon is sincerely asked.

Jesus' teaching on inclusiveness went against the social norms that the disciples knew. They were struggling to understand, and they felt inadequate for the task that Jesus asked of them. They clearly needed more of something to do these things; they thought it was faith that they were missing.

Habakkuk protests vigorously to God. He cannot deal with the violence, the ruin, the misery, and he cries out for help. God instructs the prophet to write down the vision so everyone can see it and regain their hope. They must wait for the vision's fulfillment—something the rash cannot do, "but the just one, because of his faith, shall live."

Paul writes to Timothy from prison and in his hardship he too repeats the vision, "the gift of God" for Timothy. He tells his disciple to "stir into flame" the gift he already has, the love and courage of his witness of the Lord. He tells Timothy (and us) that this is a rich trust that dwells within each of us.

Jesus' response to the disciples uses the ridiculous to teach the obvious. Why would anyone transplant a mulberry tree into the sea? And only one mustard seed is needed for a great bush. Jesus tells them they have all the faith they need to do the things he has been teaching them. They can indeed transform the world around them; the vision is not unreachable.

◆ What is the gift of faith in each of the readings?

◆ In what ways is faith found in qualities rather than quantities?

◆ What events in life challenge your faith the most? How do you manage to wait for the vision?

READING I *2 Kings 5:14–17*

Naaman went down and plunged into the Jordan seven times at the word of Elisha, the man of God. His flesh became again like the flesh of a little child, and he was clean of his leprosy.

Naaman returned with his whole retinue to the man of God. On his arrival he stood before Elisha and said, "Now I know that there is no God in all the earth, except in Israel. Please accept a gift from your servant."

Elisha replied, "As the LORD lives whom I serve, I will not take it"; and despite Naaman's urging, he still refused. Naaman said: "If you will not accept, please let me, your servant, have two mule-loads of earth, for I will no longer offer holocaust or sacrifice to any other god except to the LORD."

RESPONSORIAL PSALM
Psalm 98:1, 2–3, 3–4 (see 2b)

R. The Lord has revealed to the nations his
      saving power.

Sing to the LORD a new song,
  for he has done wondrous deeds;
his right hand has won victory for him,
  his holy arm.   R.

The LORD has made his salvation known:
    in the sight of the nations he has revealed
      his justice.
He has remembered his kindness and
    his faithfulness
  toward the house of Israel.   R.

All the ends of the earth have seen
  the salvation by our God.
Sing joyfully to the LORD, all you lands:
  break into song; sing praise.   R.

READING II *2 Timothy 2:8–13*

Beloved: Remember Jesus Christ, raised from the dead, a descendant of David: such is my gospel, for which I am suffering, even to the point of chains, like a criminal. But the word of God is not chained. Therefore, I bear with everything for the sake of those who are chosen, so that they too may obtain the salvation that is in Christ Jesus, together with eternal glory. This saying is trustworthy:

If we have died with him
  we shall also live with him;
if we persevere
  we shall also reign with him.
But if we deny him
  he will deny us.
If we are unfaithful
  he remains faithful,
    for he cannot deny himself.

GOSPEL *Luke 17:11–19*

As Jesus continued his journey to Jerusalem, he traveled through Samaria and Galilee. As he was entering a village, ten lepers met him. They stood at a distance from him and raised their voices, saying, "Jesus, Master! Have pity on us!" And when he saw them, he said, "Go show yourselves to the priests." As they were going they were cleansed. And one of them, realizing he had been healed, returned, glorifying God in a loud voice; and he fell at the feet of Jesus and thanked him. He was a Samaritan. Jesus said in reply, "Ten were cleansed, were they not? Where are the other nine? Has none but this foreigner returned to give thanks to God?" Then he said to him, "Stand up and go; your faith has saved you."

Practice of Hope

Today's First Reading and Gospel present us with miraculous healing stories, and the refrain for the Responsorial Psalm sums up the impact of these healings: "The Lord has revealed to the nation his saving power." ◆ The Sacrament of the Anointing of the Sick was revised following the Second Vatican Council and offers a beautiful source of healing for the faithful, yet is still not widely understood and appreciated in our Church. Visit www.olphtoronto.com/Sacraments/OLM_Anointing _English.pdf to read a very helpful description of the sacrament as it is currently celebrated in the Church. ◆ Many parish communities invite members to share in the ministry to the sick and homebound. With training you could share the love of God for the sick through this work of mercy. Inquire at your parish about the possibility. ◆ Jesus reminds us all about the necessity of gratitude for all of the ways God blesses our lives. Do a self-check: when is the last time you offered words of gratitude during prayer time?

Download more questions and activities for families, Christian initiation groups, and other adult groups at http://www.ltp.org/t-productsupplements.aspx.

Scripture Insights

From the early stages of his public ministry, Jesus' path takes him to the place of his Death and Resurrection. On the way, he encounters those seeking compassion and healing. Today Jesus is in between Samaria and Galilee, a place where interesting things can happen.

Similarly, Naaman is out of place—a foreigner in the land of the Israelites—yet he asks the holy man, Elisha, to cure his leprosy. The reading begins just as Naaman does what Elisha has instructed: he plunges into the Jordan and is cleansed. Elisha refuses the man's offering, saying that God's mercy and love are free. Naaman returns home, taking some dirt from the land of the holy man with him; his act of gratitude is to connect the land of the holy man with his own.

In today's Gospel, Jesus is on a journey to Jerusalem. The ten lepers approach Jesus as he is entering a village. They are required to stay outside the community, but they call to Jesus, asking for healing. Jesus does indeed heal them, and Luke says he does so, not when he hears them call to him, but when he *sees* them. In the Scriptures, whenever Jesus "sees" it means that he sees deep within the person; he sees who they really are. He sees with the heart of compassion and understands where their (our) cry is coming from. This encounter with Jesus is the beginning of new life. And yet it is only the "foreigner" who seems aware of the deeper significance of the healing and returns to give thanks.

There are many in-between places and times in our lives—when we may not be sure of our true place or the life ahead of us. At those times we cry out to the Lord: "Have pity on me; take care of me; show me what I am to do." We can be sure that Jesus "sees" us, understands our "in-between" state, and wants to heal us.

◆ Apart from leprosy, what connects Naaman and the Samaritan?

◆ What has caused you to cry out to the Lord?

◆ What effect has gratitude had in your life?

October 16, 2016

READING I *Exodus 17:8–13*

In those days, Amalek came and waged war against Israel. Moses, therefore, said to Joshua, "Pick out certain men, and tomorrow go out and engage Amalek in battle. I will be standing on top of the hill with the staff of God in my hand." So Joshua did as Moses told him: he engaged Amalek in battle after Moses had climbed to the top of the hill with Aaron and Hur. As long as Moses kept his hands raised up, Israel had the better of the fight, but when he let his hands rest, Amalek had the better of the fight. Moses' hands, however, grew tired; so they put a rock in place for him to sit on. Meanwhile Aaron and Hur supported his hands, one on one side and one on the other, so that his hands remained steady till sunset. And Joshua mowed down Amalek and his people with the edge of the sword.

RESPONSORIAL PSALM
Psalm 121:1–2, 3–4, 5–6, 7–8 (see 2)

R. Our help is from the Lord, who made heaven
        and earth.

I lift up my eyes toward the mountains;
    whence shall help come to me?
My help is from the LORD,
    who made heaven and earth.   R.

May he not suffer your foot to slip;
    may he slumber not who guards you:
indeed he neither slumbers nor sleeps,
    the guardian of Israel.   R.

The LORD is your guardian;
            the LORD is your shade;
    he is beside you at your right hand.
The sun shall not harm you by day,
    nor the moon by night.   R.

The LORD will guard you from all evil;
    he will guard your life.
The LORD will guard your coming and
            your going,
    both now and forever.   R.

READING II *2 Timothy 3:14—4:2*

Beloved: Remain faithful to what you have learned and believed, because you know from whom you learned it, and that from infancy you have known the sacred Scriptures, which are capable of giving you wisdom for salvation through faith in Christ Jesus. All Scripture is inspired by God and is useful for teaching, for refutation, for correction, and for training in righteousness, so that one who belongs to God may be competent, equipped for every good work.

I charge you in the presence of God and of Christ Jesus, who will judge the living and the dead, and by his appearing and his kingly power: proclaim the word; be persistent whether it is convenient or inconvenient; convince, reprimand, encourage through all patience and teaching.

GOSPEL *Luke 18:1–8*

Jesus told his disciples a parable about the necessity for them to pray always without becoming weary. He said, "There was a judge in a certain town who neither feared God nor respected any human being. And a widow in that town used to come to him and say, 'Render a just decision for me against my adversary.' For a long time the judge was unwilling, but eventually he thought, 'While it is true that I neither fear God nor respect any human being, because this widow keeps bothering me I shall deliver a just decision for her lest she finally come and strike me.'" The Lord said, "Pay attention to what the dishonest judge says. Will not God then secure the rights of his chosen ones who call out to him day and night? Will he be slow to answer them? I tell you, he will see to it that justice is done for them speedily. But when the Son of Man comes, will he find faith on earth?"

Practice of Faith

The message in today's readings is clear: be persistent in faith. No matter what difficulties we face, we must continue to trust that God is moving in the world in ways we may not see. ◆ The Church remembers St. Paul of the Cross this week on October 20, whose life story is a lesson in perseverance and courageous patience. Learn about the modern ministry of the Passionist Community founded by Paul by visiting www.thepassionists .org. ◆ Catholic Relief Services oversees an amazing microfinance initiative that helps poor people from all over the world translate small ideas into successful ventures within their communities. Read how it works, about the millions of people lifted up, and how you can help at www.crs.org /microfinance. ◆ Today's Responsorial Psalm expresses a calm, steady trust in the Lord. Make this psalm part of your prayer each day this week.

Download more questions and activities for families, Christian initiation groups, and other adult groups at http://www.ltp.org/t-productsupplements.aspx.

Scripture Insights

In today's Gospel parable, the widow elicits great empathy from listeners and readers. The Hebrew word for *widow* is related to a word that means "one who has no voice," but her voice is her only hope to achieve the justice she desires.

This parable is often presented as a teaching on the effects of persistent prayer. The thinking is that if we ask God often enough for whatever we want, then God will eventually answer and grant what we ask. But this would seem to equate God with the unjust judge, and it casts us as pious whiners. That may not be what Jesus intended.

Through her persistence the widow persuades the judge to grant her request, though he does so grudgingly. He is unlike God, who desires to see that justice is done "speedily."

The First Reading offers another insight into the effects of prayer. With Moses, it is the support of others that allowed him to be in touch with God. The role of the community is an important element in the prayer of the people of God.

For Paul, keeping in touch with the Lord happens by being faithful to the Word of God, which imparts wisdom. This wisdom is then expressed in action; especially in preaching and doing "every good work." The purpose and result of prayer is not just for personal gain, but is intended to give strength to others who would become disciples of the Lord.

Rather than changing God's mind, prayer changes us, little by little, even when it seems that the challenges (inner and outer) are too much. We do not lose heart, much less turn to injustice ourselves. We do not become weary, for we are constantly in touch with God. Ultimately the unjust, whether one person or many, who neither fear God nor respect human beings will not withstand the power of God working through us.

◆ How do these readings help you understand the dynamics of your own prayer life?

◆ In what circumstances have you been or encountered the widow?

◆ What is the biggest challenge to praying without becoming weary?

READING I *Sirach 35:12–14, 16–18*

The LORD is a God of justice,
  who knows no favorites.
Though not unduly partial toward the weak,
  yet he hears the cry of the oppressed.
The LORD is not deaf to the wail of the orphan,
  nor to the widow when she pours out
      her complaint.
The one who serves God willingly is heard;
  his petition reaches the heavens.
The prayer of the lowly pierces the clouds;
  it does not rest till it reaches its goal,
nor will it withdraw till the Most High responds,
  judges justly and affirms the right,
and the LORD will not delay.

RESPONSORIAL PSALM
Psalm 34:2–3, 17–18, 19, 23 (7a)

R. The Lord hears the cry of the poor.

I will bless the LORD at all times;
  his praise shall be ever in my mouth.
Let my soul glory in the LORD;
  the lowly will hear me and be glad. R.

The LORD confronts the evildoers,
  to destroy remembrance of them from
      the earth.
When the just cry out, the LORD hears them,
  and from all their distress
      he rescues them. R.

The LORD is close to the brokenhearted;
  and those who are crushed in spirit he saves.
The LORD redeems the lives of his servants;
  no one incurs guilt who takes refuge
      in him. R.

READING II *2 Timothy 4:6–8, 16–18*

Beloved: I am already being poured out like a libation, and the time of my departure is at hand. I have competed well; I have finished the race; I have kept the faith. From now on the crown of righteousness awaits me, which the Lord, the just judge, will award to me on that day, and not only to me, but to all who have longed for his appearance.

At my first defense no one appeared on my behalf, but everyone deserted me. May it not be held against them! But the Lord stood by me and gave me strength, so that through me the proclamation might be completed and all the Gentiles might hear it. And I was rescued from the lion's mouth. The Lord will rescue me from every evil threat and will bring me safe to his heavenly kingdom. To him be glory forever and ever. Amen.

GOSPEL *Luke 18:9–14*

Jesus addressed this parable to those who were convinced of their own righteousness and despised everyone else. "Two people went up to the temple area to pray; one was a Pharisee and the other was a tax collector. The Pharisee took up his position and spoke this prayer to himself, 'O God, I thank you that I am not like the rest of humanity—greedy, dishonest, adulterous—or even like this tax collector. I fast twice a week, and I pay tithes on my whole income.' But the tax collector stood off at a distance and would not even raise his eyes to heaven but beat his breast and prayed, 'O God, be merciful to me a sinner.' I tell you, the latter went home justified, not the former; for whoever exalts himself will be humbled, and the one who humbles himself will be exalted."

Practice of Charity

The Lord is a God of justice, asserts our First Reading from Sirach, and our Responsorial Psalm echoes, "The Lord hears the cry of the poor." Our Catholic social teaching affirms a worldview that gives preferential treatment to the poor. The question for us is: do we hear the cry of the poor? ◆ The citizens of the United States are preparing for a national election to call forth a new leader. How do the teachings of our Church, founded on the Word of God, influence our discernment about choosing elected officials? The United States Conference of Catholic Bishops provides guidance in a document entitled *Forming Consciences for Faithful Citizenship*. Read this brief document prayerfully to learn how to approach citizenship through the lens of faith. Find it at www.usccb .org/issues-and-action/faithful-citizenship/. ◆ Plan a gathering of parishioners or simply meet with a friend to discuss how the principles of faithful citizenship might be applied to the current situation. ◆ Listen carefully to those seeking office to discern who truly desires to serve all citizens of the land, including the poor and vulnerable.

Download more questions and activities for families, Christian initiation groups, and other adult groups at http://www.ltp.org/t-productsupplements.aspx.

Scripture Insights

Today's readings center on the experience of prayer. We sing and speak in prayer and we pray silently. We offer prayers of petition, praise, and thanksgiving. Prayer is our conversation with God. When we pray, and what we say when we pray, says a lot about who we are and who we think God is.

In Sirach we hear that "the prayer of the lowly pierces the clouds;" in the psalm we sing, "The Lord hears the cry of the poor." It's not that the lowly and the poor are closer to God by being poor and lowly, it's that they turn to God and not into themselves.

This is precisely the point of the parable. The Pharisee has lived a virtuous life, doing more than the Law requires of a devout person. The tax collector was, by reputation and practice, despised and fraudulent, and he readily admits he is a sinner.

The conclusion of the parable reverses the expectations of Jesus' audience. The Pharisee turns inward and does not seek anything from God; it appears that he only wants God to hear him report on all the pious things he's done. His put-down of the tax collector is intended to make himself even better in the eyes of God. The favor Jesus gives to the tax collector rests on his turning outward to God, who alone can be merciful and lead him to a transformed life.

Perhaps there is a little of the Pharisee in each of us; we can so easily be judgmental. We might well boast of our good deeds; even Paul declares, "I have competed well; I have kept the faith." Later in the reading, though, Paul gives the credit for his efforts to the Lord.

And we are also like the tax collector when we are honest and humble. The Lord hears the cry of all of us; our prayers pierce the clouds seeking the mercy of God.

◆ How does the parable help you to center your prayer?

◆ What do you think Paul means when he says, "I am already being poured out like a libation?"

◆ What spiritual wisdom do you find in the First Reading?

READING I *Wisdom 11:22—12:2*

Before the LORD the whole universe is as a
grain from a balance
or a drop of morning dew come down upon
the earth.
But you have mercy on all, because you can do
all things;
and you overlook people's sins that they
may repent.
For you love all things that are
and loathe nothing that you have made;
for what you hated, you would not
have fashioned.
And how could a thing remain, unless you
willed it;
or be preserved, had it not been called forth
by you?
But you spare all things, because they are yours,
O LORD and lover of souls,
for your imperishable spirit is in all things!
Therefore you rebuke offenders little by little,
warn them and remind them of the sins they
are committing,
that they may abandon their wickedness and
believe in you, O LORD!

RESPONSORIAL PSALM *Psalm 145:1–2, 8–9, 10–11, 13, 14 (see 1)*

R. I will praise your name for ever, my king
and my God.

I will extol you, O my God and King;
and I will bless your name forever and ever.
Every day I will bless you;
and I will praise your name forever
and ever. R.

The LORD is gracious and merciful,
slow to anger and of great kindness.
The LORD is good to all,
and compassionate toward all his works. R.

Let all your works give you thanks, O LORD,
and let your faithful ones bless you.
Let them discourse of the glory of your kingdom
and speak of your might. R.

The LORD is faithful in all his words
and holy in all his works.
The LORD lifts up all who are falling
and raises up all who are bowed down. R.

READING II *2 Thessalonians 1:11—2:2*

Brothers and sisters: We always pray for you, that our God may make you worthy of his calling and powerfully bring to fulfillment every good purpose and every effort of faith, that the name of our Lord Jesus may be glorified in you, and you in him, in accord with the grace of our God and Lord Jesus Christ.

We ask you, brothers and sisters, with regard to the coming of our Lord Jesus Christ and our assembling with him, not to be shaken out of your minds suddenly, or to be alarmed either by a "spirit," or by an oral statement, or by a letter allegedly from us to the effect that the day of the Lord is at hand.

GOSPEL *Luke 19:1–10*

At that time, Jesus came to Jericho and intended to pass through the town. Now a man there named Zacchaeus, who was a chief tax collector and also a wealthy man, was seeking to see who Jesus was; but he could not see him because of the crowd, for he was short in stature. So he ran ahead and climbed a sycamore tree in order to see Jesus, who was about to pass that way. When he reached the place, Jesus looked up and said, "Zacchaeus, come down quickly, for today I must stay at your house." And he came down quickly and received him with joy. When they all saw this, they began to grumble, saying, "He has gone to stay at the house of a sinner." But Zacchaeus stood there and said to the Lord, "Behold, half of my possessions, Lord, I shall give to the poor, and if I have extorted anything from anyone I shall repay it four times over." And Jesus said to him, "Today salvation has come to this house because this man too is a descendant of Abraham. For the Son of Man has come to seek and to save what was lost."

Practice of Hope

The Church celebrates the Solemnity of All Saints on November 1, lifting up all the holy men and women who have gone before us into glory. It is a holy day of obligation. On November 2, the Commemoration of All the Faithful Departed (All Souls' Day), the Church lifts up in prayer all of our beloved dead. Through all of November, the month of our faithful departed, the Church on earth unites in prayer with the Church in heaven. ◆ Many parishes enshrine the "Book of Names of the Dead" somewhere in the church space. Make a point to write the names of your beloved dead in the parish book. ◆ Place candles, mementos, and pictures of your beloved departed in a special place in your home for the month of November. ◆ Plan a special trip to the cemetery to visit the resting place of deceased relatives or friends. Bring supplies to tend the gravesites and prepare a special blessing prayer.

Download more questions and activities for families, Christian initiation groups, and other adult groups at http://www.ltp.org/t-productsupplements.aspx.

Scripture Insights

For several weeks the Sunday Gospels have reminded us of what it means to be disciples. The passages from Luke recounted the teachings, parables, and examples of Jesus' ministry that shape and direct our efforts at being faithful disciples. As we near the end of Ordinary Time the readings shift the focus from our behavior to the action of God in the world and in our lives.

The author of Wisdom speaks of God as the Lord of the cosmos. God looks upon the world as the harvester regards the single grain that falls from the balance, the scale that measures the harvest. For the harvester every grain is important, and the author of Wisdom says that God looks upon the whole world with the same attention and care. The second analogy portrays the same attentiveness; God sees the world as though it were a single drop of dew. This is a God of immeasurable care and compassion.

In Luke's story of Zacchaeus, Jesus fulfills that very role; he "has come to seek and to save what was lost." There is something amusing and even ridiculous about the plight of Zacchaeus. He is no ordinary tax collector (a group despised by the citizens), he is the *chief* tax collector. He must have been slightly embarrassed—a person of his position having to climb a tree to see Jesus. But he sets aside any personal inhibitions and climbs up.

Then an amazing thing happens. Jesus announces that he is coming to stay at his house. Jesus becomes both guest and host at the table of a sinner.

When we gather for liturgy we believe that we encounter the Lord in the Word, in the elements of the sacrament, in the priest, and in each other. At the Eucharistic liturgy the Lord is both guest and host. He becomes the meal and the host at our Eucharistic table, and in that event of communion we are transformed.

◆ What are the two promises exchanged in the Gospel account?

◆ What phrase from the First Reading is spiritual wisdom for you?

◆ What does the conversation between Jesus and Zacchaeus mean for discipleship?

READING I *2 Maccabees 7:1–2, 9–14*

It happened that seven brothers with their mother were arrested and tortured with whips and scourges by the king, to force them to eat pork in violation of God's law. One of the brothers, speaking for the others, said: "What do you expect to achieve by questioning us? We are ready to die rather than transgress the laws of our ancestors."

At the point of death he said: "You accursed fiend, you are depriving us of this present life, but the King of the world will raise us up to live again forever. It is for his laws that we are dying."

After him the third suffered their cruel sport. He put out his tongue at once when told to do so, and bravely held out his hands, as he spoke these noble words: "It was from Heaven that I received these; for the sake of his laws I disdain them; from him I hope to receive them again." Even the king and his attendants marveled at the young man's courage, because he regarded his sufferings as nothing.

After he had died, they tortured and maltreated the fourth brother in the same way. When he was near death, he said, "It is my choice to die at the hands of men with the hope God gives of being raised up by him; but for you, there will be no resurrection to life."

RESPONSORIAL PSALM
Psalm 17:1, 5–6, 8, 15 (15b)

R. Lord, when your glory appears, my joy will
    be full.

Hear, O LORD, a just suit;
    attend to my outcry;
      hearken to my prayer from lips
        without deceit. R.

My steps have been steadfast in your paths,
    my feet have not faltered.
I call upon you, for you will answer me, O God;
    incline your ear to me; hear my word. R.

Keep me as the apple of your eye,
    hide me in the shadow of your wings.
But I in justice shall behold your face;
    on waking I shall be content in
      your presence. R.

READING II *2 Thessalonians 2:16—3:5*

Brothers and sisters: May our Lord Jesus Christ himself and God our Father, who has loved us and given us everlasting encouragement and good hope through his grace, encourage your hearts and strengthen them in every good deed and word.

Finally, brothers and sisters, pray for us, so that the word of the Lord may speed forward and be glorified, as it did among you, and that we may be delivered from perverse and wicked people, for not all have faith. But the Lord is faithful; he will strengthen you and guard you from the evil one. We are confident of you in the Lord that what we instruct you, you are doing and will continue to do. May the Lord direct your hearts to the love of God and to the endurance of Christ.

GOSPEL *Luke 20:27–38*

Shorter: Luke 20:27, 34–38

Some Sadducees, those who deny that there is a resurrection, came forward and put this question to Jesus, saying, "Teacher, Moses wrote for us, *If someone's brother dies leaving a wife but no child, his brother must take the wife and raise up descendants for his brother.* Now there were seven brothers; the first married a woman but died childless. Then the second and the third married her, and likewise all the seven died childless. Finally the woman also died. Now at the resurrection whose wife will that woman be? For all seven had been married to her." Jesus said to them, "The children of this age marry and remarry; but those who are deemed worthy to attain to the coming age and to the resurrection of the dead neither marry nor are given in marriage. They can no longer die, for they are like angels; and they are the children of God because they are the ones who will rise. That the dead will rise even Moses made known in the passage about the bush, when he called out 'Lord,' the God of Abraham, the God of Isaac, and the God of Jacob; and he is not God of the dead, but of the living, for to him all are alive."

Practice of Hope

The readings this week and for the rest of November invite us to ponder what happens to us in our passing over from earthly life to death. In response to these scriptural themes, the Church continues to keep holy the month of our faithful departed through all of November. ◆ Many parishes invite members to assist in the ministry of care offered to families at the time of funeral planning and during the early days of mourning. Prayerfully consider if you are called to serve the bereaved in your faith community and inquire how you can help. ◆ Some parishes keep a list of all the names of members who have died in the past year. During November, loaves of homemade bread are delivered to grieving families with a sprig of rosemary and a letter of consolation. Make and deliver your own "bereavement breads" for people in your life who are grieving. ◆ Election Day in the United States is Tuesday. Set aside time to pray for all candidates for elected office, all election officials, and all citizens who seek to exercise their rights of citizenship in hope and faith.

Download more questions and activities for families, Christian initiation groups, and other adult groups at http://www.ltp.org/t-productsupplements.aspx.

Scripture Insights

The readings for the last three Sundays of the liturgical year focus on the mystery of the resurrection of the dead. Today's First Reading, the grisly story of the martyrdom of the seven brothers in Maccabees, opens a conversation on belief in the resurrection. The covenant between God and the Chosen People included God's promise of care and salvation and a life of faithfulness by the Israelites. The issue in the text is whether this relationship extended after death. The responses of the seven brothers indicate that they firmly believe God will raise them up. Their hope and trust in God will give them the strength to endure their death.

The scenario outlined in the Gospel presents the unlikely situation of seven brothers marrying the same woman and all dying without offspring. The question of the Sadducees is based on the premise that life on earth carries on in a similar way after death. Jesus' response indicates that the social conventions and relationships of this life are changed after death. He does not explain what life after death will be like, other than that it will be different; the limitations of this life will be transformed. The resurrection of the dead is a matter of faith in the God of the living.

The Second Reading reminds us that it would be short-sighted to think of the resurrection as only involving the moment of death. The life of the faithful disciple is always in preparation for a new life with God in eternity. Paul encourages the early community of believers to live in the belief that the Lord Jesus gives them the strength to live in hope and to do good works. The grace of God the Father has come to them through Jesus Christ and they will endure in the love of God just as Jesus did.

◆ In the Gospel, how is Jesus' approach to the issue different from that of his questioners?

◆ What elements of hope do you find in the passage from Paul?

◆ What specific parts of the psalm might be helpful to someone facing death?

READING I *Malachi 3:19–20a*

Lo, the day is coming, blazing like an oven,
  when all the proud and all evildoers will
    be stubble,
and the day that is coming will set them on fire,
  leaving them neither root nor branch,
  says the LORD of hosts.
But for you who fear my name, there will arise
  the sun of justice with its healing rays.

RESPONSORIAL PSALM
Psalm 98:5–6, 7–8, 9 (see 9)

R. The Lord comes to rule the earth with justice.

Sing praise to the LORD with the harp,
  with the harp and melodious song.
With trumpets and the sound of the horn
  sing joyfully before the King, the LORD.   R.

Let the sea and what fills it resound,
  the world and those who dwell in it;
let the rivers clap their hands,
  the mountains shout with them for joy.   R.

Before the LORD, for he comes,
  for he comes to rule the earth;
he will rule the world with justice
  and the peoples with equity.   R.

READING II *2 Thessalonians 3:7–12*

Brothers and sisters: You know how one must imitate us. For we did not act in a disorderly way among you, nor did we eat food received free from anyone. On the contrary, in toil and drudgery, night and day we worked, so as not to burden any of you. Not that we do not have the right. Rather, we wanted to present ourselves as a model for you, so that you might imitate us. In fact, when we were with you, we instructed you that if anyone was unwilling to work, neither should that one eat. We hear that some are conducting themselves among you in a disorderly way, by not keeping busy but minding the business of others. Such people we instruct and urge in the Lord Jesus Christ to work quietly and to eat their own food.

GOSPEL *Luke 21:5–19*

While some people were speaking about how the temple was adorned with costly stones and votive offerings, Jesus said, "All that you see here—the days will come when there will not be left a stone upon another stone that will not be thrown down."

Then they asked him, "Teacher, when will this happen? And what sign will there be when all these things are about to happen?" He answered, "See that you not be deceived, for many will come in my name, saying, 'I am he,' and 'The time has come.' Do not follow them! When you hear of wars and insurrections, do not be terrified; for such things must happen first, but it will not immediately be the end." Then he said to them, "Nation will rise against nation, and kingdom against kingdom. There will be powerful earthquakes, famines and plagues from place to place; and awesome sights and mighty signs will come from the sky.

"Before all this happens, however, they will seize and persecute you, they will hand you over to the synagogues and to prisons, and they will have you led before kings and governors because of my name. It will lead to your giving testimony. Remember, you are not to prepare your defense beforehand, for I myself shall give you a wisdom in speaking that all your adversaries will be powerless to resist or refute. You will even be handed over by parents, brothers, relatives and friends, and they will put some of you to death. You will be hated by all because of my name, but not a hair on your head will be destroyed. By your perseverance you will secure your lives."

Practice of Faith

Today's readings point us toward doing the "work" of Christ. In contemporary society, we tend to work 24/7 and rarely take a true day off. The Church affirms that Sunday, "The Lord's Day," be a day of worship, rest, and recreation. The third commandment instructs us to keep the "Sabbath Day" holy. Honoring the Sabbath is truly the "work" of Christ. It is time to take a new look at this practice of our faith. ◆ Read this article with wonderful and realistic ideas for keeping the Sabbath: www.lifelongfaith.com/uploads/5/1/6 /4 /5164069/livingwell_-_keeping_sabbath.pdf. ◆ Try fasting from work, technology, and shopping for one Sunday. Instead, take a hike, a long drive, or a nap. Notice how much more effective you are at your work on Monday, having honored the spirit of the Sabbath. ◆ Invite special friends over on Sunday to enjoy the sabbath with your household. Fast from hurried eating and enjoy a delicious, leisurely Sunday dinner (that you prepared on Saturday afternoon).

Download more questions and activities for families, Christian initiation groups, and other adult groups at http://www.ltp.org/t-productsupplements.aspx.

Scripture Insights

Today's Scriptures continue to focus on the end-times, the fulfillment of God's plan of salvation. This moment is often referred to as the Day of the Lord. At that time God appears in power and majesty, completing the mission of Jesus Christ with justice and righteousness.

Descriptions of this time appear in several places in Scripture, including today's passage from Malachi. It is important to note that such depictions use metaphorical language; they are not literal scenarios. Malachi uses the image of a blazing fire, an image often used as a sign of God's intervention in human affairs; for example, the pillar of fire that led the Israelites to freedom.

In the Gospel, Jesus speaks of the destruction of the Temple—a magnificent structure revered by the Jewish people. The Temple was actually destroyed by the Romans some decades later, and it is unlikely that Jesus was predicting such an event. Jesus then speaks about the "signs" that will precede the end-time. Again, many of these events came about in later years; we experience some of them in our own time. But Jesus cautions that these cosmic events must be understood carefully; they are not to be seen as literal indications of the Day of the Lord.

In the midst of both descriptions there is a strong element of hope and redemption. Malachi proclaims that the sun of justice will arise for those who fear (are in awe of) the name of the Lord. And Jesus promises those who are persecuted that not "a hair on your head will be destroyed."

Paul's instruction to the early Church is also encouraging. He offers his own example of ministry as a model for others, asking them (and us) to live in harmony and never to be a burden on others or be distracted by other people's affairs. His message is simple: stay focused on the work of the Lord.

◆ What similarities and differences do you find in the First Reading and the Gospel?

◆ What does the Second Reading tell you about problems the community was facing?

◆ Are these readings about the end-time encouraging or frightening to you?

READING I   *2 Samuel 5:1–3*

In those days, all the tribes of Israel came to David in Hebron and said: "Here we are, your bone and your flesh. In days past, when Saul was our king, it was you who led the Israelites out and brought them back. And the LORD said to you, 'You shall shepherd my people Israel and shall be commander of Israel.'" When all the elders of Israel came to David in Hebron, King David made an agreement with them there before the LORD, and they anointed him king of Israel.

RESPONSORIAL PSALM
Psalm 122:1–2, 3–4, 4–5 (see 1)

R. Let us go rejoicing to the house of the Lord.

I rejoiced because they said to me,
  "We will go up to the house of the LORD."
And now we have set foot
  within your gates, O Jerusalem.   R.

Jerusalem, built as a city
  with compact unity.
To it the tribes go up,
  the tribes of the LORD.   R.

According to the decree for Israel,
  to give thanks to the name of the LORD.
In it are set up judgment seats,
  seats for the house of David.   R.

READING II   *Colossians 1:12–20*

Brothers and sisters: Let us give thanks to the Father, who has made you fit to share in the inheritance of the holy ones in light. He delivered us from the power of darkness and transferred us to the kingdom of his beloved Son, in whom we have redemption, the forgiveness of sins.

He is the image of the invisible God, / the firstborn of all creation. / For in him were created all things in heaven and on earth, / the visible and the invisible, / whether thrones or dominions or principalities or powers; / all things were created through him and for him. / He is before all things, / and in him all things hold together. / He is the head of the body, the church. / He is the beginning, the firstborn from the dead, / that in all things he himself might be preeminent. / For in him all the fullness was pleased to dwell, / and through him to reconcile all things for him, / making peace by the blood of his cross / through him, whether those on earth or those in heaven.

GOSPEL   *Luke 23:35–43*

The rulers sneered at Jesus and said, "He saved others, let him save himself if he is the chosen one, the Christ of God." Even the soldiers jeered at him. As they approached to offer him wine they called out, "If you are King of the Jews, save yourself." Above him there was an inscription that read, "This is the King of the Jews."

Now one of the criminals hanging there reviled Jesus, saying, "Are you not the Christ? Save yourself and us." The other, however, rebuking him, said in reply, "Have you no fear of God, for you are subject to the same condemnation? And indeed, we have been condemned justly, for the sentence we received corresponds to our crimes, but this man has done nothing criminal." Then he said, "Jesus, remember me when you come into your kingdom." He replied to him, "Amen, I say to you, today you will be with me in Paradise."

Practice of Faith

The Solemnity of Our Lord Jesus Christ, King of the Universe brings us to the last Sunday of the liturgical year and we conclude our long period of Ordinary (counted) Time. Next Sunday we turn the page to the First Sunday of Advent. In the midst of this transition, those living in the United States celebrate the national holiday of Thanksgiving. ◆ This holiday week is often filled with travel and preparations, but take some time to also prepare for Advent. Bring out your Advent wreath, purchase fresh candles, clear a place for the household nativity set, and find an Advent calendar. Be ready to dedicate your home to the season of Advent next weekend. ◆ Think ahead about the spiritual practices you will follow during the season of Advent. What practices of faith can help you counteract the secular demands of the holiday season? ◆ Be ready to incorporate private and family prayer time into your Thanksgiving celebrations. Find out when your parish celebrates Mass and make arrangements to attend. Find a meaningful prayer to offer before eating Thanksgiving dinner. Dedicate your own prayer time this week to giving thanks for all the many blessings of your life.

Download more questions and activities for families, Christian initiation groups, and other adult groups at http://www.ltp.org/t-productsupplements.aspx.

Scripture Insights

Today's Gospel passage from Luke may seem a rather curious choice for this solemnity. It is from the Passion narrative that is proclaimed on Palm Sunday. Although we think of Christ as our king, he rejected that title throughout his life. The sign on the Cross that proclaimed him King of the Jews, while in fact true, was intended to be ironic. His entire public ministry was in many ways the opposite of the common image of a king. He spent his life not overpowering but empowering. He went about healing and unifying, forgiving and making others whole again—without exceptions.

This sort of king was feared by the secular authorities because he got inside of people's hearts, their spirits, their soul, and he promised life with God, forever. The leaders were threatened by a charisma they didn't understand. When you don't understand, you become fearful and resentful.

The Scripture passages give us several clues about the kind of kingship Jesus assumes. He is heir to the house of David, who had been a shepherd boy before he was anointed king. Like David, Jesus is the anointed one of God. Paul tells the Colossians that the kingdom bestowed on Jesus by the Father is universal in scope; for "in him all things hold together." In a particular way, Paul states, Christ is head of the Church as one who brings salvation to all by shedding his blood.

On the Cross he died the way he lived, extending the gift of forgiveness and eternal life to one more sinner. Forgiveness from a king is a powerful gesture; you don't really know if you deserve it, yet it comes freely and your life is changed. That's what happens to us in the Sacrament of Reconciliation. The kingship of Christ that we celebrate today was defined by his integrity; what he preached in life, he died doing.

◆ What images of Christ as King are found in the readings?

◆ How is Christ as King an image for you in prayer?

◆ What do you understand to be the relationship between the Church and the Kingdom of God?